JOIN OUR ONLINE BOOK CLUB!

Book club members receive free books and the hottest pre-release novels. To join our exclusive online book club and discuss *Her Father's Daughter* with likeminded readers, please visit:

Books.click/DuboisBookclub

* * *

We look forward to see you in our bookclub family!

"Her Father's Daughter brings a turbulent era to vivid life. All the conflicts and complexities of British India and Czarist Russia are mirrored in Dubois's story. It's breathlessly exciting and heartbreaking by turns—an emotional and historical page-turner." —**Publishers Weekly**

* * *

"Painstakingly researched, beautifully hewn, compulsively readable—this enlightening literary journey takes us from Russia to India via South Africa and Great Britain, revealing remarkable historical details, dark family secrets, and bringing to life two of the men who shaped our world as we know it. A must read." —**O, The Oprah Magazine**

* * *

"A triumphant, controversial, and fascinating plunge into the complexities of a mentor-mentee relationship at the turn of the 19th century. You'll never look at Gandhi or at Tolstoy the same way again." —**Daily Mirror**

* * *

"Author Caroline Dubois had performed tireless research. Whether it is detailing Tolstoy's life as a reluctant count with many serfs, or recounting the world of Gandhi as a young inexperienced lawyer in the racist South Africa and India, Dubois clearly has done the homework. The result is breathtaking." —**USA Today**

* * *

"This is a stunning historical novel that will keep you up late, hoping the engaging story never ends. Highly, highly recommended!" — **Washington Post**

* * *

"A compelling, page-turning narrative. *'Her Father's Daughter'* falls squarely into the groundbreaking category of fiction that re-examines history from a fresh, psychological point of view. It's smart, thoughtful and also just an old-fashioned good read." —**Christian Science Monitor**

* * *

"A powerful story for readers everywhere. Dubois has brought readers a firsthand glimpse into one of history's most fascinating eras. A novel that brings to life what these two great men have endured in order to bring their light to the world. I was moved to tears." **—New York Post**

* * *

"Extremely moving and memorable. . . *Her Father's Daughter* should appeal strongly to historical fiction readers and to book clubs that adored Anthony Doerr's *All the Light We Cannot See* and Caroline Hannah's *The Nightingale*." **—Miami Herald**

* * *

"Inspired by the actual correspondence between the two giants, Dubois has woven together the stories of Gandhi, Tolstoy, as well as of Tolstoy's daughter Tatiana, into a riveting story that reveals the bravery, cruelty and hope at the beginning of the 20th century. This is a part of history that should never be forgotten." **—Los Angeles Times**

* * *

"This is the kind of book I wish I had the courage to write—a profound, unsettling and thoroughly captivating look at mentorship and love through the dark lens of racial oppression." **—People**

* * *

"Dubois skillfully weaves Tolstoy's daughter's tale with the correspondence of a yet-to-be-known shy Indian lawyer, Mahatma Gandhi. Through Gandhi's eyes, the daughter is to learn a valuable lesson in forgiveness. *Her Father's Daughter* portrays the lives of three astonishing figures into a story of extraordinary moral power set against the harrowing backdrop of imperialism and oppression." **— The New Yorker**

* * *

"Riveting. . . Dubois moves effortlessly across physical and ethical battlegrounds, and across the territory of the heart and soul. I find it hard to recall the last time I read a novel that moved me so deeply." **— PopSugar**

* * *

"Fascinating read… A student-teacher story that will make your heart sing. Tolstoy and Gandhi come to life authentically, directed by

Dubois's detailed research and glittering prose." —**The Augusta Chronicle**

* * *

"A gem… Entirely original, *Her Father's Daughter* is a book you set aside like a fine wine and wait for the chance to reopen and savor it."
." —**BookPage**

* * *

"If you enjoy history and friendship, courage and love, you will find this book a page-turner. Dubois has given us a strong and passionate story filled with historical facts, and you will find it hard to put this book down." —**Kirkus Reviews**

* * *

"Movies and books tell the separate stories of Tolstoy and of Gandhi, but very few mention their unique relationship. Caroline Dubois has delved into the lives and times of the two giants and created a tearjerker, but the journey is as lovely as could be." —**Time Magazine**

* * *

"They say truth can be stranger than fiction. Indeed, the real relationship between Leo Tolstoy and Mahatma Gandhi is just that: so moving and emotional you could hardly believe the authentic letters Dubois weaves into the story. Historical fiction at its best!" —**Bustle**

* * *

"Readers will find it hard not to laugh a little and cry a little more as desperate Gandhi reaches out to disillusioned Tolstoy just in the nick of time. A masterpiece." —**Real Simple Magazine**

* * *

"Superb… A searing story with a breathtaking, beautiful ending." —**Huffington Post**

* * *

"An enticing read for history buffs... genuinely heart-wrenching. The memorable cast of Tolstoy, his daughter Tatiana, and Mahatma Gandhi makes for spellbinding reading." —**San Francisco Chronicle**

* * *

CLAIM YOUR GIFT!

Thank you for purchasing this novel. For a special behind-the-scenes e-book, including historical background on which *Her Father's Daughter* was based please visit:

https://books.click/Daughter

* * *

This e-book companion includes group discussion ideas, unique photographs and much more!

HER FATHER'S DAUGHTER: A NOVEL OF A TOUCHING FATHER-DAUGHTER RELATIONSHIP

A Novel

By Caroline Dubois

TABLE OF CONTENTS

PART ONE.. 4

PART TWO 177

EPILOGUE 463

PART ONE

Based on true documents.

All quotes from letters, diary entries, books and articles are directly based on the original documents.

ROME,
DECEMBER 1931

Tatiana Tolstoy-Sukhotin stood near the window, waiting.

The 67-year-old countess stared at the street below thinking, 'When will he arrive? The telegram said he'd arrive at three...'

She sat down on the couch in her little apartment. A moment later she got up and walked back to the window, thinking wistfully of the snow she loved in her childhood. She missed the snow.

The newspaper on her coffee table showed his photograph on the front page: those odd round spectacles, the brown skin, the smile with several teeth missing.

She wanted to be upset with this man for not arriving on time, but she found herself instead smiling back at the face covering the newspaper's front page.

She leaned forward and looked at the article again: *"Gandhi Arrivando questa mattina a Roma."*

She read the title again. Though she had only lived in Italy for a few years, she could understand Italian fairly well. It was very similar to Latin, of which she had an adequate knowledge. Her father had taught her well.

"Gandhi Arriving in Rome This Morning," she translated to herself, "The Indian leader to visit Prime Minister Benito Mussolini in the evening. In the morning he will be greeted by the naval cadets, and then taken to meet with government officials, including the Minister of Foreign Affairs, Mr. Dino Grandi. In the afternoon, prior to visiting Il Duce, Gandhi will be visiting the Tolstoy Museum in Rome."

She was glad the address was not mentioned. The last thing she wanted was a throng of people and the hideous reporters with their cameras. She had suffered because of them throughout her life, always chasing her father. At that moment she remembered with perfect clarity when her father was dying at the stationmaster's home in that forsaken place. She shivered remembering how the press nearly broke into his room there. What a terrifying experience.

She shuddered slightly—the memory of her father brought her pain. She looked at the drawing on the wall that she drew many years ago—22 years ago, to be exact. A portrait of her father in the year before his passing. Her father looking lost in his thoughts, almost daydreaming, his large white beard dissolving into the dark background.

She looked at the clock nervously. If he doesn't come soon, she thought, there will be no visit to the "Tolstoy Museum."

For the past two days she had been cleaning the downstairs room feverishly. The "museum" was one room, a small room she rented from the building's owner, which she dedicated to her father's legacy. It was all she could afford. But it was better than nothing.

Her father, with his socialistic ideals, left his works in the public domain. And even though her late mother was eventually able to win the rights back, as soon as the Communists took over, all the money was gone.

As she peeked out the window, she was surprised to realize how excited she was. This was only natural. She had followed Gandhi's career for over twenty years. It would be exciting for anyone to meet such a revered and celebrated leader.

But that was not it, she knew. She had met many leaders throughout her life. The fame did not move her.

It was her excitement to meet this one man. The one person about whom her father spoke with such admiration. To whom her father wrote his longest letter in his last months, when he would write no more than a paragraph to others. To the young Gandhi he wrote three full pages.

What was it about Gandhi that her father had recognized long before the Indian leader was famous? And how had her father come to admire the young Indian lawyer living in South Africa?

It was rare for her father to speak with so much admiration of anyone really. Her father criticized the

Czar, scolded the Patriarch of Moscow, rebuked the army's generals. He laughed at other authors, he criticized almost every artist, including Chekov and even Shakespeare. He mocked his own children, and she was not spared from that.

And yet, this one Hindu, this one little man, somehow elicited only compliments from her father. How she had longed for that kind of approval from him.

But her father's approval was not to be.

She found herself fidgeting with her fingers like a schoolgirl, and tried to calm herself, but her thoughts kept drifting to her father.

"My Father," pencil drawing by Tatiana Tolstoy, 1909.

YASNAYA POLYANA, RUSSIA DECEMBER 1892

Tatiana, age 29, stood in her father's study near the window waiting for him. Her eyes were fixed on the snowy trail leading into the woods.

He was late. Again. Now they might not be able to go through the many letters he had received that day. She glanced at the desk. She had arranged the letters in three meticulous piles. Forty-three letters altogether. She had read them carefully, like her mother had trained her so many years before. But now she understood the process better than her mother. This was perhaps why her father had dismissed her mother from the task.

Next to the letters, Tatiana had prepared the family's stationery in advance, her English fountain pen and her journal. Everything was there, except for her father.

She heard her siblings running around downstairs in the family room. She still needed to mend five-year-old Vanya's trousers, and to help nine-year-old Alexandra with her homework. She also needed to help 14-year-old Michael with his approaching examination in mathematics, and 16-year-old Andrey with his literature assignment. Her 22-year-old sister Masha was away from the estate on one of her romantic escapades, and asked Tatiana to create some pretext as to why she wasn't there.

Tatiana also needed to tend to her brother Lev, now 24, who had returned from university after having what the doctor called a "nervous breakdown." Lev was now in the house, but refused to see his parents or siblings. Tatiana was the only one he would allow into his room.

She kept looking through the window at the white terrain, and snow-covered birches. A small crowd began collecting there. The old porter, Abrasha, must have let them in.

Tatiana was happy that at least she did not have to take care of her two other brothers, Ilya, who was married and living near Tula, and Sergei, who worked as a bank manager and lived in Tula itself. They, for now, did not need her.

But the others did. And when she added her two parents—who, in fact, needed her even more than the children—then she felt the heavy burden once again. Her days seemed to be filled with people needing her help, and she was exhausted.

The clock struck the hour and somehow it made her sad. It seemed that every hour she was awake she was helping a family member. She felt that she was losing a part of herself.

She heard steps in the hallway behind her, "Tatiana

Tolstoya!" She heard her mother scolding her, "Stop fidgeting with your fingers like that!"

Tatiana brought her hands down at once, "Yes Mama!"

Her mother peered into the study, "Has he not come yet?"

Tatiana shook her head. What was her mother doing *here*? Papa had forbidden her from coming near his study. This was the whole purpose of Tatiana doing the paperwork with her father, to get Mama *away* from him.

Tatiana stiffened as she watched her mother enter the room. She tried to ignore her mother, wishing she'd leave quickly. The last thing she wanted was another quarrel between her parents. She wanted to say something to her mother about that, but refrained. Tatiana knew very well that her mother was only waiting to be scolded, and would then use the opportunity to lash out at her daughter. No. Tatiana would not give her the pleasure.

Sophia Tolstoy walked closer to the window, near her eldest daughter, seeing the small crowd gathering in the yard. "Why did Old Abrasha let them in again? I have told him a thousand times not to let the people past the gate!"

Tatiana murmured, "But Papa told Old Abrasha to allow them in when he comes back from his afternoon walk. Papa told me he pities them for coming so far and then being rejected."

Sophia snorted. "Pities them! He enjoys all the *attention*, that's why!"

Tatiana closed her eyes, not wanting to enter into an

argument. When she opened her eyes again she noticed a movement in between the trees down the trail. Yes. It was him.

Leo Nikolayevich Tolstoy, 65 years of age, made his way out of the woods carrying a small bundle of chopped lumber in his arms. His face, covered with an overgrown white beard and bushy eyebrows. His erect posture belied his weathered, ragged appearance.

A murmur passed through the people waiting for him. Tatiana could hear their voices through the closed window, "Count Tolstoy!" "Here he comes! Count Tolstoy!"

Her mother looked through the window, but made sure to stand behind the white drapes. She pouted her lips and muttered, "Here he comes with those silly peasant clothes and that stupid hat! Pathetic! He looks like a *muzhik*, a poor peasant! And the worst kind at that!"

Tatiana did not respond.

"And why does he insist on chopping lumber! I told him a thousand times that he need not do that, and that our serf can do a much finer job than he!"

Tolstoy walked by the people, nodded, his thick eyebrows frowning. He walked to the shed attached to the house and dropped the lumber there. He then returned, reluctantly, to shake the people's hands. One of the women handed him a book to be signed. Tatiana, even from the distance, recognized from the blue cover it was *Anna Karenina*. One of the men eagerly handed him a copy of the red, thick, *War and Peace* to sign.

Tolstoy signed the books, looking away from the

people and their staring eyes. He pretended not to hear the one who was speaking words of praise in a very loud voice. He then nodded, his face blank, and headed to the entrance to the house.

Tatiana and Sophia heard the door closing downstairs, and nine-year-old Alexandra calling, "Papa! Papa! Look at my drawing!"

But Tolstoy muttered something to Alexandra's nanny and began climbing the stairs.

Tatiana glared at her mother, hoping that the look would encourage her to leave.

Sophia looked at her daughter defiantly, unwilling to move an inch. She stood there for a long moment. Then, suddenly, as the heavy steps in the stairway came closer, she ran out of the room and to the bedroom as if nothing had happened.

Tatiana braced herself, anticipating a quarrel. She heard her father's steps stopping. But then there was no sound. Her father must have decided to ignore what he saw. He walked into the room and closed the door.

He sat on his couch, throwing his muzhik hat on the desk. "Oh, Tanya, Tanya…" he sighed and looked at his daughter.

"Papa. You are late. Forty-three letters arrived this morning. We'd better begin promptly if—"

"Have you looked at the manuscript?"

Tatiana looked away, not wanting to meet his eyes. The thick, 300-page manuscript titled *The Kingdom of God is Within You* was lying on the desk, covered by the three piles of letters. "Papa, why don't we start with the letters?"

Her father waved his hand dismissively and looked out the window.

Tatiana understood this to be a "Proceed if you so wish." She took the first letter in her hand, "An older woman," she said, "raving about Anna Karenina."

Tolstoy did not look at the letter.

Tatiana nodded, "I will answer to her cordially."

She looked through the following letter and decided to put it aside. She did it also with the third letter and the fourth. She looked for a specific letter from France. She found it and said, "This one is from a man from France," she looked at her father with hope.

Tolstoy glanced at her, *"And?"*

She looked at the letter, "He speaks about the brilliance of *War and Peace* and asks if there is any metaphor in the use of—"

Tolstoy interrupted her, "In the use of sky? Such as when Prince Andrei is wounded and Pierre recognizes his love for Natasha, and both men look up to the sky etc. etc. etc.?"

Tatiana looked down and nodded. How did her father know?

Tolstoy took a deep breath, "This was rehashed so many times in the past few weeks. Someone must have written about it in some stupid literary magazine and now every second person wants to show it as his own brilliant idea!"

Tatiana nodded, put the letter carefully aside, and

went through the other letters, hoping to find something that could soothe her father's temper.

Her father looked at her disapprovingly, "Any of them about my recent book on vegetarianism?"

There was in fact *one letter*, but it was a negative one. Tatiana did not want her father to see it. "No, Papa," she murmured.

"Any letter about *A Confession* or about *A Criticism of Dogmatic Theology*?"

Tatiana shook her head.

"How about," he looked desperately at the window, his voice raising, "my book about the Gospels, or *Church and State* or *My Religion*?"

Tatiana shook her head slowly, not daring to look at him.

Her father got off the couch and looked through the window in disbelief, "No letter about *What Is to Be Done?* or my treatise *On Life,* or my book on intoxication? Or *The Love of God and of One's Neighbor?*"

Tatiana looked down, afraid to respond and upset her father.

"I don't understand!" Tolstoy exclaimed and pointed at the letters with both his hands, "What are all these about?"

She answered quietly, "Twenty-nine of them are about *War and Peace,* ten are about *Anna Karenina...*" and there were two more. There was the letter she did not want him to see, the critique of *On Vegetarianism*. She would have shown it to her father, but the writer of the letter only wrote one paragraph, in which he quoted the

Bible about animals given to mankind, and finished with a salacious insult. No, she thought, she would not show it to him.

But there was a hope he would like the last letter. She looked at him and tried to smile. She often left the best for the end, but today the "end" came rather quickly. "There was one letter," she smiled, "from a man writing about *The Death of Ivan Ilyich*—"

Tolstoy waved his hand dismissively. He walked back to his couch and sank down.

Tatiana looked through the letters. Was there anything she missed? She knew there was not.

"Now tell me," he looked at her, "what did you think of the *manuscript?*"

Tatiana's lips tightened. She moved the pile of letters and looked at her father's handwriting on the front page, *"The Kingdom of God Is Within You."*

How she had tried to read it!

She had read through many pages, hoping to find a paragraph that would grab her. But all of it sounded so drab. It was also extremely repetitive. It could not be compared to his literary works. While they were masterpieces, this could hardly be read! It was filled with never-ending sentences such as:

> "As early as the time of Constantine the whole comprehension of the teaching was reduced to a résumé confirmed by the worldly power—a résumé of disputes which took place in a council—to a creed of faith, in which it says, I believe in so and so, and so and so, and finally, in the one, holy, catholic, and apostolic church,

that is, in the infallibility of those persons who call themselves the church, so that everything was reduced to this, that a man no longer believes in God, nor in Christ, as they have been revealed to him, but in what the church commands him to believe...."

Not only were the sentences too long and the content dull, but Tatiana knew well, the work would be scrutinized by the Church, as it was quite blasphemous.

Her father looked at her with dismay, "Well, Tanya! Tell me already!"

"I found it," Tatiana said slowly, "very... *invigorating*...."

"Liar!" her father said at her, "Don't think me a fool!"

Her cheeks reddened. What was it about him recently? He had become even more short-tempered than she had remembered. She breathed in, "I am not lying to you, Papa. I did find the writing quite... *passionate*...."

He looked at her, his eyes glaring.

Tatiana tried looking back at him, but his glare was so forceful she had to look down.

"Tanya, you too are nothing but a product of our society!"

Tatiana embraced herself, thinking, 'And now he will begin his rant...' she thought.

"And our society," he said, "is filled with errors. The quote-unquote 'cultured' people of the 'higher' classes try to drown the consciousness of the people, to blind

16

them to the necessity of changing the present order, which is nevertheless becoming clearer and clearer!"

She nodded obediently.

"However, life," her father continued, "only develops and becomes more complex, intensifying the contradictions and sufferings of men! Take, for example, military service."

Tatiana nodded. She had heard it all before. And the manuscript was filled with this very point, rehashed again and again.

"Senseless people"—her father continued with passion—"think that military service and the ever-increasing arming, and the consequent increase of taxation and of state debts, are an accidental phenomenon! That they are a result of some political condition of Europe! And they believe that, were the political considerations changed, so would the arming. They disregard the need for an internal change first!"

His eyes stared at her. She met his gaze, trying to hold her eyes steady and not look down.

"Military service is nothing but an inner contradiction," Tolstoy continued, passionately waving his hand, "which has *stolen* its way into the social concept of life! The social concept of life consists in this very fact, that the meaning of life is to be subordinated to the aggregate without any thinking—"

Tatiana tried smiling, "Papa, I have read the manuscript—"

"Well then what do you think? Am I talking to myself?!"

She bit her tongue, "Papa, it is quite filled with wisdom…."

He looked at her, his glare softening a little, "Yes?"

"Yes," she said slowly, "I think it is most admirable." She hesitated. How much she would have liked him to return to writing fiction again! "But I do think, Papa, that you could—if you wanted—deliver the *same* message using your brilliant talent for prose literature—"

Her father would have none of it. "Enough, Tanya, enough! You sound like your mother!"

This was an insult Tatiana could not bear. "Papa! I am telling you the truth!"

Her father was upset. His lips pouted like a little boy, "Do you not think that people could *benefit* from this?" he looked at the thick manuscript into which he poured his whole soul for the past two months. He dedicated endless hours to it, quoting endless sources about the military, pacifism and the evolution of the Church. Most importantly, he wrote about his new theory—never yet practiced by whole groups—of "nonviolence." He attributed its inception to Jesus Christ and his doctrine of "turning the other cheek." He looked at his eldest daughter, his eyes growing larger, "Can't people find this useful?!"

"Papa," Tatiana said quietly, taking a deep breath, "I have marked some paragraphs." She opened her journal, "If you were indeed to publish it, these paragraphs should be… *edited*."

"Which paragraphs?" her father asked, his thick eyebrows raised, deep wrinkles appearing in his tall forehead.

Tatiana looked at her journal, "Such as this, Papa. You write about Petr Chelchicky…"

"The brilliant Petr Chelchicky!" Tolstoy exclaimed, "A man in the fifteenth century who dared to state the lies of the Church he was a part of!"

Tatiana took a deep breath, "Yes…. Well, you say that his, and I quote, 'fundamental idea is this, that Christianity, having united with the power in the time of Constantine and having continued to develop under these conditions, has become absolutely corrupt and has ceased to be Christianity.'"

Tolstoy fired, "Correct!" He tightened his fist, "Good for Chelchicky!"

Tatiana coughed gently and continued, "You write, Papa, about his book, that it was, and I quote, 'one of the extremely few that have survived the inquisition of books Christianity has carried.'"

"Of course, Tanya!" Tolstoy said, "It was a real auto-da-fé, and it continues to this day!"

Tatiana sighed, feeling helpless, "You write, 'All such books, which are called heretical, have been burned together with the authors, so that there are very only but a few ancient works which arraign the departure of official Christianity from the original Christian values.'"

"Correct!"

"But, Papa," Tatiana said quietly, her eyes looking at her father as if she was speaking to a child, "You cannot write *that*. Not *this* way. It is too… vilifying, of the Church—"

"Too what?!"

She knew she was trapped. But she longed to help him. He was heading toward destruction, and she knew it. With such accusations, the book would be banned by the State. She had to help him. "Vilifying, Papa," she said, "it can be read as defamation—"

"It can be read as the truth!"

"But Papa, I cannot see how the Czar or the Church would allow this to be published—"

"So, you want me to lower my head like Galileo? Shall I not state the truth like Martin Luther? Shall I sit in silence, allowing—"

"Papa! That is *not* what I am saying!"

"What are you saying then, Tanya?!" Tolstoy said, folding his arms on his chest defiantly.

Tatiana tried to calm herself down, "I am just trying to help you, Papa. With some modifications, at least the book could get *printed*, that is what you *want*, no?" She looked at the quotes she wrote in her journal, "But when you write, Papa, 'Nowhere nor in anything, except in the *assertion* of the Church, can we find that God or Christ founded anything like what churchmen understand by the Church....'" She looked at her father, "It just will not be accepted this way...."

Her father looked at her, mumbling quietly to himself, "What have I *done*? What have *I* done?"

Tatiana could not hear him, "Papa, I cannot understand what you are saying. Speak clearly please."

Tolstoy shook his head, "I have raised a complacent, good-for-nothing, little aristocrat! Without any

20

independent thinking or the ability to question the state of things!"

His words hurt her. She pouted her lips, looking at him in disbelief.

He continued, "My own daughter! Incapable of thoughts that are not in perfect alignment with the prevailing doctrine of the day however corrupt that doctrine may be!"

Tatiana couldn't bear it any more. She covered her face with her hands, "Papa! Please! I am just trying to help!"

But her father would not listen, "You, Tanya, are nothing but a little brat, an ignorant fool!"

Tatiana felt anger building in her. Here she was, *dedicating* her *life* to help her father. Here she was, now 29-years-old, trying to save this old man from his own demise, from the hole he was digging with his own hands. Here she was, still single after she had received two marriage proposals from two men she was fond of, and whom her father dismissed without any consideration! Here she was, trying to help her old father, who rarely if ever said, "Thank you," or spoke a kind word. Here she was, doing all this for him, and this was his response?

He kept mumbling to himself.

She peeked at him through her hands, "Papa! Stop torturing me! Do you want to review these paragraphs or…?"

This upset him even more. He got up and yelled, "Review these paragraphs! Review my *writing*! My *soul*, my *blood* spilled on the paper! And you want to '*review*' it so that some corrupt bishop somewhere will not get upset?!"

Tatiana wanted to respond. But at that moment her father grabbed his muzhik hat and stormed out of the room.

She heard his quick steps down the stairs. She heard little Alexandra exclaiming joyfully, "Papa!"

And then she heard the house door slamming.

Tatiana sat there, wanting to cry.

She heard, down the hall, the door to her mother's bedroom opening.

Sophia peered through the door. Seeing that her husband was gone, she entered, glanced at Tatiana, and then headed to the window. Seeing Tolstoy disappearing into the woods, she said, "At least I am not the only one upsetting him—"

Tatiana could not stand her presence. "Leave me alone Mama!"

Her mother looked at her with alarm, her eyes widening. She raised her chin, straightened her back and walked out of the room, grunting, "Uh!"

Tatiana slouched in her chair and closed her eyes tightly, trying not to cry. He was becoming impossible and so was her mother. She should leave. Soon. She should get married and leave. This was becoming a mad house.

Tatiana Tolstoy, age 19, 1883.

Tolstoy, wearing his peasant hat and clothes, age 69, 1897.

Tolstoy children, from left to right: Ilya (age 4), Lev (age 1),
Tatiana (age 6) and Sergey (age 7), 1870.

ROME,
DECEMBER 1931

Tatiana looked through the window at the empty street. She turned to check the clock. It was already four. He was an hour late.

She went to the couch and sat down heavily. Her body ached; she was not young anymore. Cleaning the room and all the artifacts downstairs for the past two days had taken its toll. Had her daughter been in town she would have helped her. But she, her little baby and her husband gone to Milan.

She scolded herself for letting her mind wander into old memories. She preferred to stick to the few sweet memories, rather than recall, yet again, the painful times.

When she was a child it was all different. She was nine when her father began working on his new novel. "Tanyushka!" he would call, "It is a new and exciting story!"

"What it is about, Papa?"

Her father grinned, "It is about a girl called Anna Karenina...."

For the next four years her father would work on that novel. And no one could enter his study on the second floor.

That is, only she was allowed to enter.

She would sneak into the room, and sit in the divan next to his desk. He would write, back then with feather and ink, and sometimes read passages to her. She would not understand it all. She was young. She loved how passionate her father was as he read to her the sentences he carefully crafted.

"Tanyushka!" he would say, "Do you like it?"

"I do, Papa!"

He would smile at her.

Sometimes she would even say, "Papa, I do not think Anna is doing the right thing" or "Papa, I am afraid the end will not be good!"

And her father would look at her with admiration, exclaiming, "You are my little genius, Tanyushka!"

She even remembered how once—overjoyed by her comment—he began dancing in the study, pulling her from the divan and waltzing with her.

But that was a rare event. Most of the time he was busy and distant and over the years his temperament only got worse.

Tatiana's musings were interrupted by a noise. Looking out the window, she squinted to determine the source. Her eyes had suffered over the years from working on her father's manuscripts, letters and diaries.

As the noise increased, she could make out three black cars coming towards the house, which slowed as they drew closer.

She hurried to the door, picked up the key to the museum room, and ran down the stairs.

Opening the heavy door of the building, the cold December wind chilled her. Four army officers exited the first car. One of them headed to her, "Tolstoy Museum?"

"Tolstoy Room," Tatiana corrected him.

He looked at her briefly, his eyebrow raised, then nodded at the other men. One of them went to the second car and opened the door. An Indian man, who did not seem like Gandhi, got out of the car. Then a woman wearing a white tunic and a white veil, looking like a nun. But just then, when Tatiana did not know what to make of it, the small man got out of the second car, wrapped in his white shawl, bowing gently to the driver and to the army officers. Tatiana gasped. It was Gandhi.

One of the army officers led the small procession to the building, and Tatiana could see how Gandhi was saying something to the nun and the other Indian man.

Tatiana offered her hand for a handshake as they approached her. Gandhi grinned, "Oh dear!" he exclaimed, "You must be her!"

Tatiana smiled back, "And you must be him!"

Gandhi shook her hand and nodded his head.

She quickly shook the hands of the others.

Gandhi pointed at the woman, "This is my friend, Mirabehn, and this fellow," he pointed at the man, "is Mr. Madan Mohan Malaviya."

The man smiled cordially, "You can call me Madan."

Tatiana nodded and smiled, "Why don't you all come in? It is cold out here!"

Gandhi smiled and nodded, then gestured for Mirabehn to walk inside first, and then for Mr. Madan. He then insisted that Tatiana would walk in first, along with the guard, and he entered last. The three other guards remained outside.

Inside the hallway, Tatiana unlocked the door of a small room and turned the light switch on, "Welcome to the Tolstoy Room," she said, stressing the word "Room."

She smiled apologetically to the three of them as they walked inside.

The woman, Mirabehn, was the bluntest. She looked around the room, expecting to find a door into another room, then realizing this was all there was. "It is so..." she looked for words, "cozy!"

Mr. Madan smiled and nodded, "Most definitely."

Gandhi smiled and nodded too. Tatiana was already used to it. She could see the initial disappointment on people's faces the moment they entered the room. She wanted to apologize, but she forced herself not to. This, after all, was the result of the actions of the one person they were all admiring. Her father. Tolstoy, with his commitment to the peasant life and his loathing for material things, made sure to release the rights to many of his works, denying his children future royalties from his work. This, along with the Communist revolution, left Tatiana not much to support herself with, except a prestigious surname.

The small "museum" was therefore established from Tatiana's *own* money. Some of that was from her late husband, who died fifteen years before from her own translations and academic papers and from the Russian lessons she gave in Rome. But it was not much. This was all she could afford.

Gandhi smiled at her, pointing at the display, the letters on the wall, the photographs, and at the desk in the corner, "You have created all this?"

Tatiana smiled. He was trying to be kind. "Yes," she said.

He murmured, "Remarkable!"

She smiled. Standing near the entrance, she saw how Mirabehn and Mr. Madan were reviewing the photographs on the walls but ignoring the letters and memorabilia. But Gandhi was still standing not far from the entrance, looking at the first display of photographs from her father's youth and from the family's estate, Yasnaya Polyana. The way Gandhi stood there, his hands behind his back, looking at the photos ever so slowly, touched Tatiana.

It was for the few like him that she had established the Tolstoy Room. The few who *cared*.

In the past Tatiana would begin pointing at things, lecturing, explaining excitedly. But as she aged, she found that sort of narration exhausting. And she had also learned that most people were not interested. For that reason, she and her daughter had prepared a small plaque next to each artifact, letter or photograph, explaining the item. She learned to talk only if the visitors *asked* something, and she was glad to answer. But most people never asked questions.

Gandhi still stood by the first display. He murmured to himself, "Yasnaya Polyana."

Tatiana hesitated. But then she said, "Yes. It means," she explained, *"'Clear Glade,'* as in an empty circle amid trees."

Gandhi looked at her, his eyes shining, "I did not know that! Fascinating!"

She smiled and stepped back, standing near the door. She did not want to bother the visitors. Gandhi now proceeded to the second wall, reading each line, studying every picture. He then stopped near a photo of Tolstoy's eldest children. Four of them stood there in 1870. Tatiana even remembered the day she and her brothers went to the photographer in the town of Tula, an hour ride from their estate. She was six years old.

She noticed Gandhi reading the description, and she anticipated what he was about to say.

"This is you!" Gandhi exclaimed, pointing at the photograph.

Mirabehn and Mr. Madan hurried to walk back and look at the photo, a little embarrassed they had missed this detail.

Tatiana smiled at Gandhi, "How perceptive of you to notice."

Gandhi nodded and looked at the photograph. Tatiana looked at it too. Sergey, the first born, sat on a chair. Tatiana and Ilya, stood near him, with baby Lev in between them. Tatiana's arm was placed around her baby brother, guarding him. Even at that young age, she was her siblings' second mother.

Mirabehn and Mr. Madan quickly lost interest. Mr. Madan by now had finished going through the display, and went and sat in an old Russian armchair near the entrance. Tatiana looked at him and smiled as he sat down. In a way, she preferred that. She wanted people not to feign interest. If you were not interested, that was fine. Don't *act* as if you were.

She had learned this disdain for pretense from her father. Her mother always insisted on feigning whatever it was, for the sake of cordiality.

Mirabehn now, too, seemed tired and disinterested, and hovered near the second and only other chair in the room. Tatiana nodded at her. But Mirabehn did not understand the nod. Tatiana therefore smiled, "Please, sit."

Mirabehn smiled a large and appreciative smile, lifted her white tunic and sat down with a quiet sigh.

Yet Gandhi, who looked older than both Mirabehn and Mr. Madan, kept standing there, reading the little plaques, looking at the photographs with the greatest of interest. In a way, he reminded Tatiana of her father: unaware of the others, disinterested, completely absorbed in what he was doing. He now moved along the first wall, his hands behind his back, reading intently.

Tatiana remained standing there quietly, glancing at him, trying not to stare. She had been so stressed about his visit that only now was she beginning to appreciate it. It was real. Gandhi, Mahatma Gandhi, the great Indian leader, the great follower of her father, was in her presence.

But there was something so unassuming about him. In that way, he was very different than her father. Whenever her father was in a room you could *feel* it. Even with your eyes closed you could feel the air of importance, the gravity of his presence.

Gandhi was not like her father. There was a diminutive quality about him. He was not interested in talking or winning her over, nor of winning over the others in the room. He was interested in studying the display, in collecting information, without creating any fuss.

He finally turned to the second wall. As he did, he noticed Mirabehn and Mr. Madan slouched in their chairs. He looked at them, and then at Tatiana. He smiled at her. She smiled back.

He then walked to her. "Would you excuse us for a moment, Mrs. Tolstoy-Sukhotin?"

"Please," she said, "call me Tatiana." She looked around the room, "Of course."

She exited the room into the building's entrance, standing near the guard.

This was a little strange for her. She had never left *anyone* in the room on their own. All that was important to her was in that room, except for her father's diaries, which she kept upstairs.

She heard Gandhi murmuring, "I can see that you are tired. Why won't you two continue to the hotel, and

I will join you later?"

They both disagreed strongly. Mirabehn jumped. "Mahatma, I'm sorry, I'm perfectly capable—"

"I know you are," Gandhi responded, "but we had a long day, a long train ride, and quite too much time with those naval cadets! I would appreciate your presence at the dinner with Mussolini. So why won't you go back to the car and ask to be taken to your hotel?"

The conversation went back and forth. Tatiana listened intently. She was surprised to hear Gandhi finally telling them, "I have looked forward to this meeting for many years. I would appreciate some privacy with Tolstoy's daughter."

Mirabehn would not hear of it, and was adamantly against the idea. But after another minute, she and Mr. Madan suddenly exited the room.

Tatiana pretended not to hear the exchange, then heard a flustered Mirabehn say, "Mrs. Tolstoy, we shall leave for a short while." She then whispered, "Please do not take too long, as the Mahatma needs to rest before the meeting this evening."

Tatiana nodded, "Of course."

Mirabehn glanced worriedly at Gandhi, and then looked at Tatiana, raising her eyebrows, "Please help us make it brief."

Tatiana did not like that comment. Nevertheless, she smiled cordially, as the guard opened the heavy door. They then spoke to the three guards outside. The door closed behind them.

Tatiana walked back to the room silently. Gandhi

was now near the second wall. He kept going slowly through the display.

She wanted to keep standing, but she was tired too. Not from anything physical as much as from the sheer excitement since she received the first telegram three days ago.

She quietly walked to the chair closest to the door and sat down.

Gandhi finally arrived at the desk in the corner of the room, which replicated Tolstoy's desk.

He looked at her wide-eyed, "Is this... the *real* desk?"

Tatiana smiled, "The real desk is still at Yasnaya Polyana. This is a replica."

"Of course," he said quickly, "how silly of me."

Nevertheless, she saw him stroking the desk gently, looking at the manuscript inside the glass display.

She got up and said, "The manuscript, however, is the authentic manuscript."

His eyes grew larger. He looked through the glass at the original paper, at the rapid handwriting. He murmured, "I do not have many worldly possessions, Mrs. Tolstoy—" he corrected himself, "Tatiana."

She smiled back at him as he continued, "But the few letters I have received from your father are amongst my most cherished relics!"

She smiled at him and nodded. She wanted to say more, to tell him that the correspondence was also very meaningful for her father. She wanted to say that she had personally been there when her father read

Gandhi's first letter. She wanted to say that ever since her father's death she followed Gandhi's career in interest.

But she said nothing. She did not want to interrupt him. He went slowly through the third wall: Photographs of Tolstoy in his last years; photographs of his sickness at that terrible train station. Tatiana sighed as she looked at the photographs. She remembered those last days very clearly. All too clearly.

Gandhi looked at her and smiled empathetically, "It must have been terribly difficult."

She was a little surprised by his comment. Then she nodded, "Yes. It was."

He looked quietly at the last photographs.

She realized that he was one of the only people to have looked at each piece in the room.

He turned to her then, and exclaimed, "What a wonderful display you have created!"

She smiled and bowed her head gently, "It means a great deal coming from you."

He looked toward the hallway at the guard standing there. Gandhi whispered to her, "They follow me everywhere!"

She tittered.

He sighed and said quietly, "I would have liked to spend some time with you in private. Is there any place where we could chat a little?"

She looked at the guard, then at Gandhi, and then again at the guard. "My apartment is upstairs," she said quietly.

Gandhi's eyes lit up. "Could we…?"

She shrugged her shoulders and looked at the guard.

Gandhi nodded, walked into the entrance and said, "Kind Sir. The Missus and I shall now go upstairs. You may wait here or in the car as you wish."

The guard gulped, "But Sir—"

Gandhi smiled and shook his head, "Thank you for your kind service. I will return to the car on my own."

Tatiana looked at the baffled guard. Gandhi looked at her and raised his eyebrows decisively, "Shall we?"

She nodded, quickly turned off the light in the room, closed the door and locked it, and then proceeded to climb to the first floor. Gandhi followed her. She glanced over her shoulder and saw the guard looking at them from the gap between the two staircases.

She opened the door to her apartment. "It is rather small and a little messy, Mr. Gandhi, please forgive—"

"Nonsense," he said as he entered, "and please, call me Mohandas." He looked around, "What a beautiful home you have." He looked with interest at the many bookcases lining the walls, "You are a woman of letters, Miss Tatiana."

She closed the door behind them, "Are you certain the guard will be pleased?"

"I am certain that he will *not*." Gandhi smiled. He walked across the small living room to the window and glanced at the guards below, "But I am certain that *I* will be pleased."

Tatiana smiled at him. She was nervous to have him in her apartment.

He looked at the two couches, "May I?"

"Of course," she mumbled, "please forgive me...."

He sat down and smiled, "I'm so pleased to be away from those guards! They have been on my tail since the train crossed the border this morning!"

"They must be concerned," Tatiana said. She stood near the entrance, not knowing if she should sit down too.

Gandhi shrugged his shoulders, "They are not concerned. They are fanatical! And," he shook his head disapprovingly, twisting his face as if he had tasted something sour, "the ceremony given to me in the army base—"

Tatiana smiled, "The navy cadets?"

Gandhi looked at her, surprised, "How do you know?"

She pointed at the newspaper on the table.

He glanced at the newspaper and nodded. "The army general showed me hundreds of children, hundreds of tender, kind children, and you know what they were carrying?"

"Rifles?" she guessed.

He looked at her with disbelief, "Indeed! This does not give me a good impression at all! May I ask you what your impressions of your Mussolini are?"

She looked at the door worriedly. Mussolini had been in power for five years, and it was said his intelligence agency was everywhere.

Gandhi recognized her look, "Of course, forgive me. I do not wish to put you in an uncomfortable situation. Please ignore my question."

She grimaced. She had much to say about Mussolini, who spoke with promising words, captured the masses, and yet managed to restrict the freedom of speech and the power of the free press.

But Mussolini's behavior was not foreign to Tatiana. Even back in Russia, over the course of her entire life, the Tsar's agents were constantly sent to Yasnaya Polyana to spy on her father. Generally, people were wary of sharing their true opinions. And after the October Revolution and the rise of the Communists, it became even worse.

"May I ask," Gandhi said, interrupting Tatiana's thoughts, "and I do not wish to be intrusive…. But I've learned that one of your siblings lives in America, while another brother lives in Switzerland, and another in Prague, and yet others are in France. Why is that so?"

Tatiana took a deep breath. She sat down on the couch, facing Gandhi. "Surely, Mr. Gandhi—"

"Mohandas, please."

She nodded. "Surely you are aware of what has been taking place in my country."

Gandhi nodded, "But I would like to hear it from you. I hear a lot of news that I fear has been written by the government itself."

She nodded and leaned back against the couch, "Well, the new regime seems to be raising the flag of high morals and beautiful slogans. But they seem to be not much better than the Czar. Actually, perhaps worse, what with Lenin's brutality and the treatment of the old aristocracy."

Gandhi looked sad. "This is what I had feared." He paused for a moment, "Well, your father expected it."

Tatiana looked at him, surprised, "My father? How so?"

He smiled, "In '*After the Ball,*' he alludes to it clearly."

Interesting, Tatiana thought. '*After the Ball*' was one of her favorite short stories. In it, her father depicted a ball, filled with beautiful music and dancing, led by one "Colonel B." After the beautiful ball, Colonel B. is found flogging a soldier who had deserted the army. The contrast between the kind and pleasant Colonel during the ball, and the blood-thirsty Colonel after the ball was especially harsh. She wondered what Gandhi meant by his comment. "Could you elaborate please?"

"During the ball," Gandhi said, "the Colonel—I forget his name…."

"Colonel B."

"Indeed, Colonel B. Well, during the ball he is a model of social grace and standing. Yet later," he sighed and smiled a sad smile, "during the flogging, he presides over the other soldiers committing violence in a ruthless manner."

Tatiana nodded and closed her eyes for a moment. It was an interesting comment.

Gandhi looked at her quietly. "Well, I am sorry to hear this is the plight of Russia. I have heard your father's name mentioned many times in association with the revolution. But this was not what he had hoped for."

Tatiana appreciated his words. Though she had read many articles about Gandhi, she had not really known his attitude toward the bloody regime in her homeland. Was Gandhi an idealist, like all the others who fell in love with the revolution and turned a blind eye to the injustice it brought? Or was he sober, seeing the revolution for what it was? His comment made him appear more settled and wiser than she had thought.

Gandhi must have seen her face, as he said, "One must always look at the core of things, at the volition and motives, and not stick to slogans and empty propaganda."

She bit her lip and nodded knowingly. She liked him.

Suddenly they heard a knock at the door.

Tatiana stood up and went to open the door. Two guards stood there. She glanced at them and then looked at Gandhi.

Gandhi jumped off the couch, "Yes?"

"Sir," said one of them, who must have been the more superior of the two, "we've been instructed to guard you at all times and in all places."

"I understand," said Gandhi, "but now I must repose before the dinner with your Prime Minister. So I do suppose your duty is well fulfilled outside the apartment."

"Sir," the officer said again, "we've been instructed to guard you at all times and in all places."

Gandhi was a little irritated. He looked at Tatiana and then back at the guard, "I do not suppose you find danger in leaving me with this kind lady!"

The officer said nothing. There was a long pause and then the officer said, "Sir, I do apologize, but these are the instructions we have received."

Tatiana said, "It is fine, Gandhi—Mohandas—one of them can—"

"No," Gandhi said in a somewhat childish manner, "I do deserve a moment of peace and quiet!" He looked at the officers and lowered his voice, "I do appreciate your concern and your 'instructions', but I do not suppose that if I and the lady were to… indulge in *carnal knowledge* you were to keep an eye on us, am I correct?"

Tatiana stopped herself from bursting into laughter.

The officer looked blunt, "*Carnal*—what?"

Gandhi shook his head, "Knowing each other in the *biblical* sense…?"

The officer's face lit up and his eyes widened.

Gandhi nodded, "Now, if you'd excuse us!"

And with that he closed the door. He came back triumphantly to the couch, "See?"

Tatiana laughed, looking at his victorious face. He now indeed reminded her of her father!

Gandhi leaned back against the couch, "Now, where were we?"

Tatiana looked at his sandals, realizing he must be cold. Crazy, she thought, sandals in this weather of December. She suddenly realized she did not offer her guest anything to drink. "Would you like some tea?"

"Oh, that would be splendid!"

She smiled and walked to the kitchen.

To her surprise, he followed her to the kitchen. He lingered near the entrance to the small kitchen and smiled, "I do not wish to miss a moment with you."

She smiled and poured water into the copper kettle and placed it on the stove. Trying to make polite conversation, she asked, "How was your stay in England?"

"Oh, the people were very kind. But the government," Gandhi took a deep breath, "let's just say that they have still a long way to go."

She nodded sympathetically. She had read in the newspapers of the failure of the Round Table Talks about the future of British India.

"Are you…" she hesitated, "disappointed?"

"Oh, not at all," he said, "I am not." He seemed thoughtful. "Eventually India will become Indian. It will fall into our hands like a ripened apple falling from a tree. We just have to be patient."

Interesting, she thought. She appreciated his hopefulness but perhaps he was a little naïve.

"Besides," he continued, "it gave me an excuse to visit Europe, which I have not done for sixteen years. And it gave me the excuse to meet you!"

Tatiana blushed. His comment somehow made her uncomfortable. She wondered why she felt so uncomfortable. Was it because it felt like flattery? Or because it sounded like an exaggeration?

"You realize, Tatiana," he said, "that you are the closest person to Tolstoy who is still alive?"

Tatiana looked flustered. She did not like this comment either. "That is not true," she said as the kettle steamed. "There is my little sister, Alexandra, and my brothers. And there is Vladimir Chertkov, my father's publisher. I do not think—"

He smiled, "Indeed, indeed. Yet Alexandra is twenty years younger than you, and she only helped your father in his last years. You were there all along."

Tatiana shrugged her shoulders, "Only until I was married. And in his last years Alexandra—"

"But you were with him until you were married, at thirty-three years old if I am not mistaken, and still visited and helped him often. I have read several biographies about your father. And as for your brothers, they were never his *assistants*. You *were*. And you would remember the transition from his literary years to his more philosophical and social writings, which Vladimir Chertkov, with all due respect, would not."

She tried to look calm as she poured the hot water into the teapot. "Earl Grey?" she asked.

He smiled and sheepishly said, "I would prefer something herbal."

She nodded, "Of course." She had to admit to herself that she would too. She took out some chamomile, her favorite. She glanced at him standing clumsily near the entrance to the kitchen.

She had to admit to herself that he *was* correct. Ever

since the death of her mother over a decade earlier, she had become the person who had best known her father. Her older brother, Sergey, was never as involved with her father's writings. And her younger siblings, including Alexandra, did not know her father as well as she did.

She thought of Masha, who had died twenty-five years earlier. Masha would have been the second to have understood Leo Tolstoy. Her father had always loved Masha the best. He had even written it in his diaries.

That thought made her heart ache. She forced herself to smile and took the tray into the living room.

Gandhi reached his hands, "Please, let me."

Tatiana insisted, "I am fine, Sir."

As they walked to the couches, Gandhi sensed that she had stiffened. "I am sorry," he said as they sat down, "I hope I did not say anything to upset you."

She was surprised by his frankness. She herself did not quite know what had upset her so much. She looked at Gandhi and tried to smile. She saw that forgotten passion in him which she used to see in visitors at the family's estate when she was younger. People waiting to hear her father's words, to devour any thought he had, to hear him cough, to see him sneeze. She thought this was ridiculous at the time.

She noticed the silence and said, "Well, Mr. Gandhi—excuse me, *Mohandas*—how did you first encounter my father's writings?"

Gandhi grinned. "Well, that is an important question. I am sure every person who ever read your father's great works remembers the moment of that first encounter."

She tried smiling. She suddenly remembered that she promised the lady, Mirabehn, not to keep Gandhi for long. But he seemed so comfortable, and to be enjoying himself.

"Your father," he said, "came to me at exactly the right moment. It was when I had a humiliating experience. And out of that madness and darkness, his light came and shone brightly on me."

She looked at him as he closed his eyes, remembering, and told her the story.

TRANSVAAL COLONY
SOUTH AFRICA,
JUNE 1893

The train sped through the mountains. Mohandas Gandhi, a 24-year-old Indian lawyer, looked through the window at the mountains. It was a strange land, South Africa.

He had arrived in South Africa three days before. As the train stopped and loaded more passengers for the overnight ride to Johannesburg, he noticed that the air coming from outside was bitterly cold. Strange, he thought. South Africa, he had imagined, must be warm. But as the train climbed into the higher altitudes leading away from the shore of Natal Colony, the air quickly became colder.

His thoughts drifted to home. He hoped that his experience as a lawyer in South Africa would be better than the one he had back home in India, where he once stood up in court and was unable to utter a word. He then repaid the client and asked for another lawyer to represent the client instead. What an embarrassing experience.

Therefore, when the offer to serve as a mediator between two Indian merchants in South Africa came his way, Gandhi grabbed it at once.

The train stopped in some town, a few people disembarked, some boarded the train. A chilly wind came from the doors once again.

Passing by his compartment, one European man glanced at Gandhi in dismay. Gandhi quickly smiled back.

A few moments later that European passenger returned with the train conductor. The two Europeans looked at Gandhi disapprovingly. The conductor muttered, "Come along!"

Gandhi hesitated. Was the conductor speaking to him? But then, there was no one else in his small compartment. "Excuse me?" Gandhi mumbled.

The conductor shouted, "Come along! You must go to the van compartment!"

Gandhi was surprised, "But I have a first-class ticket, Sir," he said and pulled out his ticket.

"That doesn't matter," the conductor said, "no colored people are allowed in first class!"

Gandhi was flustered, "Sir, I was permitted to travel in this compartment at the Natal Colony, and I insist on staying until I reach Johannesburg!"

"No, you will not. If you do not leave willingly I shall call a police constable and force you out!"

Gandhi nearly cried, "Please, gentlemen," looking at the passenger standing behind the conductor, hoping for his help. Both looked at him crossly. "I am a lawyer," Gandhi said and took two visiting cards from his purse, "M. K. Gandhi, certified in London," he handed them the cards.

The conductor glanced at the card and snorted. "Very well. I shall call the police constable then!"

Young Gandhi felt helpless. "I have not committed any sin, Sir! I have *paid* for this ticket!"

The conductor shrugged his shoulders and walked away, the passenger joining behind him quickly.

Gandhi hoped this was all. He looked through the window, and sighed. 'Strange place', he thought. When he studied in England he had never encountered such behavior. Even in India an Indian was permitted to travel in first class compartments! He should write a letter of complaint once he reached Johannesburg.

The train began slowing down. As the train stopped in the station, the conductor came along with a tall police constable. The police constable lifted Gandhi in the air. Gandhi protested and shouted as he was dragged through the train's corridor, "Please Sir! Leave me alone! I have paid for my ticket!"

A second later he was thrown onto the platform.

As the train began leaving the station, the conductor threw Gandhi's luggage onto the platform.

Gandhi was speechless. The train disappeared.

It was bitterly cold. Gandhi stood up, cleaned himself off, took his luggage and slowly made his way into the waiting room.

The ticket office was closed. Gandhi looked at the schedule. The next train was not until tomorrow morning.

He sat there and shivered.

He missed his home terribly. He especially missed his wife Kasturba who had warned him not to take the offer in South Africa. Should he have listened to her?

The taste of the humiliation was bitter.

In the following weeks, the young lawyer kept writing to train officials, demanding an apology, which never came.

His fellow Indians living in South Africa, including his employer, asked him to calm down.

But he could not.

He was shocked at how other Indians in South Africa were not outraged. Many of them told him of similar experiences, especially in the Transvaal Colony.

But none of them wanted to do anything about it. They were afraid the government would take away their visas. So they remained silent.

But Gandhi was soon referred to one young European who shared the same thoughts. His name was Herman Kallenbach. The two met in Johannesburg, and Gandhi was pleased to see a European agreeing that the discrimination had to stop. Herman sighed and said, "The problem with the current administration here is that they have forgotten the teachings of Christ."

Gandhi nodded and looked at Herman, wishing to hear more of his thoughts.

But Herman asked instead, "Tell me, Gandhi. Have you read any of Tolstoy's works?"

"Tolstoy?" Gandhi asked sheepishly, "I have tried. I have tried reading both '*War and Peace*' and '*Anna Karenina*', but have failed—"

"No, I'm not talking about his literary works," Herman assured him. "I'm talking about his social writings."

"Social writings?" Gandhi asked, puzzled.

Herman reached for his valise and pulled out a book titled, *The Kingdom of God is Within You.*

Gandhi took it and flipped through it. He saw the name of Jesus mentioned several times. He gently closed the book and handed it over to Herman, "Thank you, dear friend, but you see, I am a little apprehensive about this kind of book. I am a *Hindu*."

Herman laughed, "And I'm a Jew! This is not a book aiming to convert anyone." He pushed the book back at Gandhi. "Just have a look at it, I think you will find it interesting."

Apprehensively, Gandhi took it. "I'll have a go at it on my next trip to Johannesburg."

Sitting in the third-class compartment of the overnight train heading from the Natal Colony to the heart of the Transvaal Colony, Johannesburg, Gandhi pulled the book from his luggage. He had three other books with him, but wanted to give the book with the strange title a chance first. He looked at it,

The Kingdom of God is Within You

By Leo Tolstoy

Translated from Russian by:

Aylmer Maude

Gandhi opened the first page and began reading,

> "Nearly a decade ago, in 1884, I wrote a book under the title, *'My Religion.'* In this book I expounded on what my religion is.

> In expounding my belief in Christ's teaching, I could not help but express the reason why I do *not* believe in the ecclesiastic-clergymen faith, which is generally called 'Christianity', and why I consider it to be a delusion."

Gandhi sat up. This was interesting. A Christian calling Christianity a 'delusion'?

> "Among the many deviations of this teaching of Christ, I pointed out the chief deviation, namely, the failure to follow one basic Christian precept: the commandment of non-resistance to evil.

Gandhi paused and looked at that word, "non-resistance." It felt to him like a translated word. "Non-resistance." He had never heard of it before. He continued reading, feeling a little ignorant.

> "This failure to follow the commandment of non-resistance to evil shows the distortion of Christ's teaching in the doctrine of the established Church.

At the time I knew very little, like the rest of us, as to what had been done and preached and written in former days on this subject of non-resistance to evil."

Gandhi smiled. So he was not the only one.

"In this book, first I shall tell of the information which I received concerning the history of the question of non-resistance to evil, then of the opinions on this subject which were expressed by clergymen; and finally, those deductions to which I was brought by both and by the historical events of recent times."

Gandhi flipped the page to the first chapter, which did not have a title. He read:

"Among the first answers to my book '*My Religion*' there came some letters from the American Quakers. In these letters, which expressed their sympathy with my views concerning the unlawfulness for Christianity of all violence and war, the Quakers informed me of the details of their so-called sect, which for more than two hundred years has in fact professed Christ's teaching about non-resistance to evil, and which has used no arms in order to defend itself.

Having proved, by a whole series of considerations and texts, that war, that is, the maiming and killing of men, is incompatible with a religion which is based on love of peace and good-will to men, the Quakers affirm and prove that nothing has so much contributed to the obscuring of Christ's truth in the eyes of the pagans and impeded the dissemination of

> Christianity in the world as the deliberate ignorance of this commandment by men who called themselves Christians."

Gandhi looked up from the book. Tolstoy's words were harsh. He denounced Christians who use violence as 'men who *called themselves* Christians.'

Gandhi continued reading with a growing interest.

> "Christ's teaching, which entered into the consciousness of men, not by means of the sword and of violence, but by means of non-resistance to evil, can be disseminated in the world only through humility, meekness, peace, concord, and love among its followers."

For the following night Gandhi devoured the 300-page book. He read quickly, not understanding everything, but sensed the words had special gravity. After arriving in Johannesburg, he quickly mailed his friend Herman in the Natal Colony,

> "Dear Herman,
>
> Your book left an abiding impression on me! Such independent thinking, profound morality, and truthfulness! Other books I have read seem to pale into insignificance.
>
> We have much to speak about when I return on Friday.
>
> Obediently yours,
>
> M. K. Gandhi."

When Gandhi returned to Natal at the end of the week he hurried to visit Herman's home. The two talked well into the night. Gandhi gushed about the clarity of the message. "If this is Christianity," he said and pointed at the book, "you can count me as a Christian!"

Herman laughed. "Me too! These kinds of books need to be circulated more. Instead, the stupid government has ban them!"

"No!" Gandhi gasped.

"Yes!" Herman laughed, "In Russia the book was completely censored by the government. They had to print the book in Germany. This is a translation of the German translation of the Russian original!"

Gandhi was shocked, "How could the Russians do it? Every Christian—every person, in fact—must read this book!"

Herman smiled. He had never seen his Indian friend so excited.

Gandhi (standing) with his two friends and supporters in South Africa, Sonia Schlesin (left) and Herman Kallenbach (right).

ROME,
DECEMBER 1931

Gandhi's eyes shone as he looked at Tatiana. "Your father's book opened a whole new world to me," he said.

Tatiana smiled. His excitement was contagious.

"I then continued to read," Gandhi said, "everything I could find. I began with *'My Religion'* of course, and found that book, too, fascinating! I continued to *'A Confession'*, then *'A Criticism of Dogmatic Theology'*, *'The Gospel in Brief'*, then *'Church and State.'*"

Tatiana nodded.

"Wait," Gandhi smiled, "I then read 'What Is to Be Done?', and 'On Life', and 'The Love of God and of One's Neighbor', and of course 'Why Do Men Intoxicate Themselves', as well as 'The First Step: on

Vegetarianism'... Am I forgetting anything? I read whatever I could put my hands on!"

Tatiana laughed. It was amusing to see him talking with such zeal and remembering all those titles. "Mr. Gandhi—"

"Mohandas," Gandhi corrected her.

She smiled at him, "Mohandas, I might want to hire you as an assistant to our little museum room. You surely know a lot, and I could use some help."

He grinned, his toothless smile going from ear to ear, "Miss Tatiana! That would be my utter pleasure!"

She smiled at him.

The conversation died down. She looked at his cup, "You have not finished your tea!"

He promptly took the cup of tea and sipped it in its entirety, then exclaiming, "A Tolstoyan tea!"

"Hardly," she said as she went to the kitchen to boil some more water, talking loudly so he could hear her, "It may be more of an *Indian* tea than a *Tolstoyan*! The spices come from India."

Gandhi followed her to the kitchen, "Then a Tolstoyan-Indian tea!"

She looked at him, standing in the entrance to her small kitchen. There was something so endearing about him.

She poured more water into the kettle and placed it on the stove.

He looked at her with curiosity, "Tell me, Tatiana, was your father as..." he searched for words, "as loving and caring as I imagine?"

She bit her lip and look away. These words, 'loving' and 'caring' would not be the first ones she'd use to describe her father.

Gandhi continued, "I mean, in his writings, his love exudes every page. And his wisdom," he closed his eyes, quoting Tolstoy, *"Everyone* thinks of changing the world, but no one thinks of changing *himself."*

Tatiana nodded politely, leaning against the counter.

Gandhi continued quoting, his eyes closed, "'Love is *life*. All, everything that I understand, I understand only because I love! Everything is united by it alone! Love is God, and to *die* means that *I*, a particle of love, shall return to the general and eternal source!"

He opened his eyes and stared at Tatiana, "Such great wisdom! And so much ahead of its time!"

Tatiana smiled cordially. Gandhi went on, quoting, "'When you love someone, you love the person *as they are*, and *not* as you'd like them to be!'"

He stepped into the kitchen, exclaiming pompously, "'*Seize* the moment of happiness! Love and be loved! That is the only reality in the world, all else is folly!'"

Tatiana tried smiling. Somehow his words made her feel uncomfortable.

"Tell me," Gandhi exclaimed and stepped towards her, "Was he as loving as I imagine?"

Tatiana closed her eyes tightly.

"Please!" Gandhi pressed, "Do tell me!"

"Enough!" Tatiana shouted suddenly. "Enough I

pray you!"

Leo and Sophia Tolstoy, c. 1905.

Tolstoy family: From left to right- Michael, Leo Tolstoy, Little Vanya, Lev, Andrey, little Alexandra, Tatiana, Sophia, Masha (standing), 1894.

Tolstoy, age 74, after illness, with daughter Tatiana, age 38, 1904

YASNAYA POLYANA, RUSSIA
JUNE 1897

"Papa! I beg you!"

Tolstoy looked at his disobedient 31-year-old daughter. "Tanya! I will not permit you to commit this mistake!"

"But Papa!" Tanya cried, "I love him!"

"Love?!" her father exclaimed, "Love is but intoxication! Believe me, you'd be better *without* love!"

"But, Papa!" Tatiana stuttered, "You... You have said the *same* of my other suitors! And Mr. Sukhotin is a *fine* man, a caring, loving man! He is not less than Obolensky, and you let Masha marry him!"

"That was my greatest mistake and I shall not repeat it!"

"Papa! Don't you want me to be happy?! Sukhotin loves me! He is kind, caring—"

"He is an old widower, Tanya!"

"He is only fifty years old, Papa! And I'm now thirty-one, I cannot wait any longer!"

She looked at her father, "Papa, he *loves* me!"

"Tanya! What do you even know of love?!"

"Papa!" Tatiana burst into tears, "I know of love! He loves me and I love him! And so *what* if he is older?! You were sixteen years older than Mama!"

"And what a mistake *that* was! Tanya!" he screamed at her. "Marriage is not needed for a fine girl like you!" he softened his voice, trying to appeal to her senses, "Why won't you remain unmarried, like your Aunt Maria? She is happy."

"Papa, I don't want to be a nun in some forsaken convent! I want to be loved! I want to be married!"

"Married! A bright girl like you should not become the *possession* of some ignorant fool!"

"He is not an ignorant fool!" Tatiana said through tears.

"He has six children, Tanya! I will not permit you to ruin your life in this way! And my word is *final!*"

"Papa!" Tatiana exclaimed and ran out of his study, through the corridor, down the stairs.

Sophia emerged in the corridor and ran downstairs after her daughter, "Tanya! Wait!"

"Leave me alone Mama!"

"Tanya, please! Stop!"

Tatiana ran outside into the woods. She hated her father. She ran and ran, and finally, at a bare spot between the trees, she fell onto her knees, weeping.

Her mother soon arrived there, panting. "Tanya! Tanyushka…!"

"Leave me alone Mama!"

Sophia looked at her daughter sobbing, her shoulders rattling. "Tanyushka…."

"Why can't Papa just let me *go*, Mama!" Tatiana cried through her tears, "He wants me to become an old spinster!"

"No, he does not, he loves you, Tanya—"

"No he does not! He does not love me and he does not love you either! He is *incapable* of loving!"

"No he is not!"

"You said it yourself, Mama! You said it yourself!"

"I…" Sophia Tolstoy searched for words, "I must have been upset when I said it…."

Tatiana continued to weep piteously.

Her mother, still panting from the run, searched for words, wishing to say something encouraging. She knelt down to show warmth and comfort her daughter, but she did not know how.

"I will speak to him, Tanya."

Tatiana looked at her mother through her tears, "Will you, Mama?"

Sophia nodded. "I will."

Their shouting was heard throughout the house.

Tatiana sat at the edge of the staircase, listening to her parents' quarrel in her father's study upstairs. Thirteen-year-old Alexandra sat next to her older sister on the stairs holding her hand.

They could hear their father's hoarse voice, yelling, "I will not let her make the same mistake as Masha!"

Her mother tried calming him down, "But Masha is happy, Leo!"

"Happy?! Happy?! A life of slavery, being bound to a man, is that happiness?! She should have stayed *here*, what was wrong *here*?!"

Sophia tried soothing him, "Sukhotin does not live very far, it's a four-hour train ride. She could visit often…."

"I will not let her marry this bald, ignorant, good-for-nothing man! Why do you think his wife died on him? She preferred *dying* over *living* with *him*!"

On the staircase downstairs, Tatiana shrieked. She shook her head with amazement. She looked at Alexandra, who shook her head as well.

Their mother said something to their father, which they could not decipher.

Tolstoy yelled in response, "Why does she need him? What can he give her that we cannot? She is fed well here. She is taken care of, what else does she need?!

Why does she want to sell herself into servitude? I simply cannot comprehend such stupidity!"

"She is a grown child, Leo!" Sophia exclaimed, then lowered her voice.

Her words became incomprehensible from downstairs. Tatiana and Alexandra tried to decipher the words. Then their father's voice came loud and clear: "I forbid it! How can she be so selfish! What will become of me?! Who will help me with my writings and correspondence!"

Tatiana's eyes grew larger, looking at Alexandra, "The selfish fool!"

Sophia's voice responded forcefully, "I can help you, Leo Nikolayevich Tolstoy! I have helped you before and I can still—"

"You are useless Sophia! The girl speaks English, French and German, much better than you or I, and is now well versed in all of the correspondence—"

"But I've taught her. I can become acquainted—"

"You are useless, Sophia! She has a *critical* mind. I could not last without her!"

Downstairs, Tatiana's eyes began to well up. Alexandra tried to calm her older sister down. But Tatiana buried her face in her hands and sobbed, muttering, "I hate him! I hate him!"

It took two full years to convince her father. Tatiana did everything, from trying to appease him, to fighting and insulting him, to avoiding speaking to him and remaining in her room for days.

Tolstoy too, tried everything he could to dissuade his daughter, even to threaten Mr. Sukhotin. Once he even threatened to cut Tatiana out of his will. This threat, however, did not go well.

"You!" Tatiana screamed at him, "You old fool! The prophet of the abolition of private property, threatens with this?!"

Tolstoy did not respond. Seeing the reason in her argument, he embraced himself as his daughter gushed, "I don't need your filthy money! Sukhotin is well off enough on his own!"

Finally, on November 14th, 1899 her parents took her to be wed at the small church in Tula.

It was snowing, and her father wept. He mumbled, "How can you do this to me, Tanyushka!"

Tatiana did not respond to him. She knew he was beyond reason.

Years later, after both her parents had died, Tatiana found an old letter from her mother to her aunt:

> "You cannot imagine how grief-stricken and sick at heart both Leo and I were while accompanying Tanya to the ceremony.... It was all so gloomy, just like a funeral, not like a wedding! When Tanya came up to say good-bye to Leo, he wept so hard it was pitiful to look at him."

Years later she also found the following entry in her father's journal, written a week after the wedding. His words brought anger to her, even years after he had died:

> "Tanya has gone away—God knows why—with Sukhotin. It is pitiful and offensive."

The diary entry went on to state:

> "For seventy years my opinion of women has done nothing but sink steadily, and yet it must go lower still. The problem with women? One thing is sure! It is not solved by *allowing* women to run one's life, but by *preventing* them from destroying it!"

ROME,
DECEMBER 1931

Gandhi stared at Tatiana. Her reaction to his question shocked him.

She was ashamed of losing her temper. "I am sorry," she said.

"No, I am sorry," Gandhi murmured, "I did not... wish... to stir up old memories."

Tatiana looked away and sighed. The water in the kettle was boiling. "My father, Mr. Gandhi—"

"Mohandas," Gandhi corrected her gently.

"Mohandas," she said without a smile, "was a *complicated* man. He was..." she searched for words, "he was a *complicated* man."

Gandhi nodded. "I see."

They said nothing else. Tatiana took the kettle off the stove, poured the water into the teapot and placed it on the tray. Gandhi did not ask to take the tray from her. He walked out of the kitchen first, and she followed him silently into the living room.

They sipped their tea in silence. Outside, the light of day slowly became softer. Evening was coming.

Gandhi then said quietly, "I do not mean to be intrusive, but, I beg you, Tatiana, please explain to me what you mean by 'complicated'?"

Tatiana took a deep breath and looked away, but Gandhi continued to gaze at her, waiting for an answer.

Her shoulders dropping, she let out a deep breath and began to speak. "When I was a child, about ten years old, my father used to teach me and my brothers some mathematics, Greek and Latin. Masha was too young to join us, so it was me and my three brothers. Papa—father—was so..." she searched for the right word, "he was so *harsh* sometimes. He was a true disciplinarian. I loved him, but I was also," she looked at the patterns of the carpet, "I was also afraid of him."

Gandhi said nothing.

Tatiana sighed and looked at Gandhi's large eyes, "I'm sorry. I do not know why I am telling you this."

"No, please, continue," Gandhi said quietly.

She sighed again. "My father... He was a *tough* man, filled with ideals. Ideals about proper education, about proper living, proper conduct, morality. He believed that everyone deserved a good education. He even insisted on teaching the children of the serfs how to read and write." She smiled, "He insisted on it, though many of the serfs could not see the use of it for their children. Nevertheless, my father used to go to their little cabins, gather the children, tearing them away from their playing, and would teach them. He never let any of us—his own children—come along, because he did not want us to intrude?"

Gandhi nodded slowly.

Tatiana smiled. "Once, we received a telegram from my father's publisher in Moscow. It was about an advance for a book my father was writing. I believe it was 'Anna Karenina', which was published then in installments in some magazine."

Tatiana looked at the window, "My mother sent me to find him and call him to come home immediately, so that we could respond to the telegram before the post office in the nearby town closed. We knew he was teaching at the time, so I ran through the fields to the serfs' cabins to search for him."

Gandhi listened intently.

"I finally came to the cabins of the serfs across the fields. I asked where my father was, and I was directed to one of the cabins. I entered. He was sitting there, with some ten children, younger than me. He was not happy to see me. 'What is it Tanya?' he barked at me.

"'Mama called for you,' I said, 'we received a telegram from Moscow about an *advance*, Papa!'"

Tatiana's eyes became moist.

"He then told me, 'That is not important, Tanya. It can wait.' I then proceeded to stay there, sitting down quietly at the edge of the cabin. He did not oppose it. Then—"

Tears appeared in her eyes. She closed her eyes tightly. "Then he continued with the lesson. And he *praised* the children. He *laughed* with them, and made silly little skits for them to remember the letters he was teaching."

Her chin began quivering.

Gandhi was unsure what to do or say. He said nothing.

"You see," Tatiana said and looked at him, "With us—with his own children, with *me*—he never praised, he never said a good word. But it was fine with me because I thought that was the way he *was*, you understand?"

Gandhi nodded.

"But seeing him with those children," Tatiana continued, "with the peasants, being so jolly, and loving, and friendly…. He even allowed them, at the end of the lesson, to hug him, and he let some of them climb on his back. None of us ever climbed on his back…."

Tears streamed down her cheeks. She got up and took a handkerchief from a desk drawer. She wiped her eyes, with her back to Gandhi.

She scolded herself for crying. Why did she need to bring up these memories?

Gandhi sat perfectly still, perfectly silent, hanging on every word.

Tatiana turned around and looked at him, "You must think me *mad*, or *selfish*, for not being *happy* for these children…."

"Not at all," Gandhi murmured. "It must have been

painful for you if he treated them in a different way than he treated you."

Tatiana nodded, "I was so *hurt*... seeing that he was *capable* of being this way. Not strict, not scolding, not blaming and calling me stupid all the time."

Her chin quivered.

Gandhi got up and wished to put his hand on her shoulder. But he did not dare. He stood in silence.

She wiped her eyes again, "I'm sorry. Forgive me. It's just.... You *insisted*, asking me about how he was.... You see, he *was* loving, he *was* caring, just not to...."

Her face twisted with pain. She tried stopping her river of tears. Once she succeeded she shook her head, breathed in, and said, "I am sorry. I did not mean to act this way."

"No," Gandhi said and sat down, inviting her with his hand to sit back down, "thank you for honoring me, Tatiana, with your truth. I never *met* your father. I only *imagined* how he was. I thank you for sharing your memories with me."

Tatiana walked back to the couch and sat down, the handkerchief tightly bundled in her fist. She smiled, "Now," she took a deep breath in, "where were we?"

Gandhi smiled at her and leaned back on the couch, saying nothing.

Tatiana looked at the teapot, "We must drink the tea before it gets cold." She poured the tea and Gandhi held his with both hands. Tatiana continued, "You were telling me how you had first heard of my father's writings."

Gandhi smiled. He sensed she was trying to change the subject. "Well," he said, "as I told you, I went on to read anything I could by your father. Eventually, I was so moved by *'The Slavery of Our Times'* and his other writings, that I wished to simplify my life. I managed to establish a small farm at which we practiced Tolstoyan values, as well as the teachings of John Ruskin."

Tatiana nodded. Her father's followers were often followers of the British Ruskin as well.

"My wife and four sons moved into this farm with me," Gandhi reminisced, "as well as several families from the Natal Colony in South Africa. It was a sort of an ashram, a communal living. We called it 'Phoenix Settlement.'"

Tatiana saw his shiny eyes and smiled.

"It was then," Gandhi continued, "that I was trying to bring your father's ideas into practice. All members of the community were instructed to read *'The Kingdom of God is Within You'* and some of your father's other writings," he smiled sheepishly, "it was mandatory reading."

Tatiana nodded with a gentle smile.

"And we built a flour mill and an oil press. We also established a small newspaper to educate the wider Indian community in South Africa." He sighed, "And it was not long before we ran into trouble with the government."

"Oh," Tatiana said.

Gandhi nodded.

INDIAN OPINION

No. 48—Vol. 8   SATURDAY, NOVEMBER 26TH, 1910   Registered as a Newspaper

COUNT TOLSTOY AND PASSIVE RESISTANCE

A MESSAGE TO THE TRANSVAAL INDIANS

WE have received for publication the following translation of a recent letter of Count Tolstoy's to Mr. Gandhi:—

Kotchety, Russia, Sept. 7, 1910.

I received your journal, and was pleased to learn all contained therein concerning the passive resisters. And I felt like telling you all the thoughts which that reading called up in me.

The longer I live, and especially now, when I vividly feel the nearness of death, I want to tell others what I feel so particularly clearly and what to my mind is of great importance—namely, that which is called passive resistance, but which is in reality nothing else than the teaching of love uncorrupted by false interpretations. That love—i.e., the striving for the union of human souls and the activity derived from this striving—is the highest and only law of human life, and in the depth of his soul every human being (as we most clearly see in children) feels and knows this; he knows this until he is entangled by the false teachings of the world. This law was proclaimed by all—by the Indian as by the Chinese, Hebrew, Greek and Roman sages of the world. I think this law was most clearly expressed by Christ, who plainly said that "in this only is all the law and the prophets." But besides this, foreseeing the corruption to which this law is and may be subject, he straightway pointed out the danger of its corruption, which is natural to people who live in worldly interests, the danger namely, which justifies the defence of these interests by the use of force, or, as he said, "with blows to answer blows, by force to take back things usurped," etc. He knew, as every sensible man must know, that the use of force is incompatible with love as the fundamental law of life; that as soon as violence is permitted, in whichever case it may be, the insufficiency of the law of love is acknowledged, and by this the very

law is denied. The whole Christian civilisation, so brilliant outwardly, grew up on this self-evident and strange misunderstanding and contradiction, sometimes conscious, but mostly unconscious.

In reality, as soon as force was admitted into love there was no more, and there could be no more love as the law of life, and as there was no law of love, there was no law at all, except violence—i.e., the power of the strongest. So lived Christian humanity for 19 centuries. It is true that in all times people were guided by violence in arranging their lives. The difference between the Christian nations and all other nations is only that in the Christian world the law of love was expressed clearly and definitely, whereas it was not so expressed in any other religious teaching, and that the people of the Christian world have solemnly accepted this law, whilst at the same time they have permitted violence, and built their lives on violence, and that is why the whole life of the Christian peoples is a continuous contradiction between that which they profess and the principles on which they order their lives—a contradiction between love accepted as the law of life and violence which is recognised and praised, acknowledged even as a necessity in different phases of life, such as the power of rulers, courts and armies. This contradiction always grew with the development of the people of the Christian world and lately it reached the highest stage. The question now evidently stands thus: either to admit that we do not recognise any religio-moral teaching and we guide ourselves in arranging our lives only by power of the strongest, or that all our compulsory taxes, court and police establishments, but mainly our armies, must be abolished.

This year in spring, at a scripture examination at a girls' high school at Moscow, the teacher and the bishop

present asked the girls questions on the Commandments, and especially on the sixth. After a correct answer, the bishop generally put another question, whether murder was always in all cases forbidden by God's law, and the unhappy young ladies were forced by previous instruction to answer, "Not always"—that murder was permitted in war and in execution of criminals. Still, when one of these unfortunate young ladies (what I am telling is not an invention, but a fact told me by an eye-witness), after her first answer, was asked the usual question, if killing were always sinful, she, agitated and blushing, decisively answered "always" and to all the usual sophisms of the bishop she answered with decided conviction, that killing always was forbidden in the Old Testament and forbidden by Christ, not only killing, but even every wrong against a brother. Notwithstanding all his grandeur and art of speech, the bishop became silent and the girl remained victorious.

Yes, we can talk in our newspapers of the progress of aviation, of complicated diplomatic relations, of different clubs and conventions, of unions of different kinds, of so-called productions of art, and keep silent about what that young lady said. But it cannot be passed over in silence, because it is felt, more or less dimly, but always felt, by every man in the Christian world. Socialism, communism, anarchism, Salvation Army, increasing crime, unemployment, the growing insane luxury of the rich and misery of the poor, the alarmingly increasing number of suicides—all these are the signs of that internal contradiction which must be solved and cannot remain unsolved. And of course solved in the sense of acknowledging the law of love and denying violence. And so your activity in the Transvaal, as it seems to us, at the end of the world, is the most essential work, the most impor-

A copy of "The Indian Opinion," 1910, edited by Gandhi

PHOENIX SETTLEMENT, NATAL COLONY, SOUTH AFRICA, SEPTEMBER 1906

The 36-year-old Gandhi looked at the article he had written, dissatisfied.

A month ago, his old friend Herman, now living with him and the other fifty residents at the farm, told Gandhi, "You always mention Tolstoy in your articles in *Indian Opinion.*' But some people may not know who Tolstoy is."

"That is impossible!" Gandhi responded.

Herman laughed, "You should not forget that only a decade ago you only thought of him as the author of *'War and Peace'* and nothing more."

"But surely everyone had read *'The Kingdom of God'* and some of his other writings!"

Herman smiled, "I wouldn't be so sure."

Following that conversation, Gandhi asked his acquaintances, and to his amazement many people in the larger Indian community admitted to a very limited knowledge about the great Russian author.

One older Indian said that he heard that Tolstoy was a rich count. Another Indian thought that he was a general in the Russian army.

These answers infuriated Gandhi, so he sat down to write an article for his magazine. He realized he had a mission to *teach* the people who Tolstoy *was*.

He now read through the draft of the article again, wanting to make it perfect before being published:

"COUNT LEO TOLSTOY

It is believed that, in the western world at any rate, there is no man so talented, learned and as ascetic as Count Tolstoy. Though he is now seventy-eight years old, he is quite healthy, industrious and mentally alert.

Tolstoy was born of a noble family in Russia. His parents had enormous wealth, which he inherited. He is himself a Russian nobleman, and has, in his youth, rendered very good service to his country by fighting gallantly in the Crimean War. In those days, like the other noblemen of his time, he used to enjoy all the pleasures of the world, kept mistresses, drank and was strongly addicted to smoking. However, when he saw the carnage and bloodshed during the war, his soul wept."

Gandhi frowned at the last sentence. He took his pen and erased it, instead writing,

> "However, when he saw the carnage and bloodshed during the war, his mind brimmed over with compassion."

Gandhi liked this expression better. He went on reading his article, pen in hand.

> "His ideas changed; he began a study of his own religion and read the Bible thoroughly. He read the life of Jesus Christ, which left a deep impression on his mind. Not satisfied with the current Russian translation of the Bible, he studied Hebrew, the language in which it was originally written, and continued his research into the Bible.
>
> It was also about this time that he discovered in himself a great talent for writing. He wrote a very effective book on the evil consequences of war. His fame spread throughout Europe. To improve the morals of the people he wrote several novels which can be equaled by few books in Europe. The views expressed by him in all these books were so very advanced that the Russian clergy were displeased with him, and five years ago, in 1901, he was excommunicated from the Orthodox Church."

Gandhi read this and sighed. He remembered reading of the excommunication five years earlier. What a folly! What ignorance the Church had shown, to denounce rather than embrace this great man!

He went on reading:

> "Disregarding all this, Tolstoy continued his efforts and began to propagate his ideas. His writings had a great effect on his own mind. He gave up his wealth and took to a life of poverty.

He has lived like a peasant for many years now and earns his needs by his own labor. He has given up all his vices, eats very simple food and has it in him no longer to hurt any living being by thought, word or deed. He spends all his time in good works and prayer."

Gandhi nodded. It was satisfactory. He then looked at the list he wrote. Lists, he learned, were important in educating the masses. Many people felt more interested in short sentences than in long paragraphs. And so Gandhi followed the essay with the following list:

"TOLSTOY'S MAIN BELIEFS:

1. In this world men should not accumulate wealth;

2. No matter how much evil a person does to us; we should always do well to him.

3. No one should take part in fighting;

4. It is sinful to wield political power, as it leads to many of the evils in the world;

5. Man is born to do his duty to his Creator; he should therefore pay more attention to his duties than to his rights;

6. Agriculture is the true occupation of man.

Gandhi was satisfied with the list. He looked at the following two paragraphs, closing the essay:

"These views he has very beautifully supported by examples from various religions and other old texts. There are today thousands of men in Europe who have adopted Tolstoy's way of life. They have given up all their worldly goods and taken to a very simple life. Tolstoy is still writing with great energy.

Though himself a Russian, he has written many strong and bitter things against Russia concerning the Russo-Japanese War. He has addressed a very pungent and effective letter to the Czar regarding the war. Selfish officers view him with bitterness, but they, and even the Czar, fear and respect him. Such is the power of his goodness and godly living that millions of peasants are ever ready to carry out his wish no sooner than it is spoken."

Gandhi looked at the article with satisfaction. This will educate his people, he thought.

His wife, Kasturba, came into his study. "Mohan," she said softly, "Herman is here for you."

"Oh, let him in!" Gandhi said cheerfully.

Kasturba looked at him worriedly, "But don't forget the lesson you promised the children in half an hour."

He looked at her reassuringly, "Yes my commander!"

She laughed and exited the room.

A minute later Herman entered Gandhi's study carrying the newspaper. Gandhi noticed his friend's face was forlorn. "Herman, is everything alright?"

Herman did not say a word, but placed the newspaper on Gandhi's desk.

Gandhi looked at the newspaper's headline:

"Government of the Transvaal Colony Legislates Anti-Indian Law"

Gandhi's heart skipped a beat, but he kept reading.

"The Asiatic Registration Act of the Transvaal Colony was approved yesterday by the Colonial Secretary, General Jan Smuts. The law aims at the Asian workers in the Transvaal region, including the cities of Pretoria and Johannesburg. Under the Act every male Asian has to register himself and produce on demand a certificate of identity."

Gandhi looked at Herman, "That is not that bad."

Herman looked grim, "Read to the end."

Gandhi kept reading.

"Under the Act, every Asian man, woman or child of eight years or upwards is required to register. For identification purposes the Registrar may note important marks of identification upon the applicant's body."

Gandhi's eyes widened.

"According to the new law, unregistered persons and prohibited immigrants could be deported without a right of appeal if they fail to comply with Act."

Gandhi looked at Herman.

Herman nodded. "One of my German friends told me some European merchants have been begging the government to enact this law."

"Begging? Why?"

"Competition," Herman said bluntly, "competition from the Indian and Chinese merchants have grown this past decade," he looked at Gandhi knowingly. "Nothing like deportation of the competition to drive profits back to the European businessmen."

Gandhi shook his head. "We must stop this."

Herman sighed, "It's government legislation, backed up by London, Mohandas. It won't be easy."

Gandhi immediately set to write a petition to the Colonial Secretary, General Jan Smuts. The next edition of the *Indian Opinion* had articles written about the Asiatic Act. The Indian community was outraged, and so was the Chinese community, as the Asiatic Act also applied to them.

Gandhi tried to calm the community. "Anger won't help us," he said to his friends. But it was not easy to calm people when it was written that policemen were allowed to enter the houses of "Asiatic people" without a court order, and to perform a body search on the inhabitants.

Sensing that this was likely to result in violence, and that it was only a matter of time until someone from the Indian community killed a British policeman, Gandhi called for a large meeting of the Indian and Chinese communities.

The replies were so quick to come, from hundreds who wished to participate in such a meeting, that Gandhi soon realized that a large venue must be found.

With money collected by the heads of the community, Gandhi proceeded to book the *Imperial Theatre* in Johannesburg, where a thousand people could sit comfortably.

When the day came, Gandhi was nervous.

Kasturba tried to reassure him, but to no avail.

"What if I stammer? I have never spoken in front of such a large audience. What if I cannot speak? What will the community think of me?"

"You will do fine, Mohan," Kasturba said calmly, "Think, why did you call the meeting in the first place?"

"To decide on what to do. For the sake of the community!"

"So stop thinking about your stammering and about your appearance. It does not matter. Think of the community instead," Kasturba said, nodding her head knowingly. "Forget about what they think of you, Mohan! Think instead of their needs. Of the community at large."

Gandhi looked at Kasturba. "I will try."

The theatre was filled with people. Gandhi looked nervously at Herman, "How many people do you think are here?"

"Some three thousand."

"Three thousand!" Gandhi gasped. "But there are only seats for—"

Herman pointed at the balconies, "Look up there."

Gandhi looked up and saw people crowding, crammed in the mezzanines.

Herman saw Gandhi looking rather pale. "Mohandas," he said, "do not worry."

Gandhi tried to smile. He looked at the audience.

Many of the men were sitting with their hands crossed over their chest. They were much older than his 36 years.

Apart from the many Indians, both Hindu and Muslim, there were a few representatives of the Chinese community sitting in the front rows, as well as a handful of white Europeans sympathetic to the cause, including Herman and some of his friends.

Though Gandhi invited the Colonial Secretary to attend, General Smuts was not foolish enough to appear. There were, however, five police constables sitting in the front row. They looked displeased with the terrible noise made by the crowd.

Herman looked at the excited audience and then at Gandhi, "I think you should begin."

Gandhi nodded. He climbed the stage, taking the two-page resolution, he and a few others had drawn up prior to the meeting. He lifted his hand. Soon the whole theatre became quiet.

He realized that reading the resolution right away would be unwise. He should say a few words instead, and explain the rationale of the resolution. "Dear friends," Gandhi mumbled, "We gathered here today in order to express our protestation—"

One man from the mezzanine stood up and shouted, "Speak up!"

Gandhi nodded, his eyes widening, "We gathered here today," he shouted, "to express our protestation to the new Asiatic Act."

A sound of dismay passed through the crowds, some booing and shouting.

Gandhi looked at the three reporters, sitting near the stage. He did not want them to get an impression of an unruly crowd. He closed his eyes and spoke, feeling his heart beating fast. "We, citizens of the British Empire, feel violated by the new law. We have written a petition, and the Colonial Secretary wrote to our delegation that the matter was 'under consideration' and that they would give us a definite reply." Gandhi's eyes glared, "Despite this, two days later, they brought the Bill before the Legislative Council in London, and passed the Bill as it was."

Everyone in the audience booed. Gandhi quickly motioned for the audience to calm down. He looked up at the British flag, hung above the stage. His voice rattled, "Since my childhood, I have been told that under this Union Jack, I shall always find protection! And justice! That is exactly what we now ask for!"

People nodded.

Gandhi looked at the three reporters, writing down his words. "Upon his coronation, His Majesty King Edward declared to the people of India that he would give us our rights and preserve our status just as Her Majesty Queen Victoria had done! Does not that promise *extend* to the Majesty's Colonies as well? Does not that promise include Johannesburg, Pretoria, and the whole Transvaal Colony?"

People nodded. Gandhi looked at the delegation of Indian community leaders. They nodded back at him.

"For the last 13 years," Gandhi continued, "I have lived in South Africa. In the Natal Colony I exercised the right to vote and other rights as well. Nowhere except here in the Transvaal have I seen such oppression of our people. And the Transvaal is still a Crown Colony, is it not?"

People cheered, "Yes! Indeed!"

Gandhi continued, "But it is not the time for speeches. Neither is this the time for petitions, as we have seen how our petitions are treated."

A murmur of dismay passed through the crowd.

"Now," Gandhi continued, "is the time for action. What shall we do against a bill which allows any policeman, without any warrant, to enter each of our houses, and perform a physical search on our children, our daughters and our wives, being allowed to do so under the law of this flag!"

A huge cry swept through the audience. A few men stood up, one of them shouting, "The British will only understand when we kill a few of them and teach them a lesson!"

Some cheered in response.

Gandhi took a deep breath, gesturing for everyone to sit down. "But," he said calmly, "it is time for us to be wise."

The audience became quiet.

"Is not the government *trying* to goad us into acting *violently*? We, the community that is known for its quiet and peaceful manners?"

He saw people staring at him. He continued, "Is there not a provocation in this Asiatic Act, expecting us to *prove* that we are violent," he looked at the audience, pronouncing each word carefully, "that we are savage, that we are disloyal to the Crown?"

People began nodding their heads slowly.

"If we choose violence," Gandhi continued, "will we not simply play into the hands of those who want the Indian and Chinese communities out of the Transvaal Colony and of all of South Africa? The British police and army can deport us all in a matter of days, and end the community here - after decades of our hard work."

People nodded in agreement.

"No. We shall not play into their hands." He pursed his lips, looking intently at the audience, ignoring the police constables readying their batons in the first row.

"Dear friends," Gandhi exclaimed and looked at the balconies, "which action are we therefore left with? Must we either choose compliance with the law, and degradation of our respect in a way that proves our inferiority, or must we choose violence instead, bringing our own demise?"

Silence ensued.

"Luckily, there is another option. That is the option of resistance, but not a violent one."

His eyes shone. He had thought about this idea for years now. He had preached about it in small circles, and written about it in his magazine. He had lived it in his mind's eye. Now was the time to put it to the test.

"We must resist," he continued, "but in a *peaceful* manner. We must not submit to the law, but suffer the consequences."

One man shouted at Gandhi from the back of the theatre, "They will put us all in jail!"

Gandhi anticipated that comment, "Yes. They might.

But for me, there is great pride in going to jail with our heads raised high rather than submitting to an unjust law with our heads held low."

People nodded. One person stood up and pointed at Gandhi. "He is right!"

Gandhi smiled for a brief moment. He did not anticipate that response.

"Friends," Gandhi said, "we will prove to the British government and to the *entire* world, that the Asiatic community is one of honor! It is loyal to the Crown, and is loyal to the *principles* on which the Crown is based! And when those in power *deviate* from those eternal principles of justice, we shall help them see their own folly!"

People nodded. Gandhi sensed their approval. He noticed Herman in the front row nodding at him.

Gandhi looked up at the balconies and continued, "If needed, we shall fill their jails with all of our men! Let our cry of justice be heard around the world until they repeal this demeaning law at once!"

One man in the balcony stood up, "But who will support my family if I am in jail?"

Some people nodded and shouted, "Yes! Who?"

Gandhi nodded. "I am the father of four children myself. We all know that *alone* we are easy to break. If each person acts according to his own whims, we shall never be able to convince the government to repeal the shameful Act. But, if we join hands together, Muslims, Hindus, Sikhs, Chinese," he gestured at the Chinese delegation, "we could succeed. You tell me: can I trust the community that if I go to jail, you all shall join hands and feed my family?"

People nodded. Then the unthinkable happened. One person stood up in solidarity. Then another, then another. Soon the whole theatre stood up, quietly.

Gandhi looked at them. Apart from the constables and the reporters, everyone was standing. Their honor was expressed. Defended.

Gandhi nodded at everyone, excited, and gestured for them to sit down. Gandhi took his time looking at the crowds seated in the balconies, "We are together in this!" he looked at the man who had asked what would happen to his family if he were to go to jail. "Your family will be supported by the community. We will forget no one."

The man in the balcony looked at Gandhi approvingly.

Gandhi took a deep breath and finally looked at the resolution document in his hand. "Prior to the meeting, the elders of the community proposed the following resolutions. If you agree to them, we shall approve them, all of us together. If you disapprove, we shall amend them. We want everyone to be unanimous with our plea."

People were quiet as Gandhi read:

> "This meeting respectfully protests against the Asiatic Act and humbly requests the local and the imperial governments to withdraw the Asiatic Act. We declare that we find it manifestly in conflict with the past declarations of His Majesty; which recognizes no distinction between all members of the British Empire.

> If this denial is unacceptable, the Asiatic community demands that a judicial inquiry which is in conformity with the British system be held.
>
> This meeting hereby authorizes the British Indian Association to send a deputation to England in order to put the grievances of the Asiatic community before the imperial government."

Gandhi took a breath in and read slowly,

> "Should the Legislative Council, the local and the imperial governments reject the humble prayer of the Asiatic community against the Asiatic Act, every person present at the meeting solemnly and sincerely resolves that, rather than submit to this tyrannical law and abide by its un-British provisions, he will prefer to go to jail until the Act is repealed."

Gandhi looked at the audience. "Those in opposition, please stand up!"

He was tense as he looked around the room.

"Those in support," he shouted, "please stand up!"

And they stood. Everyone. Gandhi had tears in his eyes.

"With this," he shouted, "the resolution is accepted. Copies will be sent to the Colonial Secretary, General Smuts, and to His Majesty's Court. God save the King!"

Everyone replied, "God save the king!"

As he came down from the stage, Gandhi had a feeling of incredible apprehension. From now on, he knew, there would be no turning back.

Mahatma Gandhi in South Africa, c.1900.

ROME,
DECEMBER 1931

Tatiana looked at Gandhi. Though it happened a quarter of a century ago, he was still excited about it.

His eyes shone as he told her, "Soon I found myself taken, for the first time in my life, to visit His Majesty's palace."

Tatiana looked at him, not understanding.

"The prison," Gandhi smiled.

"Of course," Tatiana smiled back. "My father would have been so proud."

Gandhi smiled in appreciation. "To jail, I took one book with me. Guess which one?"

Tatiana smiled, "'The Kingdom of God'?"

Gandhi smiled, "Indeed! My greatest possession! When I left the jail after my first time I gave it as a present to my warden, Mr. Nelson was his name."

Tatiana sighed. "I remember my father being excited about the news from the Transvaal Colony. He felt like he was one of your people."

Gandhi nodded, "We *sensed* it. Everyone in my cell read the book, and we discussed it each evening." Gandhi's eyes became moist. "We spoke about the importance of not submitting to an unjust law; about the redemption in being on the right side of justice."

Tatiana said, "I remember my father speaking about the Transvaal. It was in 1906, in the winter, right?"

Gandhi looked at her, puzzled, "How did you remember?"

Tatiana hesitated, taking her time before speaking, "It was a difficult time for the family, and the news about the nonviolent resisters in the Transvaal was like a ray of light for my father."

Gandhi hesitated, "May I ask why was it a difficult time for the family?"

Tatiana pointed at a large photograph hung on the wall, framed in an elaborate golden frame: a woman in her mid-thirties looking to the right, daydreaming.

Gandhi looked at the picture and then at Tatiana.

She bit her lip. "My sister. Masha."

Masha Tolstoy, c. 1900.

Tatiana (left) and Masha (right), c. 1890.

SUKHOTIN ESTATE, OREL, RUSSIA NOVEMBER 1906

Years later Tatiana would remember where she was that day.

She was in the living room, reading. Sukhotin was away for the day on some governmental trip. Olga, the nanny, was with Tatiana's baby girl.

Tatiana had longed for a baby since her marriage began six years earlier. They had tried many times. Yet again and again, the baby had been stillborn. Four stillbirths.

Finally, on her fifth year of trying, Tatiana gave birth to a healthy baby, to her great surprise, and to the surprise of the whole family.

They named the baby girl Tatiana, on Mr. Sukhotin's insistence. But soon everyone began calling her Anya to differentiate her from her mother.

Anya was a sweet little baby girl, and the year that had passed since her birth was magical. Sophia, Masha, and Alexandra all came for a long vacation, and to help Tatiana with the baby. It was not the first grandchild—there were already 15 of them—but it was the first grandchild by one of the three daughters in the family. She was special.

Masha, too, had tried to give birth, but—like Tatiana—experienced three stillbirths. Seeing little Anya, Masha was overjoyed for her older sister. "Tatiana," she would say, "you did it! You gave birth to a beautiful soul!"

That day, when Anya was with the nanny, Tatiana heard a knock at the door, and the servant Nadya running to answer it.

She heard a manly voice, "I have a telegram for Mrs. Tatiana Sukhotin."

Tatiana got up and quickly walked to the door. A telegram?

Her immediate thought was 'Who is it?'

Was it her mother? Was it her father? She grabbed the small envelope from the man and opened the printed page, her hands shaking.

"To: Tatiana Tolstoy-Sukhotin

From: Alexandra Tolstoy"

Her eyes jumped to the message:

"Tanya, we need you. Masha. Sick. Come at once."

She raised her eyes from the telegram, meeting the

eyes of Nadya. "Masha!" Tatiana exclaimed to the servant.

The post office delivery man was outside, going back to his horse. Tatiana quickly calculated. To mount the horses and get them ready would take a half hour or so. She opened the door. "Wait! I need to come with you!"

The man looked puzzled, "I am sorry, Ma'am, but I need to return to the post office at once!"

"And I need to go to the train station. It's an emergency! I'll pay you twenty rubles!"

He looked at her, undecided.

Tatiana yelled, "Thirty rubles. Wait here. It will only take me a minute!"

She spoke to Nadya, "Quick, I need my suitcase."

Nadya nodded and ran to the bedroom.

Tatiana quickly left a note on her husband's desk, written with tears in her eyes and a trembling body, *'It's Masha. Sick. I left for Yasnaya. T.'*

She hurried to the nursery. Olga was there, rocking Anya, who was sleeping. Tatiana looked at Olga and whispered, "I need to go. I don't know for how long. Take care of her. Telegram me!"

Olga's eyes widened. "Yes, Tatiana."

Tatiana stroked little Anya's head, feeling the soft hair on her tender baby's head.

Then, she took her coat and boots, and Nadya came running with the suitcase.

As Tatiana left she gave Nadya one last glance, then

whispered to her, "Take care of Anya!"

Nadya nodded.

Tatiana looked at the man. "Go!"

Five hours later Tatiana arrived at Yasnaya Polyana. She prayed throughout the entire trip.

The porter of the estate came to help her down from the carriage and pay the driver. His face betrayed the situation.

Tatiana looked at him as she came out of the carriage. "Dear Abrasha! Am I too late?"

He shook his head 'no,' and hurried to help her with her suitcase. She ran in the snow toward the house. He followed her quickly. She turned to him sternly, "Abrasha! Don't let any visitors in!"

He nodded, "The Countess had already instructed that."

Tatiana opened the house door. The maid, Natasha, jumped at her, "Tatiana!"

"Where is she?"

"She is upstairs," the maid called after her.

Tatiana ran up the stairs. She saw two doctors conversing with one another in the hallway. They looked at her. She saw the look in their eyes as she passed them and walked into the room.

The first thing she saw was Masha covered in a blanket to her chin. Tatiana did not notice her parents, her sister Alexandra, or her two brothers Ilya and Sergey, nor Masha's husband, Obolensky. She only noticed Masha, looking pale as a ghost, and thin and sickly.

"Masha!" Tatiana exclaimed, tears running down her cheeks.

Masha's eyes were closed. She opened them, not understanding who was in front of her, "Tanya? You came?"

Tatiana hugged her little sister. She noticed how frail Masha was.

She looked at the people standing, "Why didn't you call me earlier?"

Alexandra murmured, "She only came here this morning, Obolensky says she was fine yesterday."

Tatiana noticed Masha's husband at the back of the bedroom. He mumbled, "She was coughing for several days, but there was an improvement—"

"Several days?!" Tatiana shrieked. She looked at her mother, "What have you given her?"

Sophia, pale and uncharacteristically quiet, murmured, "We gave her some tea with horseradish, and some compresses."

"With mustard?" Tatiana asked, nearly shouting.

"Yes," her mother said.

At that instant Masha began coughing loudly. Tatiana's ears sharpened. It sounded like Masha's lungs were filled with liquid.

Tatiana looked at her mother, "Bronchitis?"

Her mother motioned with her mouth, "They say Pneumonia."

Tatiana glanced at Masha laying in the bed, her eyes closed, and then looked at her mother, "She needs eucalyptus extract, and a bucket of hot water."

Alexandra, who had been quietly standing in the corner, said, "Tanya, Dr. Makovitsky says she needs rest."

"I *said*," Tatiana repeated her words, looking at the helpless gathering in the room, "I need eucalyptus extract! And a bucket of hot water!"

Alexandra nodded and left the room, "I'll get it."

Tatiana touched the wall, feeling how damp and chilled it was. She looked at her brothers, "We need to warm the house more. Load the fireplace downstairs with more wood. Use oil if you need. We need to warm the room! I want the room to sweat!"

Her two brothers nodded and left the room.

Masha moved her head slowly on her pillow, "Please don't fuss about me."

Tatiana ignored her. "Mama," she looked at Sophia, "I need elecampane. We'll mix some for her with hot water to drink. And also black radish!"

Her mother went to retrieve the items.

Tolstoy looked grim. Tatiana looked at him, she knew he would be helpless with most tasks. "Papa, stay at her bedside, and massage her hands."

Her father, without a word, kneeled down and did as he was told.

Tatiana looked at Obolensky and pointed at Masha, "Massage her other hand. Later the feet, we need to stimulate her blood!"

Obolensky nodded and began massaging Masha's other hand.

Tatiana took a deep breath and exited the room. She walked to Dr. Makovitsky and his assistant.

"I'm listening!" she said.

Dr. Makovitsky sighed, "I already told your parents."

Tatiana gave him a glaring look.

He swallowed and said, "It does not look good. Her lungs are flooded. There are signs of inflammation. At least we were able to take down her fever. She had vomited twice—"

"Vomited?!" Tatiana was horrified, "Why didn't anyone tell me?"

The doctor shrugged. His eyes were sad. "Her sputum…." He breathed in, "it's rust-colored."

Tatiana grabbed his hand, "Dr. Makovitsky! We need to do everything we can! I believe she can still get out of it!"

Dr. Makovitsky nodded and tried to smile reassuringly, but she could tell that his heart was not in it.

They heard coughing coming from Masha's room.

The following three days were a blur to Tatiana. She watched her sister slowly wilt before her eyes. Her mother could not stand to watch, and ran through the house yelling at the servants. Her father sat beside Masha for hours on end, eventually climbing into bed with her and hugging her.

Masha's convulsions became worse and worse. On the second day she began spitting up blood. Her skin became blue-tinged, especially around the fingers and nose.

Tatiana relentlessly tried everything, massages, liquids, compresses… everything.

Obolensky could also not stand being there, and was hard to communicate with, speaking in half sentences, looking dazed.

On the fourth day, late at night, Masha's body gave up.

Tatiana was lying on a mattress near the bed, dozing in and out of sleep, when her father began crying, holding Masha in his arms.

Tatiana sat up at once, "Papa?"

Her father said nothing, sobbing quietly in his daughter's arms. He mumbled, "Oh God! Take me, God, not her!"

Tatiana reached and touched Masha's hands. They were cold. Tatiana screamed, "Doctor! Mama!"

The following weeks were unbearable.

Tatiana remained at Yasnaya Polyana.

Everyone seemed to lose their ability to speak. The house was quiet.

At one point, Tatiana even hoped her parents would argue about something. That would be better than the unbearable silence.

But her parents did not fight.

If anyone *did* speak their words were whispered, as if someone was sleeping.

The only ray of hope in the household was baby Anya, whom Sukhotin had brought, along with the nanny Nadya and the maid Olga. Little Anya was just beginning to stand and kept falling down. She filled the house with giggles and laughter, unaware of what happened.

Sophia slept in her room most of the day. She kept the green shutters and curtains closed. She was crying to God often about the cruelty of taking a daughter from her mother in her prime.

Tatiana heard these cries from her room and shivered.

Her father had buried himself in writing. *"The Law of Love and the Law of Violence,"* his new manuscript. He asked Tatiana to read it.

It was yet another work that Tatiana found hard to praise. It felt to her as if he had already written these words and thoughts in *all* of his other books: the principles of nonviolence, the attack on the Church, the re-examination of Jesus' writings.

As she was reading it in the drawing room, her father played with little Anya. He made faces, tickled her, hugged her and carried her on his back through the house.

Tatiana found it difficult to concentrate on the stale manuscript. She watched as Anya laughed; she watched as Anya pulled on her grandfather's white beard; she watched as her daughter fell asleep in her grandfather's arms.

Tatiana wanted to be happy for her daughter, seeing just how happy she was.

But for some odd reason she could not.

An uncomfortable feeling crept into her heart. She could not find any better word to describe it but *jealousy*. She kept brushing those thoughts away. But they came creeping back again and again. How *she'd* dreamed of having her father pay attention to her, play with her, walk with her, hug her and talk to her.

But Tolstoy seemed to be more interested in his granddaughter than in his daughter. And if he *was* interested in his daughter, it was mostly to solicit compliments from her regarding his writing. Which Tatiana found hard to give.

Tatiana wanted to return home badly. She missed Sukhotin, who did his best to take the long train ride and join her every weekend. But it was not only his presence that she missed. It was her new life. Her own place under the sun. Her refuge.

Yet she stayed in Yasnaya Polyana. The weeks became months as she helped to bring the house back to order. Her mother slowly came out of her room. The snow began melting, and the birds began chirping outside.

Her father gave his new manuscript to his publisher, Chertkov, and then started on yet another book.

Tatiana helped Alexandra with the piles of letters and paperwork. These days there were over a hundred letters arriving by mail each day, not only from Russia, but from around the world.

Many of the letters, however, were not exactly *supportive*. Christians who viewed Tolstoy's works as blasphemous cursed the old man, wishing for him to die.

These letters Tatiana and Alexandra hid from their father.

Other writers tried *arguing* with Tolstoy. Some argued that while indeed there was some truth to nonviolence, there still must be some exceptions to the rule, must there not?

One such letter came from the publisher of a newspaper called *"Free Hindustan."* The author, a Hindu named Mr. Tarak, tried to convince Tolstoy that in the case of India, violence led by the oppressed Hindus was only legitimate, given the oppressive British rule. Mr. Tarak asked Tolstoy to support the movement for independence in India, and to justify the occasional use of tactical violence on the side of the Indians against their oppressors.

Tatiana frowned at the letter. While she did not put it in the letters to be hidden from her father, she did put it in the pile of unimportant letters.

That afternoon, like all other afternoons, Tatiana and

Alexandra joined their father in his study and went over the letters together.

Tatiana and Alexandra separated the letters into three piles: the short pile of important letters, the medium pile of unimportant letters, and the third pile, by far the highest one, of words of flattery to their father regarding his early literary works.

Tolstoy always dismissed the last pile. He would not say anything, but with a brisk hand movement would signal to his daughters to put the letters away.

After they had gone over the small important pile, Tatiana quickly gave an overview of the unimportant pile.

"Wait," said Tolstoy, "tell me more about this Indian."

Tatiana pulled the letter out. "His name is Mr. Tarak—"

Alexandra jumped, "I think he had written to us before, Papa? Asking for your endorsement of the violent independence movement in India."

Tatiana nodded, "That's exactly what he is asking now."

Tolstoy hit his fist on the desk, "These Indians will simply not get it!"

Tatiana looked at Alexandra, bewildered. Her little sister shrugged her shoulders.

"They are falling into the stupid behavior of the Europeans!" Tolstoy continued and stood up, "While they *themselves* have the great tradition of Krishna and the Buddha.... Violence will lead them nowhere! They must liberate themselves from *within first!*"

Tatiana looked at the next letter in the pile, "This, Papa, is from a Russian arguing about the importance of military service, stating that if Russia would have no army, then—"

"Wait," Tolstoy said, upset, "I was not done Tanya! Give me that letter from the Hindu."

Tatiana handed him the letter.

He read through it quietly.

Tatiana heard little Anya crying somewhere in the house and stood up to leave.

Tolstoy looked at her, "Where are you going? I was in the middle!"

"Papa, little Anya is crying—"

"She has a nanny doesn't she? I was not done!"

Tatiana sighed and sat down.

Tolstoy continued, "I must explain to him, and to all of India, that they must follow the teachings of Christ, and their own teachers, and be wise rather than foolish! Imagine," he looked at Alexandra and Tatiana, "if India could get rid of colonialism and oppression in a *nonviolent* way, what a light it could shine on the world! Everyone could then learn from India! The Negroes in America, the oppressed all over Africa and Asia, even within Russia we could...."

Tatiana closed her eyes. His words were tiring for her. Perhaps it was time to go – she was beginning to feel she was losing her mind.

The following day she packed her belongings and bid farewell to her parents and sister. Alexandra was now the only sibling still living at home at the age of 23. Their father was nearing his 80th birthday and relied on her assistance.

Frankly, Tatiana could not see how her little sister could do it. She remembered how difficult it was for her when she was young, and now at age 42 it was unbearable. She could not stand her father's tyranny and her mother's pathetic cries for attention. No. This was her *past*. And she wanted to put it behind her.

As she was packing her belongings with her maid Olga, she heard her parents arguing in the dining room.

'Good,' Tatiana thought, 'it means that things are back to normal.'

Little Anya was playing with her nanny. Tatiana made her way through the house, saying farewell to her sister and then to the servants. She then came to kiss her father goodbye in his study.

Her father looked at her with dismay, "Why must you leave me again?"

Tatiana smiled, "I will be back soon, Papa!"

"Well, you can leave, Tanya. You are of no use." He looked away.

She tried to ignore his comment, "Thank you, Papa. Take care as well."

Then, as she was exiting the room, her father turned to her, "But do leave little Anya with us!"

Tatiana quickly exited the room exclaiming, "We will return soon Papa!"

She went to her mother in her mother's bedroom. She kissed her on the hand and said, "Keep sane, Mama!"

"I am trying, Tanya," her mother said lamentingly, "God knows I am trying."

As the carriage left Yasnaya Polyana, Tatiana sighed in relief. She had missed her own life, her own house. She smiled at little Anya and murmured, "Spring is here, Anyushka."

How she had wished Masha could have witnessed it.

Masha Tolstoy with her father Leo, c.1905.

ROME,
DECEMBER 1931

Gandhi said quietly, "I am so sorry to hear that. It must have been so horribly difficult to lose her."

Tatiana tried to smile, "Sooner or later we all go. But she was my father's favorite, so it was especially hard for him."

Gandhi was taken aback, "I do not suppose that she was more favored than—"

"Oh she was. His favorite. He said it himself often. And he wrote it too, in his diary."

Gandhi gulped. This did not fit with his impression of Tolstoy. "I... am... sorry to hear that."

"No," Tatiana stiffened, "the truth—the naked truth—is always the best, is it not?"

Gandhi nodded slowly.

Tatiana sighed, "After her death things were quiet for a time, but then my mother became ill."

"Ill?" Gandhi asked. He thought that Sophia Tolstoy died a decade or so *after* her husband.

"Yes," Tatiana answered, "but not in a physical sense. She became ill... mentally...."

"Oh," Gandhi murmured, "I am sorry to learn that."

"My father was sorry too," Tatiana said coldly, "his last two years were unbearable." She hesitated for a moment and then said, "What do you know of Vladimir Chertkov?"

Gandhi shrugged his shoulders, "Only that he was your father's publisher and promoter of your father's writings."

"Right," Tatiana sighed, "that too. But he became my father's best friend. And the more my father spent time with Chertkov, the more my mother retreated into her own world, imagining conspiracies, even suspecting a romantic relationship between the two."

Gandhi looked down, "So... unfortunate to hear that."

Tatiana was quiet.

Gandhi realized how little he really knew of Tolstoy. He had heard of some strains between Tolstoy and his wife, but even so found it hard to believe that Tolstoy, the loving wise sage, would have had a troubled marriage.

He began realizing that the picture was more complicated than he had imagined.

Tatiana smiled, "You see, Mohandas," she pronounced his name slowly, "things are sometimes more complex than they might appear to the outside world."

Gandhi nodded, "I presume that."

He expected Tatiana to go on speaking, but she was quiet. She looked at the clock and asked, "Are you certain that it is fine that you are staying here for so long?"

"Oh it is my pleasure, Mrs. Tol—" he corrected himself, "Tatiana."

Tatiana smiled. "So, how did you come to write to my father in the first place?"

"Well, that is the question, is it not? I had wanted to write to him for years... The nonviolent campaign which we led to abolish the terrible Asiatic Act was taking longer than I expected. I was jailed several times for 'incitement.' Many Indians in the Transvaal Colony were put in jail. And they all looked up to me. I guess," he sighed, "that I had envisioned a brief campaign, with a swift victory."

Tatiana nodded. "And it was not to be...?"

Gandhi shook his head. "We began it in 1906. Three years later, the terrible Act was still in place, many people were in jail, including some European gentlemen supporting our cause. It was hard for the community to take care of all of the families whose fathers were incarcerated...."

Gandhi looked sad. He shrugged his shoulders, "I guess I was wondering whether this method of nonviolence, was *practical*. It seemed as if the world had forgotten about us—"

"Certainly not," Tatiana said, "we heard news about

the Indians in the Transvaal all the way in Russia."

"Yes," Gandhi said, "but no *progress* was made. The government insisted on breaking us. And at one point I was about to give up...."

Tatiana raised her eyebrows. Gandhi? The great Indian activist? Give up?

Gandhi, age 40, 1909.

PHOENIX SETTLEMENT, NATAL COLONY, SOUTH AFRICA, JULY 1909

Gandhi was happy to be home after a three-month jail sentence performing hard labor. And this was the third time he had been incarcerated.

The first time he went to jail, it all seemed grand. It was exciting. He felt that he was standing up for his rights. For freedom. For his values. For justice.

The second time it was less exciting, and the prisoners were forced into hard labor.

And now, returning once again, he was exhausted, gaunt, and perhaps worst of all, began to doubt his commitment to this plan.

Kasturba, too, was unhappy. Not only had her husband been gone for a long period, but he was planning to leave again, in a week, for several *months*. He had been assigned to travel to England as the representative of the Indian community. Their task was to convince the British government to repeal the Asiatic Act.

Kasturba was especially bothered by the fact that her husband did not even know if he would be able to meet the people in power, nor how long this trip would be.

"Why do you need to do all this?" Kasturba lamented to her husband at night.

They were lying in bed, and Gandhi was quiet. This was his first day home, and it was not exactly the homecoming he had expected. Kasturba was sour all day. She was not cordial to the many visitors from the community who had come to welcome him home.

Kasturba was upset, "Soon, Mohan, your sons will forget you are their *father*!"

Gandhi said nothing.

Kasturba began crying, "It is *difficult* for me, Mohan. Think of me! Think of your family!"

Gandhi nodded and stroked her arm.

Kasturba continued, "Medvev Kapur's wife came here after she received the news of his death."

Gandhi nodded silently. Medvev Kapur, one of the activists, died in jail a month before. Gandhi, upon hearing it, was devastated. He could not eat for several days, wondering if he was responsible for the death of that man.

"She screamed at me," Kasturba continued, "yelling that Mohandas Gandhi had killed her husband! That you, with your"—she hesitated for a moment, picking her words carefully—"unwise doctrine, forced people to go to jail...."

"I forced no one to do anything." Gandhi murmured.

"I know, Mohan, but it is people's *lives* that you are meddling with. Could Medvev really *choose* to do what he wished? Had he relented and got that stupid pass from the British, don't you realize the community would have turned their backs on him?"

Gandhi was quiet. He had thought similar thoughts in recent weeks. The responsibility on his shoulders was more than he could bear.

Kasturba sighed, "Why won't you just tell everyone that you have *tried*, and that it is not worth people's lives?"

"But it's our dignity, Kasturba."

"Mohandas Gandhi!" Kasturba reproached him, "In that way you have become exactly like the British! You sound like them! You care more about your 'dignity' than about the well-being of your family, of your community!"

Gandhi bit his tongue. These were harsh words. He realized the entire burden had fallen on his wife's shoulders, including the allegations about her husband 'sending people to die.' He took a deep breath, "It must have been difficult for you, to see Mrs. Kapur...."

"It was terrible," Kasturba murmured, "she screamed at the children, too. 'Your father is a murderer!'" Kasturba sighed. "It was terrible."

Gandhi kept stroking her arm. "I am sorry," he said finally. "I am so... so... sorry...."

He began weeping quietly.

Kasturba took him in her arms. "My dear Mohan," she whispered, "my good dear foolish Mohan...."

The following days many men came to consult with Gandhi. He had also paid a visit to the Kapur family, and saw some of the people who gotten wounded in the peaceful rally organized in his absence.

In the evenings Gandhi spoke with his wife. "I don't know what to do. Sometimes I think it would be best for us to leave. We can go back to India. Or to England. It can be good for the boys if we move to England. They could get proper education there. My old friend Doctor Mehta invited us there. Perhaps we should leave here."

Kasturba could see her husband was not in his right mind.

Four days after having returned home, Gandhi whispered to Kasturba at night, "I am thinking of calling the campaign off."

To his surprise, his wife, who had been trying to convince him of doing so, said, "And letting the government win?"

Gandhi was taken aback by her comment. "I thought you wanted me to quit the campaign. I thought you—"

"I want you to do what is right," Kasturba said. "I

want you to do what is right according to your heart."

Gandhi was on the verge of tears, "But I don't know any more what is right! People are dying because of me, people are abused, families are broken! There are now two thousand people in jail, Kasturba! I cannot go on this way!"

Kasturba was quiet. "Have you tried to consult with someone?"

"That is all I do all day! Consult and consult!"

"No, with someone from outside the community."

"Herman is in jail; they would not let me see him—"

"No," Kasturba sighed, "from *outside*. How about that author, Ruska was his name?"

"Ruskin," Gandhi corrected her, "John Ruskin. He died."

"I see." Kasturba said, "You had always said you wanted to write to him."

"I know. But it is too late."

Kasturba whispered, "Then you should write to Tolstoy. You speak of him all the time. Ask him."

Gandhi laughed quietly, "Tolstoy! What... How can... Tolstoy is *busy*! And he is *old*, he must be..." he calculated in his mind, "he must be 80 by now!"

"Well, he could still read your letter and tell you what he—"

Gandhi snorted, "You do not understand! He has just written another book, '*The Law of Love and the Law of Violence.*' He might be writing another book as we speak. He does not have time to read letters, nonetheless to respond!"

Kasturba shook her head, "You said the same of Ruskin, and then he died, Mohan. This Tolstoy of yours is still alive."

"But I hear he is sick—"

"All the better then! Before he dies. You should get his opinion. Did not the whole nonviolent idea come from him?"

Gandhi was quiet, "Yes, but... I cannot write to him!"

"Why not, Mohan?"

Gandhi sensed how upset he was. He noticed the irritation growing in his chest, tingling throughout his body. Why were her words angering him so much?

He breathed in, "Kasturba, you just don't understand these things."

"All I understand," Kasturba said quietly, "is that when you receive a letter from someone consulting with you, you become pleased—"

"But he is a great author, the greatest—"

"Just answer my question, Mohan: do you become pleased when someone wishes to consult with you?"

"I suppose," Gandhi said reluctantly.

"Then he must respond the same way," she paused thoughtfully, "Do not let the opportunity slip away. He is old, and if you do not muster the courage to write to him now you will be sorry for it later."

Gandhi breathed heavily, sensing the weight of his wife's words, "I can't...." he whispered.

Kasturba smiled, "You are a courageous man, Mohan. You were not afraid to go to jail. Why are you afraid then of writing Tolstoy? Write to him, I pray you. And send him also that biography the Englishman has written about you."

"Which?" Gandhi asked, "Doke's '*An Indian Patriot in South Africa*'?"

"Yes!" Kasturba laughed.

Gandhi sat up, irritated. A year earlier an Englishman who had met Gandhi offered to write a short biography about him. Copies of the book were now sitting in Gandhi's office. He knew he could not send them to people, knowing that it would not be humble and rather boastful of him to send a book about himself.

Gandhi looked at his wife, "Kasturba, you simply do not understand *anything!*"

Kasturba, sensing her husband's irritation, laughed, "Or is it you, Mohandas Gandhi, who does not understand?"

Three days later Gandhi was all packed. It was heart-wrenching for him to say goodbye to his wife and four sons, for a few months, just having returned a week earlier from three months in jail. But he had to do it. If not for himself or for his family, then for the community, who was paying for his travels, believing in him as the possible savior of the community.

As he approached the door to kiss his sons' goodbye, Kasturba asked him, "Have you taken some copies of the book that Englishman wrote about you?"

Gandhi thought his wife to be impossible. "Kasturba!" he exclaimed, "It is not how Europeans work. If I go around giving that book to people it would be considered untactful, distasteful! Boastful!"

Kasturba disappeared into his study. She returned with three copies in her hands of J. J. Doke's *'M. K. Gandhi: An Indian Patriot in South Africa.'* She opened his suitcase and placed the copies there.

He looked at her disapprovingly. She kissed him on his forehead and whispered, "You take care. I already miss you."

Gandhi's face twisted, trying not to cry.

Gandhi proceeded to hug his four sons, standing in a line near the door, 21-year-old Harilal, 17-year-old Manilal, 12-year-old Ramdas, and 9-year-old Devdas.

His eyes watered as he hugged them and kissed each one several times on each cheek.

The other members of the Phoenix Settlement bid him farewell. The farm was not the same without him, but unfortunately, they had become used to it. For the past three years, since the beginning of the nonviolent campaign, he was often gone, either arrested or travelling for several weeks at a time to the Transvaal Colony up north.

Followed by his sons to the main road, Gandhi, with his one suitcase, took a carriage to Durban. From there he took the long overnight train to Cape Town.

On the train, he sat in the third class compartment. This, however, was no longer a nuisance to him as it was in the past. On the contrary, now he felt kinship with the poor, most of whom were Negroes. Opening Tolstoy's new book, Gandhi felt like he was practicing what the old sage had preached. He smiled kindly to the others as the train made its way to the west coast.

Arriving in Cape Town the following morning, the tired Gandhi bought a newspaper before walking to the port for the afternoon steamer that would take him on the ten-day journey to London.

He had mixed feelings. He had studied in London twenty years earlier. It was his beloved city. There he had matured, become a conscious vegetarian, met Indians preaching for the future independence of India. There he read his own culture's ancient writings for the first time: The *Bhagavad Gita*, the *Vedas* and other ancient texts. There, in the foreign land, he learned to be proud of his heritage, while at the same time trying, as best he could to become a proper Englishman. He even took some dance classes and learned to waltz.

But now the London he was headed toward was the seat of the injustices against his own people. And although Gandhi and others had tried repeatedly to change the unjust laws, the voices which came from London were dim, distant, and cold.

They offered sympathy. But not justice.

He wanted *justice*.

Not only for the Indians of South Africa, but for all

Indians. In motherland India as well.

He walked to the store with a coin of three pence, the late Queen's image minted on it. He reached for the newspaper.

And then he saw the headline.

He paled at once.

> "Political Assassination in London; Colonel William Curzon, British Advisor to the Secretary for India, Murdered by a Hindu Nationalist"

Gandhi leaned against the newspaper rack, overwhelmed.

> "At a reception held at the Imperial Institute yesterday Colonel Sir Curzon Wyllie was shot five times by a Hindu student who approached the Colonel, killing him instantly. The crime had evidently been premeditated, as in the possession of the student were found two fully loaded revolvers, a dagger, and a knife."

Gandhi's eyes began to tear. A Hindu student?

> "The murderer, named Madan Lal Dhingra, appears to have engaged Sir Curzon Wyllie in conversation, and then suddenly to have drawn his revolver and fired five shots at him. He then attempted to shoot himself. In his excitement, however, he miscalculated the number of shots, and the revolver aimed at his own head snapped without explosion. Two bystanders at once seized and disarmed him.
>
> Sir Curzon Wyllie had a very distinguished career, his last office in India being that of Resident in the West Rajputana States. At the

time of his death he held the position of political aide-de-camp to Lord Morley, Secretary for India.

Lord Chamberlain of the Household said last night, "If the perpetrators and instigators of outrages of this kind think they are going to destroy British rule in India, or drive the British people into panic-stricken reprisals, they are very much mistaken. Neither the British people, the British Government, nor the able and devoted Indians will be deflected by one hair's-breadth from their duty by the fear of death."

Lord Chamberlain further added that "We shall continue to govern India in the interests of the governed, and shall neither be frightened into granting the fanatics what they want, or what they think they want."

The murderer is said to have been affiliated with the "India House" established four years ago in Highgate, London, as the convention place of Indian radicals. The police continue to investigate the murder. The Daily Telegraph expresses the deepest possible sympathy for Lady Wyllie, who was in the building when the murder took place."

Overwhelmed, Gandhi walked to the nearby bench and sat down. He covered his face with his hands and cried. He wept for Sir Curzon Wiley. He wept for Mrs. Wiley. He wept for the Indian people, for the Hindu student's family, and even for the Hindu student himself, for having chosen the wrong path.

Finally, he wept for himself.

With this happening a week before his arrival in

London, he knew that the South African Indian case would not be well received.

Ten-days later, upon his arrival in London, Gandhi settled in the cheapest room in the Westminster Hotel. His first visit was to his friend Dr. Mehta, who had welcomed Gandhi in London twenty years earlier.

Gandhi visited Dr. Mehta in his large and fine house. The two passed some memories and inquired about each other's families.

Dr. Mehta admitted, "I have been following your career closely, I often read 'The Indian Opinion', and I am fascinated by your courage to speak the truth as it is."

Gandhi smiled, "Thank you. It means a lot to me hearing it from you."

Dr. Mehta smiled, "Well, what do you intend to accomplish in London?"

"I will try to educate members of the government about the cause of the Indian people in South Africa and ask them to repeal the Asiatic Act."

Dr. Mehta nodded, "I assume you have read about Sir Wiley's assassination?"

Gandhi nodded.

"You realize that now, with the assassination, you are unlikely to encounter open doors?"

Gandhi sighed, "I know. But I shall do what I can. I also wish to speak to these Hindu young men. I shall go promptly to the 'India House' and speak to the—"

"India House?! Have you gone mad? Those are just young hoodlums there, bringing shame upon the Indian people! Upon their brothers!"

Gandhi smiled, "True, but they *are* our brothers. I shall try and convince them that their method is not wise and—"

"Mohandas! The British government will associate you with them!"

Gandhi sighed, "The British government can do as it pleases. I have already spent much time in jail defending my beliefs. Now I believe we must not desert these students, or else, they will further lose themselves in the wrong direction."

Dr. Mehta opened his eyes disapprovingly, "You have some strange ideas, Mohandas...."

The following day Gandhi visited the *India House* and after introducing himself, asked for permission to give a lecture about nonviolence. Reluctantly, the manager, a young man called Gopal scheduled a talk for him the following evening.

Gandhi was excited when he returned to the *India House* for his talk. In the main room there gathered some thirty young men. They were mostly in their twenties, and he was now a 40-year-old. Yet he saw himself in them, and them in him.

The lecture, however, was more difficult than he had anticipated. Soon after he began talking, one of them interrupted him, shouting, "Your methods are wrong!

We've been nonviolent for two hundred years, and what have we got? The British oppression is only deepening! The British only want to diminish us!"

The other young men cheered in agreement.

Gandhi tried responding, "When you say 'The British' you oversimplify, young man. I am sure that there are *some* British who indeed want to 'diminish us', but many of them sincerely want the best interest of the Indian people—"

Another young man jumped, "It only *seems* that way," he said, "but they do nothing unselfishly! Those who are supposedly *for* the Indians are so only for the time being!"

Gandhi took a deep breath in, "Again, you do not know that to be certain. I myself know several well-meaning and honest British—"

"Who will stab you in the back when you are not looking!" said one of the young men, "My father was shot by a British soldier! And that soldier was never even taken to court for murder! For leaving a family of seven children without a father and a wife without her husband!"

Gandhi nodded sadly. He paused. "I am sorry to hear that."

The young man looked away, not looking Gandhi in the eyes. Gandhi looked around the room, thinking of how he could reach these young men. "I understand your anger at the British. Yet violence and assassinations would not expel the British from India."

"You don't know that for sure!" one of them shouted.

Gandhi smiled a sad smile, "Well, should the British leave in consequence of such murderous acts, who will rule in their place?"

"We will!" shouted another, "The Indian people!"

Gandhi spoke slowly, "From what you are saying, I deduce you think that everyone with an Indian skin is good? And that every Englishman is bad because he is simply an Englishman?"

Some of them nodded. Some, however, could see Gandhi's cynical remark for what it was.

"India," Gandhi continued, "can gain nothing from the rule of murderers—no matter the color of their skin. This violent direction would be the wrong direction to go. The rule that it would lead to would leave India utterly ruined and laid waste, because of your good intentions, wrongfully directed."

Silence followed.

Gandhi looked in their young eyes. "I know you mean well. But no act of treachery can ever profit a nation."

The one who had lost his father stood up, "Well, tell us then: if your nonviolence approach is so successful, why do we hear of our brothers in South Africa sitting in jail? And why do we hear that the oppression only grows there?"

Gandhi sighed, "You are right. I have not much to show you as to the benefit of the method I propose. But I know that on this path of nonviolence at least I can sleep peacefully at night, be it at home or in jail. Which I am afraid that your friend, the murderer of Sir Wiley, cannot."

That night Gandhi returned to the hotel depressed.

Having difficulty falling asleep, he rose and wrote a letter to Herman:

> "To: Herman Kallenbach,
>
> Volkhurst Prison, Transvaal Colony,
>
> South Africa
>
>
> Dear Herman,
>
> I think of you often. I assume that by the time you receive this letter there will remain only a month for your stay in prison. Nevertheless, I hope that you find it strengthening.
>
> I arrived in London three days ago, and have not given myself sufficient sleep yet. I have met Dr. Mehta, a very old and staunch friend.
>
> I have made it a point to see Indians here of every shade of opinion. Opposed as I am to violence in any shape or form, I have endeavored specially to come into contact with the so-called extremists. This I have done in order if possible to convince them of the error of their ways.
>
> Visiting their 'India House' this evening, I have noticed that some of the members of this party have an earnest spirit and great intellectual ability. They are certainly unsparing in their emotional devotion to the matter.

One of them spoke up to me with a view to convince me that I was wrong in our methods and that nothing but the use of violence, covert or open or both, was likely to bring about redress of the wrongs the British undertake.

Unfortunately, my attempts to convince them of our methods did not yield fruit. I could see in these young men an awakening of the national consciousness. But among them it is in a crude shape and there is not a corresponding spirit of self-sacrifice. I have noticed impatience of British Rule. The hatred of the whole race is virulent. The British statesmen are supposed to do nothing unselfishly. Distrust of British statesmen is writ large on their minds.

None of these young people disapprove of violence. Unfortunately, I have practically met no one who believes that India can ever become free without resorting to violence.

I have called on several government offices yesterday and today. It seems my mission might be even more difficult than I had presumed. Nevertheless, I hope to somehow be able to at least meet with the Leader of the House of Lords.

I do hope to write back with more cheerful news in my next letter.

Yours,

Mohandas"

ROME,
DECEMBER 1931

Tatiana looked at Gandhi with appreciation. She was beginning to understand how difficult his struggle was not only with the British, but also within his own community.

She hesitated, but then said, "Then, twenty years ago, when you came to England you had not accomplished what you hoped for. And now, coming to Rome after your Round Table Talks in London, again, you had not accomplished what you hoped for, or am I wrong?"

Gandhi smiled, "Some battles are of a longer span than a few days, or months, or even decades. One must have patience."

Tatiana pressed, "But do you really believe that the British will one day just... *leave* India?"

Gandhi smiled, "I believe they will leave their *holding*

of India. Many British will remain in India, but the regime must become democratic, with the rule of the majority."

"And this could happen without violence?"

Gandhi nodded, "Without a drop of blood."

Tatiana looked at him, wondering if he was merely a dreamer?

Gandhi continued, "What we tend to forget is that our enemy is human. For the Indians, the British are human. No British person would want to rule an entire nation if we could *show* that person the wrongdoing and the injustice of their rule."

Tatiana nodded. "Which is why you launched the salt campaign last year?"

Gandhi smiled, "I keep trying to find creative ways to attract the attention of the British to the wrongdoings that they themselves commit. The tax on salt in India is one of the most illegitimate taxes there could be, as it mostly burdens the poor, of which we have many in India." He sighed, "But when trying to draw the attention to the wrongdoing, one must do it out of love, not out of hatred. Hatred could only harbor more hatred."

Tatiana wished to believe him. "But surely you must have *some* contempt! How about toward that Colonel Dyer of theirs? Didn't he just massacre hundreds of innocent Hindus?"

Gandhi sighed.

Tatiana squinted, looking at him carefully, "Could you say that you have love toward *him?*"

Gandhi took a deep breath. "I hate what he *did*. I hate it *terribly*! But I try not to hate *him*. Your father taught that to me, 'Hate the sin, not the sinner.' Your father would meet hatred by love and self-suffering!"

This was Tatiana's turn to sigh. Was Gandhi really talking of her *father*? Her father, who had once left her mother, right when she was due to give birth, and run away? Her father, who had insulted everyone, *everyone*, with his sharp and demeaning comments?

Tatiana smiled, "I believe my father would have been very happy to see you practicing these ideals."

Gandhi's eyes lit, "Would he?"

Tatiana nodded.

Gandhi suddenly began crying. Tatiana found it a little odd.

"You…" Gandhi mumbled, "You have no idea what it means to me to hear it from you…."

Tatiana found it strange that her words could mean so much to this world-renowned leader. "I'm afraid you do not understand what *you*, Mohandas, meant to my father."

Gandhi shook his head disapprovingly, "Now you are just being kind to me…."

"No," Tatiana smiled, "you need to realize, he thought he was surrounded by fools and that most of his followers were imbeciles—"

"Did he *say* that?" Gandhi wondered out loud.

"Oh yes," Tatiana smiled.

Tatiana Tolstoy, 75, 1939.

YASNAYA POLYANA, RUSSIA, SEPTEMBER 1909

Tatiana did not really want to go back to Yasnaya Polyana. Although she missed her parents and her sister Alexandra, life there was untenable.

Her mother insisted, writing to her, "Surely you will come to our 47th wedding anniversary on September 23rd. We have not seen little Anya in ages. And your father would be very upset if you did not come. Also, Tanya, this will be the last opportunity to enjoy the summer before winter comes. I expect your attendance."

Sukhotin insisted too. "Your father is not in the best of health. We must not miss an opportunity to see him. And it will make your mother happy, too."

Tatiana reluctantly acquiesced, knowing full well that each previous visit had ended in disaster.

The family of three along with their two maids took the carriage from the Tula train station. As the carriage trudged through the birch trees, the uneasy feeling of returning to her childhood home began to grow.

The feast was planned for that afternoon. The atmosphere in the house was festive; her father seemed happy, and immediately took little Anya to tour the house with him. He listened to her stories about the train ride, and marveled at her speech.

Meanwhile, Sophia grabbed Tatiana's arm and took her aside, revealing to her daughter the "secret" news. Her father's assistant, Chertkov, was trying to have her father sign a new will, which disowned the family of all of the rights to her father's writings.

"Mama," Tatiana said firmly, "I do not wish to get involved—"

"Well sooner or later you will have to, Tanya! You cannot be an ostrich burying its head in the ground!"

But that was *exactly* what Tatiana had wished to be.

The anniversary feast, luckily enough, went well. That is, if you do not count the argument between Tolstoy and his wife. Tolstoy expressed that the meal was too lavish and festive. Sophia answered that it was a mandatory part of the celebration. Tolstoy then groaned something in response. Then Sophia shouted, "Do you want to say it out loud so that we could all hear?" Tatiana exclaimed, "Mama! Papa! Can't we just eat like a normal family?"

After the meal her father took her upstairs. "Oh, Tanya! I have been missing you!"

"Really, Papa?"

"Oh yes! With recent events in the world I find it hard to sleep at night."

As they entered the study, Tatiana longed for him to ask her about her life, about her marriage, about her daughter, about her health... anything that had to do with *her*.

Her father sat in his chair. "Look at Spain, Tanya. Hundreds of anti-war activists were killed in demonstrations by the Spanish army. And in Britain, the first political assassination in the past thirty years! And by whom? By a Hindu!"

Tatiana tried to seem interested.

"Don't tell me you hadn't heard, Tanya!"

"Papa, I have a daughter to take care of, and a husband, and a household...."

Tolstoy looked at her disapprovingly, "Since when did you become so... bourgeois? You used to care about the world Tanya!"

"I do care, Papa!" Tanya retorted.

Her father waved his hand, "I predicted this assassination!"

Tatiana looked unimpressed.

"Oh yes, Tanya! I have written to an Indian newspaper that had asked me for my *support* of their nationalistic aims and of violence! I wrote a long, twenty-page response for the editor of that newspaper, explaining to him *clearly* what the Hindus *ought* to do! And I haven't heard a thing from him!"

Tatiana sighed, "Papa, he had asked for your *support*, that is all. You shouldn't have bothered yourself with writing so much. Of course he is not going to publish it if it is against his own philosophy!"

"I shouldn't have 'bothered myself'?" Tolstoy asked, his eyes growing large.

Tatiana embraced herself. She knew that look all too well.

"I shouldn't have *bothered myself?*" Her father repeated the sentence, "Of course! I should have just kept silent at seeing how the world is falling apart, and not share the little that I have learned and know to be true! Of course!"

"Papa! I didn't say that!"

"Then what did you say, Tanya? You want me to lock myself in the house, like you do, to show no interest in the world, and to live my content life, like an ostrich with its head in the ground, while other people are suffering?"

Tatiana sighed. He was talking exactly like her mother. They were both mad. She was not willing to have this conversation. She was not a girl anymore. She was 45-years-old. She did not *have* to listen to this. She stood up.

"Where are you going?"

"To see if little Anya needs me."

"Sure! Go ahead! Leave the old fool!" her father exclaimed, "You and the rest of the world! I give my heart to you, and I receive nothing but contempt! I can choose between either the blind followers on one side or contemptuous children on the other! This is my lot!"

Tatiana walked quickly down the stairs. How she hated getting into arguments with him that way.

She shouldn't have come.

She looked at her husband, "We are leaving."

Sukhotin was surprised, "We said we'll be staying the night."

"I want to take the last train. I cannot stay here!"

Sophia and Leo Tolstoy, c.1900.

Gandhi as a lawyer, age 35, 1906.

LONDON,
SEPTEMBER 1909

"From: Dr. Mehta

To: Mr. Gandhi,

Westminster Hotel,

4, Victoria Street, London,

Mohandas,

Do come and visit me at my house promptly.

I have put my hands on a unique piece of writing which I am sure would delight you!

Come promptly!"

Gandhi held his black umbrella aloft and made his way quickly through the drizzly London streets. The smell of rain reminded him of his university years, a terrified Hindu student trying to study for the bar examination.

He wondered to himself if anything had changed. Here he was, twenty years later, still not feeling a part of the city. Still feeling like a foreigner in London. To an extent, still being terrified.

These past three months in London had not been easy. Time and again he knocked on doors, trying to meet British officials and speak to them about the unjust fate of the Indian and Chinese communities in South Africa.

Time and again he was politely declined. Insincere smiles and empty promises were all he received.

He sighed as he walked into the large yard of his friend Dr. Mehta's home. Perhaps Dr. Mehta was right when he predicted that Gandhi would encounter only closed doors.

Thoughts of relocating to London with his family came to Gandhi's mind again. Here his two young sons could receive proper education. Here the feeling of inferiority so powerfully felt in South Africa was gone. At least on the surface.

He knocked on the door and the Indian servant smiled warmly, "Mr. Gandhi! The Doctor will be happy you came!"

Gandhi smiled in appreciation. The servant took the umbrella from Gandhi and placed it in a brass umbrella stand by the entrance. He then disappeared into the back of the house.

Gandhi waited in the entrance, when a minute later Dr. Mehta came through the corridor, cheerful. "My dear friend Mohandas!"

Gandhi tried to smile, "It is good to see you, Doctor

Mehta."

"Why so somber?"

"I have been given very little attention from the government officials I have been trying to impress—"

"Well what did you expect!"

Gandhi tried to defend his view, though he felt somewhat foolish, "That they would see the wrongdoing in the current situation…."

Dr. Mehta smiled, "Well this is what I like about you! Always so optimistic! If the world was filled with *Gandhi's*, oh what a world we'd have!"

Gandhi grimaced.

"Well," Dr. Mehta lowered his voice, "I have something for you which I think you might like!"

Gandhi followed the doctor to his study, "I am certainly curious!"

Dr. Mehta laughed with pleasure. "Most deservedly!" He reached for his drawer and fetched a pile of papers bound together with string, and sat down on the wide divan. Gandhi sat next to him.

Dr. Mehta held the pages in his hand, "I received this from a friend, who received it from another friend. It is a letter, an essay of sorts, written to the editor of '*Free Hindustan.*'"

"To Mr. Tarak?"

"Exactly," Dr. Mehta smiled.

Gandhi was confused, "And he decided not to publish it?"

Dr. Mehta nodded and his eyes grew larger, "If you'd read it, you'd understand why he decided not to publish it!"

Gandhi shrugged. "Who is it by?" He was a little disappointed that *this* was the great 'surprise.' Many people wanted him to publish things in his *Indian Opinion* magazine.

Dr. Mehta said nothing and just smiled.

Gandhi repeated his question, "Who is it by?"

He looked at the headline,

> "A Letter to a Hindu:
>
> The Subjection of India – Its Cause and Cure."

There was no author name. Gandhi looked again at Dr. Mehta, "Who is it by?"

"Oh, read it, Mohandas, and then you'll see!"

Gandhi did not like the mystery. But he trusted Dr. Mehta. He began reading.

The essay began with some quotes:

> "All that exists is One. People only call this One by different names."
>
> —THE VEDAS.
>
> "God is love, and he that abideth in love abideth in God, and God abideth in him."
>
> —I JOHN iv. 16.

Finally, there was a third quote from the Vedas, and another one from Krishna. Gandhi found it a little distasteful to begin one's treatise with so many quotes. The author, he thought, must be a little *pompous*.

Nevertheless, he continued to read:

> "I have received your letter and two numbers of your periodical *'Free Hindustan'*, of which both editions interest me extremely. The oppression of a majority by a minority, and the demoralization inevitably resulting from it, is a phenomenon that has always occupied me and has done so most particularly of late. I will try to explain to you what I think about that subject in general, and particularly about the cause from which the dreadful evils you write of have arisen and continue to arise.
>
> The reason for the astonishing fact that a majority of working people submit to a handful of idlers who control their labor and their very lives is always and everywhere the same— whether the oppressors and oppressed are of one race or whether, as in India and elsewhere, the oppressors are of a different nation."

Gandhi kept reading attentively:

> "This phenomenon seems particularly strange in India, for there more than two hundred million people, highly gifted both physically and mentally, find themselves in the power of a small group of people quite alien to them in thought, and immeasurably inferior to them in religious morality."

Gandhi chuckled, "'Immeasurably inferior to them in religious morality.' Who is the *author* of this?"

Dr. Mehta motioned to his closed lips and pointed to the paper. Gandhi continued reading.

> "From your letter and the articles, it appears

that the reason lies in the dubious precepts of pseudo-religion and pseudo-science with the immoral conclusions deduced from them and commonly called 'civilization.'"

Gandhi's eyes widened. This sounded *familiar*. A little like *Ruskin*. But more so, like *Tolstoy*. Leo Tolstoy had often written about 'pseudo-religion' and 'pseudo-science.'

But Tolstoy had *never* written anything about *India*, at least not that Gandhi was aware of.

"Your letter shows that most of the leaders recognize no possibility of freeing the people from the oppression they endure except by adopting the irreligious and profoundly immoral social arrangements under which the English and other pseudo-Christian nations live today."

Gandhi skimmed through the paragraphs, feeling his heart beating faster with each word:

"However, throughout history, one thought constantly emerged among different nations, namely, that in every individual a spiritual element is manifested that gives life to all that exists, and that this spiritual element strives to unite with everything of a like nature to itself, and attains this aim through *love*."

He looked at Dr. Mehta, "This must be Tolstoy's writings!"

Dr. Mehta grinned and pressed, "Go on reading!"

Gandhi flipped through the pages, devouring the words:

"As history progressed, the recognition that love represents the highest morality was interwoven everywhere with all kinds of falsehoods which *distorted* it, that finally nothing of it remained but words.

It was taught that this highest morality was only applicable to private life—for home use—but that in public life all forms of violence, such as imprisonment, executions, and wars, might be legitimately used. This, ignoring the fact that such means were diametrically opposed to any vestige of love."

"Indeed!" Gandhi mumbled, "Indeed!"

"In your periodical you set out as the basic principle that: 'Resistance to aggression is not simply justifiable but imperative.'

I must disagree. Love, and love only, is the way to rescue your people from enslavement."

Gandhi's eyes began watering. He looked at Dr. Mehta, "Yes! That is what I've been saying!"

"Love and forcible resistance to evil-doers, involve such a *contradiction* as to destroy utterly the whole sense and *meaning* of love.

Now, in the twentieth century, you, an adherent of a religious people, deny your own heritage, and you repeat (do not take this amiss) the amazing stupidity indoctrinated in you by the advocates of the use of violence—your European teachers."

Gandhi looked at Dr. Mehta, "He is saying it all!"

Dr. Mehta smiled, "Keep reading Mohandas!"

Gandhi read rapidly, through the tears of relief and joy that were blurring his vision:

> "When the Indians complain that the English have enslaved them it is as if drunkards complained that the spirit-dealers who have settled among them have enslaved them. You tell them that they might give up drinking, but they reply that they are so accustomed to it that they cannot abstain, and that they must have alcohol to keep up their energy!
>
> What does it mean that two hundred million vigorous, clever, capable, and freedom-loving people, are subdued by thirty thousand men— not athletes but rather weak and ordinary people? Do not the figures make it clear that it is not the *English* who have enslaved the Indians, but the *Indians* who have enslaved *themselves*?"

Gandhi jumped from the divan, shouting "Eureka! Eureka!"

Dr. Mehta chuckled. "Keep reading!"

"I can't!" Gandhi exclaimed, "I can't!" His heart was pounding. Nevertheless, he kept reading, now standing.

> "As soon as men live entirely in accord with the law of love natural to their hearts, which excludes *all* resistance by violence—as soon as this happens, not only will hundreds be *unable* to enslave millions, but not even millions will be able to enslave a single individual."

Gandhi read as fast as he could, embracing each word:

> "The formula is simple: do not resist evil, but

also do not yourself *participate* in evil. Do not participate in the collection of taxes, and in the violent deeds of the unjust law courts and—most importantly—in the violence of armies and soldiers. Do that, and no one in the world will be able to enslave you."

Gandhi exclaimed, "Yes! Yes! He writes about non-participation! Non-cooperation with evil! It is stronger and more powerful than violent resistance!" He turned to the last page, disappointed that the essay was ending:

"Whether an Indian seeks liberation from subjection to the English, or anyone else struggles with an oppressor—whether it be a Negro defending himself against the North Americans; or Persians, Russians, and Turks against their own governments—what is needed is not beliefs in Paradises and Hells, in reincarnations and resurrections—one thing only is needful: the knowledge of the *simple* and *clear* truth which finds place in every soul—the truth that for our life one law is valid—the law of love, which brings the highest happiness to every individual as well as to all mankind."

The essay ended with a quote by Krishna:

"Then you will know what love has done for you, what love has bestowed upon you, what love demands from you.

—KRISHNA"

Only after reading the quote did Gandhi notice the small writing below:

"YASNAYA POLYANA, December 14th, 1908."

"It *is* Tolstoy's!" he exclaimed.

156

Dr. Mehta smiled a large smile. "What did you think?"

"What did I think?! What did I think?!" Gandhi took Dr. Mehta's hands in his hand and pulled him off the divan, "It is brilliant! Brilliant!"

Dr. Mehta laughed and sat back down. Gandhi hurried to look again at the last page. "December 1908?! How come this has been written nine months ago and I have yet to see it?!"

Dr. Mehta shrugged his shoulders. "I just received it yesterday."

"From where?"

"From a friend of a friend, somehow it got to Paris. I received it by mail."

Gandhi shook his head, "I read all the copies of *Free Hindustan* even though I'm not particularly a fan of their agenda. And I've *not* seen this essay!"

"Why of course," Dr. Mehta nodded and smiled, "For some reason, Mr. Tarak must have decided not to publish it...."

"For some reason!" Gandhi laughed, "This repudiates *everything* he preaches! It shows the poison he spreads!"

Suddenly Gandhi began crying again. He sank into the divan and buried his face in his hands.

Dr. Mehta became alarmed. "Mohandas? Are you alright?"

Gandhi kept sobbing, mumbling, "Yes... yes...."

Dr. Mehta sat there, worried. He had never seen

Gandhi that way.

After a long minute Gandhi mumbled through his tears, "It's just... that I have been thinking... of desisting...."

Dr. Mehta's eyes widened, "Desisting?"

Gandhi nodded, "Of abandoning the campaign. Of declaring it null. Of adhering to the government decree, and leaving South Africa."

"You?!" Dr. Mehta exclaimed, "The editor of *Indian Opinion*?"

Gandhi nodded. "You don't understand. The time in jail... the non-response from that General Smuts, the Colonial Secretary, who has been purposefully ignoring me, and the polite smiles of the officials here in London thinking me mad! It's been... such a burden...."

Dr. Mehta put his hand on Gandhi's shoulder. "If *you* give up, if Mohandas K. Gandhi gives up, what will become of the rest of us?"

Gandhi smiled through tears and shrugged. He looked at the essay, "This essay must be duplicated! We must translate it to Gujarati, and to Hindi too! and we need at least five thousand copies to distribute here in Britain among the young people, they must read it! And also everyone in South Africa!"

Dr. Mehta laughed. "I was thinking the same thing. How many copies do you think we need?"

Gandhi's eyes shone with excitement, "At least fifteen-thousand!"

Dr. Mehta nodded slowly. "You are the printer among us: how much would it cost to produce a little booklet like this?"

"About half a pound," Gandhi said, examining Dr. Mehta's eyes. Was he thinking of...?

"Indeed," Dr. Mehta nodded and closed his eyes, "That should be... seven thousand and five hundred pounds." He looked at Gandhi, "I was thinking of possibly contributing a similar sum, as my little token for the sake of the community—"

Gandhi grabbed both of Dr. Mehta's hands, "No!"

Dr. Mehta smiled, "Yes!"

Gandhi mumbled. "You... you are a saint!"

Dr. Mehta chuckled. "Not a saint at all. That is the little I can do!" He looked at Gandhi, "I've been thinking it over all day. There are three things that must be done first."

"What are they?" Gandhi asked eagerly. In his mind he was already envisioning the young people he had met in the India House reading the riveting essay.

"First," Dr. Mehta said, "we need to translate it to Gujarati. It is important to me for our people to—"

"I can do it!" Gandhi exclaimed.

Dr. Mehta smiled, "I was hoping so. Very well. Then, I was thinking it would be proper to have a short introduction, telling the reader a little about Tolstoy, giving a short background...."

Gandhi nodded. "I can do that!"

Dr. Mehta smiled, "Good. Then, the third thing— and the most important—is to write to Tolstoy and—"

"Write? To Tolstoy?"

"Why of course. We don't even know if he indeed wrote this—"

"He did!" Gandhi exclaimed, "I am certain of it! I can recognize his elegance in every—"

"Yes, but we must be *certain*. Also, we need to see if he indeed permits the reprinting of it. There might be some money and publication rights involved."

Gandhi's heart sank. "Indeed," he nodded slowly, "indeed. How silly of me. I should have thought of it myself." He sighed, "Well, you can write to him and explain our good intentions!"

Dr. Mehta chuckled, "*I* can write to him? *You* should write to him!"

"I…?"

"Of course! *You* are the *editor* among us. You are the *publisher* of a newspaper. What do I know about these things? I am but a doctor!"

Gandhi, his eyes widening at the mere thought, looked at Dr. Mehta. "I am not sure I can…."

"Of course you can! You have read his writings, all that I have read about him comes from your weekly magazine!"

Gandhi nodded slowly, processing the thought, "I… should… write to him…." His breath became heavy, "I should write to him." He looked at Dr. Mehta. "I should write to him!"

Dr. Mehta nodded. "Of course!" He did not see what was so puzzling for Gandhi. "Haven't you written to that General Smuts, as well as to the Leader of the House of Lords?"

Gandhi nodded and gulped.

"Then you can write to this Russian author!"

Gandhi nodded, looking stupefied.

"Mohandas? Is everything fine?"

Gandhi nodded slowly, speechless. He walked to the door, as if in a dream, "I will... let you know if he responds...."

Dr. Mehta said, "Wait! You forgot the actual essay. Send it to him, see that he confirms that it is his."

"Indeed, Indeed," Gandhi said as he took the essay in his hand. He looked pale.

"Mohandas? Are you not feeling well?"

"No... I am fine... I am perfectly... fine...."

Gandhi walked to the door. Dr. Mehta followed him and opened the door for him. "Mohandas, I am thinking that perhaps we should make not 15,000 copies, but 20,000 copies!" He looked at Gandhi, hoping to see him smiling.

"Indeed..." Gandhi said, as in a dream, "Twenty thousand, that is more than fifteen-thousand...." He pressed his hands together in appreciation, and left the house, the essay in his hand.

"Mohandas!" Dr. Mehta called after him, "You forgot your umbrella!"

Gandhi turned around, smiled and nodded, taking the umbrella, "Yes! Indeed!" He bowed his head and walked through the garden, approaching the street, and hesitated for a moment, as he'd forgotten where he was going.

Dr. Mehta watched him from the door, a little worried about his old friend. 'Some rest would do,' he thought.

Gandhi began walking on the pavement. The drizzle had stopped. The air was chilly, but refreshing. He walked slowly toward the hotel. He placed the essay inside his jacket, wanting to protect it.

'I will write to Tolstoy,' he told himself. 'Of course. That is only *reasonable*. I will write to him. Many people write to him. I am a people—that is, a *person*. I can write to him.'

The wet sidewalks glistened in the afternoon sun. 'I can write to him. Mr. Tarak of *Free Hindustan* wrote to him! What cheek he had! Asking Tolstoy to embrace his violent movement!'

He nodded to himself, feeling his heart beating fast. 'Of course I can write to him. I *will* write to him! Not for me, no! Not for Mohandas Gandhi. I would not want to bother him about *me!* I will write for our cause! Yes! So that we could make copies of this.' He put his hand on his coat, feeling the essay inside, 'Everyone must read *this!*'

It took Gandhi three days.

In his hotel room, with the curtain closed, trying to block off all distractions, Gandhi began the letter by writing:

"Dear Sir,"

No. "*Dear*"?! That was too familiar. He should just write "Sir." He wrote down:

"Sir,"

But that looked almost a little diminishing. He sighed. He should write it in *capital* letters. *Yes*. That would show his respect.

"SIR,"

Gandhi then went on to write a lengthy paragraph, excusing himself for writing the letter:

> "I am aware that those who honor you and endeavor to follow you have no right to trespass upon your time. It is rather their duty to refrain from giving you trouble so far as possible. I have, however, who am your obedient servant, taken the liberty of writing to you...."

He looked at his notebook with disapproval. It sounded too.... Apologetic. He changed the words 'Obedient servant' to 'an admirer', and followed the sentence with:

> "...taken the liberty of writing to you addressing this communication in order to have your advice."

He sighed. It sounded so insufficient. It sounded completely unsatisfactory. He should speak about what *Tolstoy* cares about. He then rewrote the paragraph, adding the words, 'in the interests of truth.'

> "I am aware that those who honor you and

> endeavor to follow you have no right to trespass upon your time, but it is rather their duty to refrain from giving you trouble, so far as possible. I have, however, who am your admirer, taken the liberty of addressing this communication *in the interests of truth* and in order to have your advice."

He sighed, got up, and then forced himself to sit back down again. He reread it and shook his head in adamant disapproval.

He then read it again, adding to the end of the paragraph:

> "...taken the liberty of addressing this communication in the interests of truth and in order to have your advice on problems, the solution of which you have made your life work."

That last bit sounded better to him, asking for Tolstoy's advice on 'problems, the solution of which you have made your life work.' It sounded respectful. It sounded like Gandhi wasn't an ignorant fool trying to waste Tolstoy's time.

He sighed. He still did not like that paragraph at all, but he decided to try and continue.

But how?

He should not simply ask: 'Can we print your essay?'

He should introduce himself first, he thought.

He nodded to himself, sighed, and wrote:

> "I take the liberty of inviting your attention to what has been going on in the Transvaal for

nearly three years."

That sounded good. But would Tolstoy know *where* the Transvaal was? Would he know it was the central region of South Africa, where the great cities of Pretoria and Johannesburg are located?

'Of course he would know!' Gandhi told himself. 'Tolstoy is versed in world politics!'

'But what if he wouldn't know?'

Gandhi gulped, and added, in brackets:

> "I take the liberty of inviting your attention to what has been going on in the Transvaal (South Africa) for nearly three years."

He then thought that it might be a little *disrespectful* to add "South Africa" in brackets. It was as if writing to someone, "I am writing to you about Rome (Italy) or about Scotland (Great Britain).

It sounded hideous.

He then erased the brackets. This would be more respectful. *Of course* Tolstoy would know of the Transvaal! The man had quoted Krishna! The man was well versed in politics, religion, the arts, morality, law… in *everything*!

Gandhi sighed. This was becoming tiring.

He continued to write, his tongue peeking from his lips in concentration:

> "We are an Indian population of nearly 13,000. We have for several years labored under various legal disabilities. The prejudice against color and in some respect against Asiatics is intense in our colony."

Good, he thought. This was now becoming informative, and *useful*, supplying the great author with details and relevant *information*. The great author would need to know those things in order to see whether he approved the distribution of his essay.

Gandhi reread the paragraph, realizing that he needed to explain a little about color prejudice. To him it was clear that the prejudice was based on rivalry between merchants. Herman attested to it, and he was not even Indian.

Gandhi nodded to himself. It was only in recent years, when the Indian community had produced some of the greatest traders and businessmen, that restrictions were beginning to emerge. When the Indians were simple workers in the mines a few decades ago, no one cared to restrict them in any way. But now that they were becoming successful in their trade and shops and taking some of the profits *away* from the Europeans, the Indian presence had begun to be a 'problem.'

He sighed and wrote,

> "This prejudice is largely due, so far as we are concerned, to Europeans becoming jealous of the growing share of our tradesmen in the local trade."

He then reread the paragraph, noticing it spoke of 'We' and 'Us' and was a little too... self-centered. He needed to bring the facts as they were: in a dry, *distant* manner, the way he had learned in law school. Be remote, be calculated, be informative—but *not* emotional. He closed his eyes, concentrated, then looked at the notebook and wrote the paragraph again:

> "There is in that colony a British Indian

population of nearly 13,000. These Indians have for several years labored under the various legal disabilities. The prejudice against color and in some respect against Asiatics is intense in that colony. It is largely due, so far as Asiatics are concerned, to trade jealousy."

He read it again. It sounded better. More succinct and to the point.

He continued writing,

"The climax was reached three years ago, with a law which the author of this letter and many others considered to be degrading and calculated to demoralize those to whom it was applicable.

The author of this letter felt that submission to law of this nature was inconsistent with the spirit of true religion. Therefore, he and some of his friends were and still are firm believers in the doctrine of non-resistance to evil."

He nodded, satisfied with mentioning Tolstoy's creed. He thought that the great author would like that. He continued,

"The author of this letter had the privilege of studying your writings also, which left a deep impression on his mind."

He sighed. This sounded *terrible*. He erased the 'author of this letter' and simply wrote 'I.' Tolstoy preached for simplicity, did he not? Gandhi thought that he needed to avoid making the letter complicated. The truth was simple. He rewrote the paragraph:

"I felt that submission to law of this nature was

inconsistent with the spirit of true religion. I
and some of my friends were and still are firm
believers in the doctrine of non-resistance to
evil. I had the privilege of studying your
writings also, which left a deep impression on
my mind.

Gandhi nodded to himself, more pleased than
before. He continued writing:

"British Indians before whom the position was
fully explained, accepted the advice that we
should *not* submit to the legislation, but that we
should suffer imprisonment, or whatever other
penalties the law may impose for its breach."

He went on to describe their current plight in the
shortest and most succinct style:

"The result has been that nearly half of the
Indian population, which was unable to stand
the heat of the struggle or to suffer the
hardships of imprisonment, have withdrawn
from the Transvaal rather than submit to the
law that they have considered degrading. Of the
other half, nearly 2,500 have for conscience's
sake allowed themselves to be imprisoned,
some as many as five times. The imprisonments
have varied from four days to six months, in
most of the cases with hard labor. Many have
been financially ruined. At present there are
over a hundred passive resisters in the
Transvaal jails."

He thought of Herman, and of some of his other
friends. He shook his head disapprovingly. He thought
of the families. It was terrible. He felt that Tolstoy
should *know* this.

"Some of these have been very poor men, earning their livelihood from day to day. The result has been that their wives and children have had to be supported out of public contributions, also largely raised from passive resisters. This has put a severe strain upon British Indians, but, in my opinion, they have risen to the occasion. The struggle still continues and one does not know when the end will come. We also notice that, in so far as the struggle has been prolonged, it has been due largely to our weakness and, hence, to a belief having been engendered in the mind of the Government that we would not be able to stand continued suffering."

He stared at the long paragraph, thinking it sufficient.

He then reread the letter from the beginning. 'Good', he thought, 'now he shall understand who we are.'

Gandhi sighed. Now he needed to explain why he decided to write the letter. He continued writing:

"I have come to London to see the imperial authorities and to place before them our position, with a view to seeking redress. Here a copy of your letter addressed to a Hindu on the present unrest in India, has been placed in my hands by a friend. On the face of it, it appears to represent your views.

It is the intention of my friend, at his own expense, to have 20,000 copies printed and distributed and to have it translated also. We have, however, not been able to secure the original, and we do not feel justified in printing it, unless we are sure of the accuracy of the copy and of the fact that it is your letter."

Gandhi looked at the paragraph. It was far from perfect. He would correct it later. He had something else on his mind, however. There was one more thing, though, that he wished to change in the actual reprinting of the essay.

In the manuscript, Tolstoy referred to reincarnation. He clearly wrote: "What is needed is not beliefs in Paradises and Hells, in reincarnations and resurrections—one thing only is needful: the law of love...."

Gandhi knew the difficulty in that sentence. Was it to be read by some of the less educated Hindus, this sentence may evoke a great deal of antagonism. Many Hindus found comfort in reincarnation.

Gandhi even told the wife of Medvev Kapur, who had died in jail, that her husband had died for a noble cause, and with such love on his lips for his incarcerators, he would surely be reincarnated as a mighty prince.

This comforted the poor lady.

Gandhi knew that if he were to print Tolstoy's sardonic comment about reincarnation, people might disregard the whole essay. Some might even call the author a heretic.

Gandhi paced back and forth in the small room. Then he gathered his courage, considered his words carefully, and wrote:

> "I must, however, venture, if I may, to make a small correction to the essay. In the concluding paragraph you seem to dissuade the reader

from the belief in reincarnation. I do not know whether you have specially studied the question. Reincarnation or transmigration is a cherished belief with millions in India, indeed in China also."

He then thought of his fellow people now incarcerated, many of whom, like the late Medvev Kapur, suffer great physical pain and the risk of death in jail. For them, the concept of reincarnation was one of the points of light in their daily struggle. Gandhi proceeded to write:

"With some of the passive resisters who have gone through the jails of the Transvaal, it has been their only solace. My object in writing this is not to convince you of the doctrine's truth, but to ask you if you will please remove the word "reincarnation" from the other things you have dissuaded your reader from."

Gandhi then reread the last two paragraphs. He changed 'I would venture to make a *correction*' to 'I would also venture to make a *suggestion*.' He also added brackets into one of the key sentences. Instead of writing:

"I do not know whether you have specially studied the question."

He modified the sentence to:

"I do not know whether *(if it is not impertinent on my part to mention this)* you have specially studied the question."

The new sentence, with the comment in bracket, sounded to him more respectful.

He looked at the page. It was unreadable, filled with corrections and arrows. He was generally pleased about that last part, but did not know whether that would go well with the great author, who most likely calculated each and every word, and would not want his writings changed in any way.

He nevertheless *had* to ask it.

There was one more small issue which troubled him. In the essay there were several quotes from Krishna. He wanted to bring them in their *original* Sanskrit for the Hindu reader, but was afraid he did not recognize some of the translations. He therefore wrote:

> "One final concern I have: in the essay you have quoted largely from Krishna and given reference to several passages. What is the title of the book from which the quotations have been made?"

He then closed the letter,

> "I much appreciate your time and attention.
>
> With respects, I remain,
>
> Yours,
>
> M. K. Gandhi."

He then read the entire letter again. It needed much modification.

Gandhi spent days trying to perfect the letter. He worried that Tolstoy might frown at poorly phrased sentences, and perhaps not even respond to an inadequately composed letter.

He changed the ending to "your obedient servant."

He changed some of the phrases to sound politer, and yet at the same time warm and familiar. But not *too* familiar.

He realized that the first paragraph, after many of the changes he made might sound a bit overbearing:

> "I am aware that those who honor you and endeavor to follow you have no right to trespass upon your time, but it is rather their duty to refrain from giving you trouble, so far as possible. I have, however, who am an utter stranger to you, taken the liberty of addressing this communication in the interests of truth and in order to have your advice on problems, the solution of which you have made your life work."

He wanted to get rid of it and jump straight to the point, informing the 81-year-old man of the happenings in the Transvaal. He imagined that Tolstoy received hundreds, if not thousands of letters each day, and that he would most likely skip such formal paragraphs, wishing to understand what the letter was really *about*.

At a bold step he decided to erase the whole paragraph, and simply begin the letter with:

> "I take the liberty of inviting your attention to what has been going on in the Transvaal..."

But then he regretted it. He liked the warm and affectionate sound that the first paragraph had, mentioning that he realized this had been Tolstoy's "life's work." Also, it expressed that he "honored"

Tolstoy. And it mentioned the "truth" which Tolstoy so passionately searched for. It showed that Gandhi was *versed* in Tolstoy's writings.

Finally, he decided to place the essential parts of that paragraph at the very *end* of the letter.

After three days of working on it, he was exhausted.

He knew that he should wait no longer. It was important for him to receive Tolstoy's answer. He knew very well that with the young Indians' hearts being filled with fear, and dedicated to violent resistance, the murder of another Curzon Wiley could happen any day. He knew how much the translation of the essay could mean to the young men, coming from the great Russian author who recognized the plight of the Indian people. Gandhi envisioned the young men hearing the wisdom coming not from the unknown Mohandas Gandhi, but from the world-renowned Tolstoy. He knew Tolstoy could succeed where he had seemed to fail.

He typed the whole letter on the hotel's typewriter, resulting in just under two pages. He signed it, his hand shaking, feeling the importance of the moment. He then attached a copy of Tolstoy's 20-page essay. He bought a large envelope, on which he wrote:

"To Count Leo Tolstoy,

Yasnaya Polyana,

Russia."

Then, fearing the nearby Kensington post office might misplace the envelope, he walked for nearly an hour, the large envelope inside his coat, to the General Post Office in St. Martin's Le Grand. There he bought five stamps, placing them carefully on the envelope, feeling a great reluctance sending it.

He thanked the teller and walked out of the post office. He felt weary and excited at the same time. He walked back to the hotel, and on the way passed through Hyde Park. He sat down on a bench watching the lake. It then began to rain. He had forgotten his umbrella. Nevertheless, he kept sitting there, on the bench, the drizzling turned into a generous pour. He watched the rain drops falling on the Serpentine Lake. He felt invincible. He had just sent a letter to Leo Tolstoy.

Tolstoy reading a letter, age 79, 1907.

PART TWO

Based on true documents.

All quotes from letters, diary entries, books and articles are directly based on the original documents.

YASNAYA POLYANA
OCTOBER 1909

It hadn't been two weeks since Tatiana left her parents' home in anger after their anniversary celebration, when she received a telegram from her mother, telling her Alexandra was sick and urging her to come.

The carriage approached the gates of her childhood home. She got out, followed by Nadya, holding little Anya. Tatiana worried about bringing her daughter with her, not wanting her to catch whatever illness Alexandra was suffering from. But she did not know how long she'd be gone. And she could not part from her daughter for too long.

Old Abrasha rushed from the porter's cabin to assist her, taking her valise.

Tatiana looked at him, "Is it serious?"

Abrasha shook his head, "The doctors said it is not. That she needs to rest for a few days, that is all."

Tatiana thanked him for the information.

At home, the house was uncharacteristically quiet. Leaving Anya with Nadya in the drawing room, Tatiana hurried to her sister's room. She was surprised to see that Alexandra was feeling rather well, resting in bed. Alexandra shouted when she saw Tatiana entering, "Sister! You have come to save me!"

Tatiana was baffled. "What is going on, Alexandra?"

"Mother, she is driving me mad!"

Tatiana sat on her sister's bed.

Alexandra continued, "She and Papa fight all the time. She has gone mad. And so has he," she whispered, "I cannot stand being here alone! Why won't you, Sukhotin and Anya move in with us for the time being?"

"Alexandra, that would be impossible—"

At that moment Tolstoy came to the door, "Tanya! Finally, I need help!"

Tatiana sighed. "Hello Papa, I am fine, thank you, how are you?"

"The doctor has recommended Alexandra to rest for several days, but did not tell me how I should, myself, deal with the hundreds of letters—"

Tatiana shook her head. "Papa, I think you need an assistant. Whatever happened to that Nikolay of yours?"

"Who, Gusev?" Tolstoy asked, "The government exiled him for assisting me in sending censored writings to publishers abroad! That stupid government is—"

At that moment Sophia walked down the hall, shouting, "Tanya? Tanya?"

Alexandra rolled her eyes, whispering to her sister, "Here it begins anew."

Their mother appeared at the door, seeing their father inside the room. She looked at him, upset, "Why didn't you tell me Tanya has arrived?"

Tolstoy groaned, "I just saw her myself!"

Sophia came to kiss her, "Tanyushka! Where is little Anya?"

"She is playing with the nanny."

Tolstoy looked irritated. "Can I at least finish my sentence?!"

Everyone became quiet. Tolstoy looked at Tatiana, "I have *much* work. I need your help!"

"Yes, Papa," Tatiana said quietly.

Tolstoy mumbled something and left the room. Sophia quickly followed him into the corridor, "Why can't you let *me* help you? I can read letters too!"

Her voice disappeared down the hallway, until they heard the door to their father's study slam shut.

Then they heard their mother shrieking, running through the corridor and into her bedroom. Then her door was slammed shut as well.

Alexandra whispered, "It's been getting worse."

Tatiana took a deep breath in.

Later, in her father's study, she was appalled by the

number of letters thrown on the desk and on the small table in the corner.

Her father whined, "I can't work here anymore!"

Tatiana murmured, "Be calm, Papa. In two hours we can clear this mess."

"No, Tanya," her father looked helpless, "your mother," he whispered, "she will not leave me alone!"

Tatiana ignored her father's comment. If there was one thing she learned early on it was *not* to get in the middle of the two of them. Her parents had always had difficulties, and Tatiana learned to stay away.

She sat down and looked at the pile of letters. She took the letter opener in her hand, and quickly began opening the letters. She attached an envelope to a letter, remembering very well past agonies in times when misplaced envelopes and letters led to her father's responses being sent to the wrong addresses.

The thought of this made her smile.

"Why are you smiling?" her father inquired.

"Oh, no reason, Papa."

Her father groaned.

Within minutes she finished opening all the letters, and now began sifting through them.

Her father looked at her, "You don't even read them?"

Tatiana gave her father a look which he recognized: her eyebrows were raised, her nostrils slightly widening, meaning, 'Do not disturb me.'

He nodded and looked away.

He had a large book in front of him. He tried to read it, but could not concentrate. Every once in a while he looked at his daughter.

She avoided his eyes and kept sorting through the letters. She had done this for years, from when she was 19 years old to the actual morning of her marriage at the age of 33. Fourteen years next to her father, every single day, including weekends.

She sighed. Only God knows how she survived.

Little Anya ran down the hallway and opened the door of the study. Tatiana was fierce, "Anya, go and play elsewhere!"

Nadya appeared at the door, "I'm sorry Tatiana." She took Anya in her arms and closed the door to the study.

Tolstoy looked at Tatiana, "Why are you so *brutal* with her?"

Tatiana's eyes widened, "Papa, do you want me to leave?"

He said nothing, groaned, and looked down at his book.

She continued going through the few dozen letters remaining. She thought to herself, 'Who are you, Papa, to tell *me* how to raise my daughter? You, who have been such a strict disciplinarian, such an awful and distant teacher, calling me '*brutal*?'

She said nothing, pushing the thoughts aside, like she always did. Any sign of weakness would often be used by her father against her. She had learned not to appear weak next to him. Not to appear like her mother.

She remembered how she had had one difficult pregnancy after another. When the third child was stillborn and she cried, her father scolded her, telling her, "Tanya! Stop crying. This is clearly a benefit for your spiritual life…"

He clearly hated when she cried or showed any sign of emotion. And so she learned never to show it to him.

Tolstoy looked at her. She felt his eyes.

"Tanya," he said softly, "do you remember how you used to come into the room? My study was downstairs in the library then. You would come there when I wrote *War and Peace*."

Tatiana nodded. The memory pained her.

Her father continued in wonderment, "You were the *only* one who could come into my room when I was writing."

Tatiana inhaled deeply. She glanced at the last letter and put it in the 'not-important-pile.'

He sighed and looked at her.

She finished arranging the piles, took her pen in hand and said, "Papa, shall we begin?"

"Already? You are quick. Alexandra takes longer…."

Tatiana nodded. "This letter is from Aylmer Maude from Britain, he is writing about—"

"Oh Aylmer! It's been a long while! I wonder how he is doing. Do you remember when he lived in Moscow and he and his wife would come to visit us?"

Tatiana clenched her jaw. "Papa, let us be efficient. He is asking for your opinion about the second volume of your biography. The second volume needs to go to print soon."

"Oh," her father sighed, "I've tried to read it, but it's so boring!"

"Well, shall I write to him to go ahead and print it? That you have given him your blessing?"

Her father looked tired. "I don't know. I promised Chertkov that I would read it and respond to Aylmer myself."

"Papa, I think you should just let it go. The way I know you, you won't get to it at all."

Tolstoy took a deep breath and waved his hand in approval.

Tatiana put the letter in a new pile.

The following hour they went through all of the important letters. Finally, there was one more.

"This is," she took the letter, "from some Hindu—"

Her father's eyes lit up, "Mr. Tarak? The editor of the 'Free Hindustan'? Finally, I've been waiting—"

"No, Papa, someone else, one Mo"—she looked at the letter—"one Mohandas Gandhi. He asks for permission to reprint what you have sent to Mr. Tarak. Can I send him an approval?"

Tolstoy mumbled, "Who is he? How many copies does he want printed?"

"He is a Hindu, from"—she glanced at the letter—

"South Africa. He wants to produce twenty thousand copies. Papa, can I send him approval—"

"Twenty thousand copies?" Tolstoy's eyes grew larger, "That is excellent! What else does he write?"

Tatiana sighed. "Papa, I'm tired."

"I am tired too, Tanya, but this is important! What does he write?"

Tatiana shook her head and looked at the letter, "He writes about what he does in the *Trans*—somewhere in South Africa…."

"The Transvaal?"

Tatiana nodded.

"Interesting," Tolstoy said, "Read it to me!"

Tatiana quickly looked at the letter, flipping to the second page,

> "A copy of your letter addressed to a Hindu on the present unrest in India has been placed in my hands by a friend. On the face of it, it appears to represent your views. It is the intention of my friend, at his own expense, to have 20,000 copies printed and distributed and to have it translated—"

"Wait," Tolstoy stopped her, "That's how he begins? No introduction? No explanation about him and his motives?"

Tatiana sighed, "Papa, we are almost done with all the letters—"

"Tanya," Tolstoy said, looking carefully at his daughter, "if you came to help me *this* way, like *this*, then

I can do it alone."

Tatiana pouted her lips. She hated when he made her feel guilty. "Sir," she read.

Her father leaned back against the back of his chair, "Where is the letter written from?"

"Britain, a hotel in London."

"Very well. Go on."

Tatiana read,

> "I take the liberty of inviting your attention to what has been going on in the Transvaal (South Africa) for nearly three years.

> There is in that colony a British Indian population of nearly 13,000. These Indians have for several years labored under the various legal disabilities. The prejudice against color and in some respect against Asiatics is intense in that colony. It is largely due, so far as Asiatics are concerned, to trade jealousy."

"Mmmm…." Tolstoy hummed, "interesting. Go on."

Tatiana kept reading,

> "The climax was reached three years ago, with a law which I and many others considered to be degrading and calculated to unman those to whom it was applicable."

"*Law*," Tolstoy muttered, "probably some discrimination *disguised* as 'law'…."

Tatiana nodded and kept reading,

> "I felt that submission to law of this nature was

inconsistent with the spirit of true religion. I and some of my friends were and still are firm believers in the doctrine of non-resistance to evil."

Tolstoy leaned forward, "Non-resistance *to evil?* This is how he writes it?"

Tatiana nodded.

A small smirk appeared on her father's face. "Go on Tanya!"

"I had the privilege of studying your writings, which left a deep impression on my mind. British Indians, before whom the position was fully explained, accepted the advice that we should not submit to the legislation, but that we should suffer imprisonment, or whatever other penalties the law may impose for its breach."

Tolstoy clenched his fist, waving it in the air, "Brave folks!"

Tatiana shook her head, but a tiny smile made its way across her face,

"The result has been that nearly one-half of the Indian population that was unable to stand the heat of the struggle and to suffer the hardships of imprisonment, have withdrawn from the Transvaal Colony to the Natal Colony, rather than submit to law which they have considered degrading. Of the other half, nearly 2,500 have for conscience's sake allowed themselves to be imprisoned, some as many as five times."

Tolstoy's eyes lit up, "*Really?*"

Tatiana continued,

> "The imprisonments have varied from four days to six months, in the majority of cases with hard labor. Many have been financially ruined. At present there are over hundred passive resisters in the Transvaal jails."

Tolstoy mumbled, "Over a hundred? Hindus? Passive resisters? Who *is* this man?"

Tatiana shrugged her shoulders and continued,

> "Some of these have been very poor men, earning their livelihood from day to day. The result has been that their wives and children have had to be supported out of public contributions, also largely raised from passive resisters. This has put a severe strain upon British Indians, but in my opinion they have risen to the occasion."

Tolstoy mumbled to himself again, "Over a hundred passive resistors! In jail as we speak!"

Tatiana glanced at her father. He looked so pleased. Something in seeing him this way reminded her of her once-young-father. Back then, when she was young, there was something less *severe* about him; he was a little more lighthearted. He was hardly the 'prophet' that now so many 'Tolstoyans' were admiring.

She continued,

> "The struggle still continues and one does not know when the end will come. We noticed that in so far as the struggle has been prolonged, it has been due largely to our weakness, and hence to a belief having been engendered in the mind of the Government that we would not be able to stand continued suffering.

I have come to England to see the imperial authorities and to place before them the position, with a view to seeking redress.

There is one thing, with reference to which I would trespass upon your time."

Tolstoy looked at Tatiana, "That is the printing matter?"

Tatiana nodded,

"A copy of your letter addressed to a Hindu on the present unrest in India has been placed in my hands by a friend. On the face of it, it appears to represent your views. It is the intention of my friend, at his own expense, to have 20,000 copies printed and distributed and to have it translated also."

"Translated?" Tolstoy asked.

Tatiana nodded.

"To Hindi?" Tolstoy mumbled to himself. He liked the thought of it, "Tolstoy in Hindi!"

Tatiana smiled for a moment, then turned serious again,

"We have, however, not been able to secure the original, and we do not feel justified in printing it, unless we are sure of the accuracy of the copy and of the fact that it is your letter. I venture to enclose herewith a copy of the copy, and should esteem it a favour if you kindly let me know whether it is your letter, whether it is an accurate copy and whether you approve of its publication in the above manner. If you will add anything further to the letter, please do so."

Tatiana looked at her father, "I think he hints of monetary compensation."

Tolstoy waved his hand dismissively, "Nonsense, I will not ask for any compensation."

Tatiana sighed. For the past few years her father had insisted again and again on offering his works for free. This had been one of the main areas of dispute between her parents. But she had decided, wisely, to remain out of it.

She continued to read, approaching the last few paragraphs,

> "I would also venture to make a suggestion. In the concluding paragraph you seem to dissuade the reader from the belief in reincarnation. I do not know whether (if it is not impertinent on my part to mention this) you have specially studied the question."

Tatiana raised her eyes in disapproval. Who was this person criticizing her father, doubting his depth of study of reincarnation? There was no one subject which her father had not studied. He could converse about anything, really. She did not like the tone of the letter.

Her father signaled for her to continue.

She read,

> "Reincarnation or transmigration is a cherished belief with millions in India, indeed in China also. It explains reasonably the many mysteries of life. With some of the passive resisters who have gone through the jails of the Transvaal, it has been their only solace. My object in writing this is not to convince you of the truth of the

doctrine, but to ask you if you will please remove the word *'reincarnation'* from the other things you have dissuaded your reader from."

Tolstoy mumbled, "That should not be a problem."

Tatiana nodded and kept reading, faster now,

"In the letter in question you have quoted largely from Krishna and given reference to passages. I should thank you to give me the title of the book from which the quotations have been made.

I have wearied you with this letter. I am aware that those who honor you and endeavor to follow you have no right to trespass upon your time, but it is rather their duty to refrain from giving you trouble, so far as possible. I, however, who is an utter stranger to you, have taken the liberty of addressing this communication in the interests of truth, and in order to have your advice on problems, the solution of which you have made your life work.

With respects, I remain,

Your obedient servant,

M. K. Gandhi."

Tolstoy nodded his head slowly. Tatiana noticed his face, wearing the familiar expression he had when something pleased him.

After a long moment he murmured, "Nonviolent resistance in South Africa… *'A Letter to a Hindu'* printed in India…" he looked at his daughter, "This is good news, Tanya."

Tatiana nodded. She was happy for her old father,

who seemed distant, pensive. She remembered often seeing him this way in the past, before he had become so zealous about his ideas, and so *attached* to *his* truth and *his* opinions.

She looked at him, not wanting to disturb the sudden calm that had befallen on him.

"Papa," she finally said, "should I respond to him, telling him that he can use the manuscript, and that he should send you a copy when it is published?"

Her father took a deep breath in, then exhaling slowly, "I think I shall write to him myself."

"But Papa," Tatiana said, "do not burden yourself."

Her father smiled and pointed at her, "This," he squinted and looked at her intently, "this reminds me of my old Tanya."

Tatiana smiled reluctantly and looked away.

Her father murmured, "Where has she gone, my old daughter?"

Tatiana sighed, "I am here, Papa."

Tolstoy nodded.

They said nothing.

Finally, her father said, "I think we are done for the day, don't you?"

Tatiana nodded.

"Now," he said, "come here and let me kiss you."

She got off her chair and leaned next to her father, as he kissed her on the forehead. The touch of his beard and mustache tickled her, like it used to tickle her when she was a little girl.

Her father nodded, "Thank you, Tatiana Tolstoya."

"Sukhotina," Tatiana corrected him with a sheepish smile.

"For me you will always be Tolstoya."

Tatiana nodded. She felt swept up in the emotions of the moment. She looked at the sorted piles of letters, "Leave these to me, Papa, I will finish them all tomorrow."

Her father waved his hand in both dismissal and gratitude. "Just give me that letter from the Hindu."

She placed the letter in front of him and left the room quietly.

Oddly, she felt a sudden urge to stay there, in the study with him. She wondered at it. Only an hour earlier she had wanted so badly to be done already. What had changed?

She knew what changed. She had seen a glimpse of her father that warmed her, a man who could create women characters with incredible realism and depth, almost as if a woman was writing. The great author who, in his twenties, rattled the literature scene with his first works, "Childhood," "Boyhood" and "Youth," all of which were told from the refreshing perspective of a child—with all the genius subtle *nuances* of a child. She saw the Papa who was sensitive, kind, aware—not the domineering, controlling, ever-criticizing patriarch.

She thought to herself that in fact she had missed her old Papa. Her heart ached as if a gulf of longing opened in it. She suddenly thought of Anya. She hurried away to find her daughter playing in the drawing room. She lifted Anya in the air, embraced her tightly. Hugging her four-year-old girl she murmured, "Anyushka! My Anyushka!"

Tatiana and Anya Tolstoy-Sukhotin, c. 1917.

ROME,
DECEMBER 1931

Tatiana and Gandhi sat in silence as the weight of their stories settled in the room.

They both felt like witnesses to something important. And they knew that they both shared similar emotions.

Tatiana wondered, what was it exactly? They both loved Tolstoy. They both admired him. Though Tatiana had uneasy feelings toward her father, and while she often criticized him in her mind, she *still* was his greatest devotee. She knew that. Not only in her early life—in her twenties and thirties—but also later, as a mother. Time and again she would leave everything behind, and take the train to Tula, hop on a carriage and head toward her father.

Yes, it was to her father that she would run, not toward her mother. Her father knew that, and she herself knew that. Everyone knew that.

Her father once said off-handedly in his last years, "Tanya, you will sort through my writings when I'm gone. Only you will know what to do."

Tatiana then tried to dismiss his comment, "That is not true, Papa, Alexandra, Sergey and Andrey and the others know just as much, and Mama can help. Everyone can."

Her father looked back at her with his all-too-familiar look, saying, 'You and I both know what you are saying is a lie.'

And while she dismissed that look, she did know that he was right.

Now, at the age of 67, with her father gone for over two decades, she *still* was his greatest devotee. She was the one who insisted on converting Yasnaya Polyana into a museum. She was the one presiding over the second museum in Moscow. And when fleeing her motherland, she was the one to organize literary salons of great Russian authors in exile, discussing her father's works. She was the one insisting on renting the small room below her apartment and converting it into a museum, wishing to have a sacred space nearby to commemorate her father.

Often she would come downstairs by herself. Although her father was long gone, and had sometimes been impossible to deal with, still she needed to feel his *presence*. She would often look at the few original manuscripts which she was able to hold onto, at his messy handwriting which only she could decipher.

Gandhi smiled at her.

She smiled back.

He said, "You must have been very close to him."

She nodded and smiled a small smile. Yes, she was.

Gandhi looked at her, "Writing to your father was a seminal moment for me."

"Really? How so?"

"It made me feel that I could somehow *help* your father in spreading his wisdom. Me, Mohandas Gandhi, could *help* your father. It was an unheard-of thought for me."

She nodded.

Gandhi closed his eyes, "I had thought of writing to him many times before. I had so many thoughts and observations to share with him over the years. I read each of his new works, year after year, marveling at his fast pace of creation, at his wisdom, always being able to put in words what I had felt true in my heart but was unable to express."

Tatiana smiled.

"I read whole passages to my wife," Gandhi said, and then sheepishly added, "she is illiterate...."

Tatiana tried to conceal her surprise. Yet Gandhi spotted her reaction and said, "Women, unfortunately, were not cherished in my society in the past. I hope it is now changing."

Tatiana nodded.

"But I've taught her," Gandhi said, "I insisted on teaching her. And she can now read and write slowly, but it is not as enjoyable for her as I would have liked for it to be. But," he closed his eyes for a moment, "I would read to her whole passages, especially from *'The Kingdom of God'* but also from other books. She really liked *'Ivan the Fool.'* She still mentions it occasionally."

Tatiana nodded, "I like that story too," she said quietly.

"You do?" Gandhi said, "It is brilliant, isn't it? Though Ivan's brothers are tempted by money and military power, the unsophisticated Ivan, with his simple way of life, eventually becomes the ruler of the country! Despite the lack of a standing army or currency! And *all* of the citizens are welcome at Ivan's table!"

Tatiana laughed, "And those who have calluses on their hands are fed first—"

"Yes, the workers!" Gandhi exclaimed, "While the intellectuals have to eat the leftovers!" he burst into laughter.

Tatiana smiled. She hesitated for a moment, not wanting to sound too arrogant, but then she said, "I copied my father's handwriting in that story and sent it to the publisher."

"You *did?*" Gandhi's eyes widened.

Tatiana smiled and looked at the window, "I was only 21, and had helped my father for two years then…. He had given me the responsibility of copying his handwriting, which was a heavy responsibility—"

"I can only imagine!"

Tatiana nodded, "And then I read the story to my little brothers. Masha loved it," she said, closing her eyes at the memory of her late sister. "She was fourteen then. And little Andrey and Michael loved it. And even Alexey, who was four years old, understood the story...."

"That is the *brilliance*," Gandhi said excitedly, "the wisdom lies in *simplicity*, in telling a complicated story in a simple way, so that even a child could understand it!"

Tatiana laughed, "You sound like my father!"

Gandhi was overwhelmed by the comparison, and shook his head in disapproval. He played with his fingers.

They sat there in silence for a moment.

Suddenly they heard a knock at the door.

Tatiana got up and walked to the door, opening it.

The two guards were there, and looked away from her into the house.

Gandhi, from the living room, saw them and exclaimed, "Behold! I am still alive!"

"Sir," one of them said, "according to our schedule you are to leave now for your tour of the Palazzo Venezia."

Gandhi looked confused, "I thought the dinner was at eight."

"Yes," said the guard, "but prior to it there is a tour of the palace scheduled for you."

Gandhi waved his hand dismissively, "I thank you, but we have yet to conclude this meeting. When I am done I shall return to the car by myself."

The guards looked confused.

Gandhi added from the couch, "Thank you very much!"

The guards nodded and turned around heading downstairs.

Tatiana closed the door. "Are you sure you don't—I do not wish to get you in any trouble…."

Gandhi smiled, "Oh, don't worry. They will come back, this just gained us a little more time."

Tatiana came back to the living room and sat down. Then she noticed the empty teapot. She got up and said, "I'll make us some more tea."

In the kitchen Tatiana waited for the kettle to boil. Her thoughts turned back to her father. The meeting with Gandhi was stirring many old memories.

When the water boiled Tatiana poured it into the kettle and returned to the living room. He looked at her, shyly and said, "If I may say, this"—he gestured at her and him—"is so enjoyable for me."

Tatiana sat down, "And for me."

Gandhi sat down. "I think that receiving the letter from your father might have been one of the most meaningful moments in my life."

"Was it?" Tatiana asked.

Mohandas and Kasturba Gandhi, c.1895.

LONDON,
OCTOBER 1909

Gandhi walked back into the hotel. He was tired after yet another unsuccessful day of trying to procure meetings with members of the House of Lords. As he approached the stairs, the receptionist called over to him, "Sir? Mr. Gandhi?"

Gandhi looked at the receptionist, surprised. The tall English man had, up until that moment, seemed quite aloof.

"Yes?" Gandhi said, walking toward the reception.

"I believe we received a letter for you."

"Oh," Gandhi said. It had only been two weeks since he had sent the letter to Tolstoy, so he knew the letter would not be from him. It was probably from someone in his family.

The receptionist turned to the wooden postal cabinet and took the letter in his hand. He handed it to Gandhi slowly, almost reluctantly. "I do not mean to seem impertinent," he said, "but do you really correspond with the great Russian author?"

Gandhi looked at the letter, disbelieving the writing on it. "From: Leo Tolstoy, Yasnaya Polyana, Tula District, Russia." The other side clearly had his name on it: "Mohandas Gandhi, Westminster Hotel, 4 Victoria Street, London W.C., Great Britain."

Gandhi was speechless.

The formerly-aloof-receptionist began speaking in a torrent of words about Anna Karenina being possibly the best novel he had read since—

"Excuse me," Gandhi mumbled finally, and took the letter. He walked up the stairway, first slowly, then faster, eventually jumping over every other stair.

In his room he put his coat and his umbrella down, placed the letter on the desk, and stared at it.

He knew the letter was most likely a polite rejection of his request. Surely that was all that it would be. Otherwise how else could he explain the rapid reply? Any *thoughtful* reply would have taken *days* or even weeks. And he was told in the post office that it could take up to ten days for the letter to arrive in Russia. And now only two weeks had passed.

His thoughts were rushing about in his head. He almost thought of not opening the letter, not yet. Would it not be more respectful to open it next to Dr. Mehta? After all he was the one to introduce him to the essay and offered the money for the—

Gandhi's hands grabbed the letter, ignoring these thoughts, opening the envelope in an instant and unfolding the one-page letter. He held it in his trembling hands and read:

"Yasnaya Polyana,

Oct. 7, 1909

To: Mr. M. K. Gandhi

Westminster Hotel

4 Victoria Street,

London, W.C.

GREAT BRITAIN

Mr. Gandhi:

Just now I have received your very interesting letter, which gives me great pleasure. May God help all your dear brothers and co-workers in the Transvaal Colony.

This fight between gentleness and brutality, between humility and love on one side, and conceit and violence on the other, makes itself ever more strongly felt here to us also— especially in the sharp conflicts between religious obligations and the laws of the State expressed by the conscientious objection to render military service. Such objections are taking place very frequently.

I have indeed written "*A letter to a Hindu*" and am very pleased to have it translated.

As to the title of the book on Krishna, that shall be communicated to you soon from Moscow.

As regards to reincarnation, of course I would

accommodate you, if you so desire, to delete those passages in question.

It will give me great pleasure to help your edition. Publication and circulation of my writings, translated into Indian dialects, can only be a matter of pleasure to me.

The question regarding monetary payment of royalties should not at all be allowed to appear in religious undertakings.

I give my fraternal greetings and am glad to have come into personal contact with you.

Leo Tolstoy"

Gandhi fell onto the bed, holding the letter in his hand, not believing his good fortune! The letter was *handwritten*. The signature looked *authentic*. The envelope indeed stated "Yasnaya Polyana." Could this be *real?*

Yes, this was a real letter. A *real* letter from *Tolstoy* to him! To Mohandas Gandhi.

He could not comprehend it. He read the short letter again, and then again, relishing each word:

"Just now I have received your very interesting letter…" *Interesting* letter? Also, Tolstoy had taken the extra moment to add the word 'very', stating "*very* interesting letter." And the rest of the sentence read, "which gives me great pleasure." could it really be that it had given him pleasure? And not only 'pleasure', but '*great* pleasure'?

Was this a mere cordiality? Or did Gandhi bring actual *pleasure* to his teacher and sage?

He read it again not believing that Tolstoy had so generously blessed Gandhi and his struggle: "May God help all your dear brothers and co-workers in the Transvaal Colony."

Tolstoy even noticed the small details, promised that someone from Moscow will let Gandhi know of the exact title of the book on Krishna from which the many quotes in *'A Letter to a Hindu'* were taken. Tolstoy even allowed Gandhi, so generously, to omit the sentence about reincarnation.

Gandhi also marveled that Tolstoy would be "very pleased" to have the essay translated. Could it be that Gandhi helping to publish the essay would indeed give "great pleasure" to the old master? Or was Tolstoy just being kind and polite?

No, Gandhi decided. Tolstoy *was* sincere. Here he wrote that "publication and circulation of my writings, translated into Indian dialects, can only be a matter of pleasure to me."

Gandhi reread the sentence, "can only be a matter of *pleasure* to me."

He read it out loud, to himself in the empty small room, "publication and circulation of my writings, translated into Indian dialects, can only be a matter of *pleasure* to me"!

He giggled. This was a letter addressed to *him!* From *Tolstoy!*

He found it hard to believe.

He paced around the room, thinking of what should be done next. He should translate the essay. He should write a preface to it. He should print it and send it to

Gokhale in Mumbai, and ask for it to be distributed....

Gandhi's hands reached again for the letter, and he read it yet again. He marveled at Tolstoy's "fraternal greetings." This means that Tolstoy sees *him*, Gandhi, as his *brother!*

This was too much to bear.

He had to *share* it with someone.

He decided to telegram his family. On the way downstairs he formulated the short message, trying to spare the cost of any additional word, while at the same time wishing to capture the enormity of the moment. He completed the telegram form at the reception desk and gave it to the tall receptionist, who was eager to converse, but Gandhi apologized, "I must pay homage to a very dear friend, please forgive me."

With the letter from Tolstoy in hand along with his black umbrella, Gandhi nearly ran through the London streets, crossing the roads somewhat dangerously, then running down the smaller streets past Hamilton Terrace. He quickly passed by the beautiful houses with their well-tended gardens without a second glance until he reached Dr. Mehta's door.

It was only when the servant opened the door with a surprised look that Gandhi realized he had come unannounced. The servant explained that Dr. Mehta was seeing a patient, but that he would soon be available.

Gandhi nodded and waited patiently in the waiting room.

Finally, nearly an hour later, and after Gandhi had managed to read the letter several more times, Dr.

Mehta appeared at the entrance, "Mohandas! What a pleasant surprise! Please forgive me for taking so long—"

"He wrote back!" Gandhi exclaimed, "He wrote back!"

"Who?"

Gandhi shouted, "Tolstoy of course!" He then whispered, a little embarrassed of shouting like that, "Count Tolstoy! He responded!"

"Favorably?"

"Favorably? Favorably?! Read!" Gandhi handed Dr. Mehta the letter. He looked anxiously at his old friend as he read the letter.

Dr. Mehta nodded, "That is very kind of him."

"Very kind?!" Gandhi exclaimed, "This is… noble! Gallant of him! And he responded so *promptly*!"

Dr. Mehta laughed, "Very kind of him."

Gandhi paced the room, "I will translate the essay, and write the introduction as you advised, but I must make some copies of it immediately! I will take some to the *India House* and show these young men exactly—"

"India House?" Dr. Mehta frowned, "Wasn't your last visit there a failure?"

"I wouldn't say it was a *failure*…."

"That is exactly what you said. You said, 'They did not understand anything. It was an utter failure', you sat right there on the divan when you said it to me."

"I… well… It may have been a *challenge*, but now,

with this," he pointed at the letter, "I *know* I can convince them."

Dr. Mehta sighed, "They say that one must pick his battles, Mohandas."

Gandhi nodded and said adamantly, "I pick this one with both my hands."

Two days later Gandhi stood in front of the large room in the *India House.*

The day before, when he arranged for the talk, Gopal, the manager of the India House, was surprised to see him. He clearly remembered the unsuccessful meeting a few months earlier, when the South African Hindu walked away from the meeting, obviously defeated.

But Gandhi returned rejuvenated, requesting a prompt meeting be called the following day.

Now, facing a crowd of over twenty young Hindus, Gandhi distributed copies of Tolstoy's essay among them. "It is written in a rather lofty English," he said, "but I assume you should all handle it fine."

The following half hour was quiet, as Gandhi insisted that each person read the *'Letter to a Hindu'* at his own pace. When a few of them finished, he whispered to them to write down any questions that they might have. Only when the last one finished reading Gandhi said:

"You are all familiar with the *'Free Hindustan'* magazine?"

They all nodded.

"Well, the editor of the magazine had written to Tolstoy, asking him for his *support* of the violent struggle for Indian independence. Now, let me be clear. Though I am a preacher of nonviolence, you and I share the *same* aspiration: An India free of foreign rule, an *independent* India, where everyone can live in peace, be valued, respected and free."

He looked at them intently, "You and I do not differ on the *end* goal. On the contrary, I am willing to give my life for the attainment of this noble goal. Do you?"

Most of them nodded, some eagerly.

"Where we differ, or," he corrected himself, "where we might have differed *thus far*, is in the *way* of procuring that goal. I, like you, once believed in the power of physical brute." He paused for a long moment. "And so did Count Tolstoy. When he was a young man of about your age, he was a soldier in the Crimean War."

Gandhi looked around the room. "Tolstoy saw people killed in front of his eyes. He saw the brutish state of men. He saw the damage violence brings to one's soul. He saw the damage that violence brings to one's *society*."

Gandhi nodded, looking into the young people's eyes, "He knew that a heart which learns to become violent, will eventually use the violence against its own people. The Russian army, violently killing others, supported a Russian society, in which violence is executed in the day-to-day life. Even coercion, lack of freedom of speech, unfair court systems—even *these* are forms of violence. Tolstoy understood that."

He paused. "But Tolstoy was willing to take the *courageous* step and to walk away from the violent doctrine, as attractive as it may have seemed to him in the beginning. He was willing to turn his back to the stature and prestige which being a commander in the army brought."

He looked around the room. He was not in a hurry. He knew very well that these young people were also moved by the stature and prestige that violence could grant them among their peers. Did he not see the previous time he was there how their eyes glittered when he mentioned the assassination of Sir Curzon Wiley? Even if they did not *say* it to him, he sensed their respect to their peer who committed the murder.

"No," Gandhi said, "Tolstoy was willing to walk away from the prestige given by others, and to turn to the truth as he knew it, the truth of his heart, which he knew was the real truth. Since then Tolstoy's life has been devoted to replacing the method of violence for removing tyranny or securing reform by the method of *non-resistance to evil*. He would meet hatred expressed in violence by love expressed in self-suffering!"

Gandhi sighed. "Five years ago, some of you may remember, Japan—without bothering to declare a war—destroyed seven ships of the Russian Fleet at Port Arthur, on the border of Russia and China. Tolstoy condemned Japan for having blindly followed the law of modern science, falsely so-called, and feared for that country 'the greatest calamities.' I venture to tell you, Tolstoy was right! Whether now, or in ten years, or in fifty years, Japan will *have* to pay for its violence. Our own religion teaches us of the law of *karma*. When one chooses violence, one is bound to suffer violence. When one," his eyes became moist, "dare to choose love and even *suffer* doing so, one is bound to receive love! We do not need to read Tolstoy in order to understand it. Our own religion and tradition teaches us that."

There was silence in the room. Gandhi continued, "It is time for us now to pause. The route that many have taken—" he paused, then adding, "that many of *us* have taken—may lead us astray. We must consider whether, in our *impatience* with English rule, we do not want to replace one evil by another—and a worse."

His last comment caused unrest, and one of the men stood up, "No rule—no rule at all—can be worse than the English!"

"Really?" Gandhi said, his voice raised. "Really? Are you *certain* of it? How about the *Americans*?"

The young men looked puzzled.

Gandhi continued, "We hear the Americans, by decree from President Andrew Jackson, through the Indian Removal Act, removed *whole* tribes of 'Indians', in many ways bringing the end of several civilizations!"

"The British have moved and relocated us too!" called one of the men, "And they still do!"

"Indeed," Gandhi nodded, "but are they the *worst* of occupiers? How about Genghis Khan? You may not know him, but I am older than you and have known him myself."

A quiet laughter passed in the room.

"Genghis Khan," Gandhi smiled, "who lived 800 years ago"—the rest of the group smiled, understanding the pun— "had much more blood on his hands than the British Empire *ever* will. Under his leadership the Mongol empire grew into the largest empire the world has ever seen. The Mongol army swept across Asia, killing its rivals with great ferocity for nearly two centuries! It is estimated that 60 million were killed by them! Do you want a Genghis Khan?"

Silence followed.

Gandhi continued. "And to those of you believing in *revolutions* and *throwing* the British out without any gradual, healthy process, then think of this: how many of you know about the Chinese famine that proceeded the end of the Yuan dynasty?"

No one raised his hand.

Gandhi nodded, "In China, following the end of the Yuan dynasty, chaos reigned, and rule passed between warring tribes, with many outlaws ruling and roaming the country. An era where no law and no judgment followed. Without an organizing regime, soon famine broke out. By the time the new Ming Dynasty took control, *30 million* had been killed by mere unrest and famine, simply because the power from the Yuan dynasty was not properly passed on."

He looked around the room. He could sense that they were with him, and had respected him for having done his homework. He pointed at the copies of the essay, "Tolstoy lays two paths clearly before us. We either choose violence, contaminating the soil of our motherland with gun factories and more blood than your mind could ever conceive of, or—" he paused—

"we dare to take the more difficult route of nonviolence. It may be a *longer* one. It will for certain be the more *difficult* one. But the end result is something that I am willing," his voice trembled, "to give my life for."

Silence followed. Some of the men moved uncomfortably in their seats.

Gandhi nodded, "If we do not want the English in India we must *pay the price*. Tolstoy indicates it."

He opened the essay and read out loud,

> "Do not resist evil, but also do not yourselves *participate* in evil: do not participate in the collection of taxes, and in the violent deeds of the law courts and—most importantly—the violence of armies and soldiers. Do that, and no one in the world will be able to enslave you."

He looked at them as he would often look in recent years at the judges in court. He would represent people from the Hindu community at courts ruled by white British judges. He could often sense the judges' innate disrespect for him just because of his appearance. Therefore, Gandhi would quote from past British rulings: quoting Lord Bannatyne, Lord Kennet, Lord Glenlee and other famous British judges. It was never his *charisma* which won him the cases, but always the attention to *detail* and the *references* he would make that would convince the judges that justice was on Gandhi's side.

Gandhi looked around the room. He sensed that his words had made an impact. Then, one of the young men raised his hand.

"Please," Gandhi said.

The man stood, "Their Bible states, in Exodus 21:23, 'But if there is any further injury, then you shall appoint as a penalty: life for life, an eye for an eye.'"

The many young men nodded in agreement as the man continued, "It says so in their sacred book! This is all they *know*, an eye for an eye!"

The young men nodded in agreement and mumbled some statements of agreement.

Gandhi waited for the murmur to quiet down and then said, quietly, "An 'eye for an eye' would only make the whole world blind."

Silence followed as the men were contemplating his comment. One of them then stood up. Gandhi recognized him from the previous talk, as the one whose father was shot by a British soldier. "But the British," the young man said, "don't *think* that we are capable of home rule, of self-governance!"

Gandhi nodded. "True. But the question we must ask ourselves is," he said quietly, "do *we* think we are capable of home rule?"

"Yes we are!" one of them shouted, and others followed, "Yes! We are!"

Gandhi nodded. "And do you represent the majority of Indians?"

This time the men were less cheerful in their expressions.

Gandhi nodded. "Some people I know may say that those present in this room—me included—are but rich and spoiled children, heirs of princes and Indian royalty, coming only from the large cities." He paused and looked around the room. "Some may say that we do not *represent* the Indian people. And that the Indian people, honestly, do not *feel* ready."

One of the quieter men stood up, "But isn't every society led by the few leading scholars and the intelligentsia?"

Gandhi nodded, "Possibly. But we must ask ourselves the question I had posed regardless: Are we *ready*? And do we *believe* we are ready? And if we are ready, then why do all of us cooperate with the regime, and enable ourselves, as Tolstoy says, to be controlled by so few?" He then looked at the essay again and quoted, *"Do not the figures make it clear that not the English, but the Indians, have enslaved themselves?"*

"I have read it," the quiet young man said, "but it only portrays the *symptoms*, but does not offer the *cure*."

Gandhi shook his head, "The cure is clear, but you may not like it! The cure is through showing the British the injustice that they cause. And the only wise way to do it, as Tolstoy clearly stated, is through non-cooperation." He paused. "I envision a time in which the brute force of the British and the sheer stupidity of their rule over a foreign people will baffle so many of them, that it would lead to their *willing* withdrawal, but"—he raised his hand, his palm facing them— "I know very well that you will say that I am a dreamer. I am certain that they said the same of Sri Gupta, our great Hindu brother who established the Gupta dynasty, uniting India in the Golden Age of our country. Did they not say of Sri Gupta, who believed in a united, large and prosperous India, that he was a dreamer? And yet, a dreamer brought to a dynasty and heritage not less prestigious than the Roman Empire, if not more." He looked at the young men's eyes, "Our Golden Age in science, mathematics, astronomy, religion and philosophy, came because of a *dreamer*."

He pointed at the essay, "I beg you to at least entertain these radical ideas. Think among yourselves if there is not *more* courage, *more* bravery, in choosing the nonviolent way of offering love and willing to suffer, over the easy violent way, which leads to nothing but more violence in the future."

Silence followed. Then, suddenly, one of the young men clapped. A few others joined him, but not everyone. Gandhi motioned for everyone to stop. "Please reserve the applause to when our nation is free," he said, "Then we could all applaud together."

Gandhi left the *India House* feeling invincible. He felt more certain of his approach than ever. He took a carriage back from Highgate to Regent's Park, from which he walked to the hotel, enjoying the cool night.

When he returned to the hotel he was pleased to find two telegrams waiting for him at the reception. One was from Moscow, from Mr. Chertkov of the Tolstoy's office, specifying the name of the book from which the references were made in Tolstoy's essay, *"Sri Krishna: Lord of Love"* by P. Bharati.

The second telegram brought an immediate smile to Gandhi's face. His son stated briefly,

"Congratulations for Tolstoy! Anticipating your

return. Mother asks if you sent him your biography."

Gandhi chuckled as he read it. This was exactly his wife, his Kasturba. He could hear her in his head, "You should have sent him the biography!"

The following weeks Gandhi tried his best to accomplish his mission in London. He was finally given a meeting with the Leader of the House of Lords, Earl Robert Crewe-Milnes.

The meeting at the House of Lords in the Palace of Westminster did not go well. Though he was cordial, the Earl explained that the Asiatic Act could not be repealed. However, he offered that the *enforcement* of the Act might be "*taken more lightly*" if Gandhi and the Indian community would quit their campaign. He explained to the small and gaunt-looking Hindu that his campaign made "too much noise" and was a "nuisance" to the Colonial Secretary General Smuts and to the Transvaal Colony's Government.

Gandhi was cordial, but was unwilling to agree to the compromise, "Please understand me, my Lord, this is a principle of the *law*, not of the *enforcement* of the law. As citizens of the British Empire, we are entitled to the same rights *under the law*."

Seeing that the Earl was unimpressed, Gandhi explained, "The Asiatic Act, which is an unjust *law*, must be repealed. Otherwise what you are offering to me is but a *temporary* solution, until again pressure is put by interest groups on the Colonial Secretary, and he shall decide to enforce the law again! We demand that the law itself be repealed, as it is unlawful."

The Earl gave Gandhi excuses dressed in flowery language, and shortly after concluded their meeting.

Returning to the hotel, Gandhi's mood was foul.

To add to this, the following day he read in the newspaper that:

> "Russian Author Leo Tolstoy is bedridden with pneumonia. The doctors warn that the author of 'Anna Karenina' and 'War and Peace', aged 81-year-old, is in a dire condition. His agent Mr. Vladimir Chertkov from Moscow stated: "Count Tolstoy is attended by the finest doctors in the Russian Empire. His family is attending to his every need. Our prayers are with the great author and with his family."'

Gandhi read the article and his heart began racing. "No!" he whispered, "Please, Lord, *don't!*"

The following day Gandhi received even more bad news,

> "Harilal is in prison again, Transvaal court ruling, hard labor for six months."

Gandhi read it and shook his head in amazement. His son! In jail! The Transvaal government was ruthless!

He became depressed. The clarity that he had achieved in London, the belief in the righteousness of the path he was taking, the victory of touching the hearts of the young men at the India House—all of it now gone. He was at a loss.

The following day, when Gandhi returned to the hotel in the evening, the tall receptionist called his name as he was about to take the stairs. "Mr. Gandhi?"

"Yes?" Gandhi asked, dreading another bad news.

"You have a guest," the receptionist said, and pointed with his eyes at a European gentleman sitting in the lobby wearing a black bowler hat. The receptionist whispered, "He says he is the translator of Tolstoy's writings, and"—his eyes widened—"that Tolstoy himself sent him to you!"

Gandhi was puzzled. Tolstoy sent this man? He thanked the receptionist and walked, hesitantly, to the gentlemen in the suit who was reading the newspaper. The man sported a neat white moustache and beard, well-trimmed.

"Sir," Gandhi murmured, "have you been looking for me?"

The man stood up. Gandhi noticed he was very tall, "Are you Mr. *Gandhi?*"

"I am him," Gandhi said.

"And I am Aylmer Maude, the translator of—"

Gandhi exclaimed, "You are Aylmer Maude! I have read your translations! *'The Kingdom of God', 'Confession', 'What is Art',* I've read all the non-fiction works—"

"Well," Mr. Maude smiled and reached his hand for a handshake, "it is my pleasure then to meet you!"

"No," Gandhi said, shaking Mr. Maude's hand with both his hands, "the pleasure is all mine!"

Mr. Maude pointed to the couch in front of him, "Please."

For several hours, the two sat in the hotel lobby, Mr. Maude sharing with Gandhi many memories of his years in Russia, reading and then meeting Tolstoy.

Gandhi could not believe that Mr. Maude had actually *met* Tolstoy. He begged Mr. Maude to tell him what Tolstoy was like.

Mr. Maude went on to tell Gandhi about Tolstoy the man. Gandhi was delighted to hear that he was just as he had imagined him: kind, grand, brilliant.

Gandhi expressed his remorse hearing that Tolstoy has been sick.

"But he is doing very well!" Mr. Maude said.

"Very well?" Gandhi said, not understanding, "but I have just recently read—"

"This kind of news appears every now and then, do not trust it! Yes, Tolstoy did have a bit of a cold, but let me assure you, he reads his letters daily."

"Really?" Gandhi asked sheepishly, "I've refrained from writing back to him, not wanting to tire him."

"Oh do not worry about that! He was good enough to send a note to Chertkov for him to telegram me, urging me to meet you at the Westminster Hotel!"

"Really?" Gandhi's eyes became moist, "He really did that?"

Mr. Maude nodded. "I presume he must have taken a

liking to you."

Gandhi's eyes widened.

"Now," Mr. Maude got up, "if it is not too late for you, I'd like to dine somewhere. Would you join me for dinner?"

Gandhi was still mesmerized by Mr. Maude's comment. Tolstoy had 'taken a liking' to him? Could it be?

"What say you?" Mr. Maude asked again.

Gandhi hesitated. He had had many negative experiences in London eating in the company of meat-eaters, who would often insist that he eat meat as well. After that the conversation would always deteriorate. He had learned to prefer having "tea" rather than a full meal with a person whom he did not know.

"What are you thinking so long?" Mr. Maude said smilingly.

Gandhi looked down, "You see, Mr. Maude, it would be my *pleasure* to dine with you, but I am a vegetarian, and in London I've learned—"

"Well I'm a vegetarian too!"

Gandhi's eyes lit. While vegetarianism was common in India, it was rare to find vegetarians in Britain. "You are?" he asked.

"Of course! I'm a Tolstoyan!" Mr. Maude smiled, "We shall go to 'The Central'!"

"'The Central'?" Gandhi's eyes lit up, "On Farringdon Street?"

Mr. Maude nodded.

Gandhi exclaimed, "My, I have not been there in twenty years! When I was a student here I used to go there all the time. What a pleasant surprise!"

Mr. Maude seemed happy, "Shall we then?"

Gandhi exclaimed, "We shall indeed! I cannot believe we are going to 'The Central'!" he looked at Mr. Maude with appreciation, "And with the news of Tolstoy feeling better, you, Sir, have just made my day!"

Aylmer Maude, British author and translator of the works of
Tolstoy, circa 1910.

YASNAYA POLYANA,
NOVEMBER 1909

Tatiana and Alexandra sorted the letters quietly. Tolstoy was resting in the adjacent bedroom. But he was feeling better. Three weeks had passed since she arrived at her childhood home following her father's sickness.

Her father improved rapidly. Now she was more relaxed about her father's state. She knew he'd get better.

What worried her more, however, was the state of her mother. Her mother would walk around the house, trying to listen in on conversations. Once, when Tatiana walked out of her own room, she found her mother seemingly dusting the paintings in the hallway. "Mama!" Tatiana exclaimed, "Are you *spying* on me?"

"Not at all, Tanyushka," her mother whispered, "I was just wondering whether your Papa was in your room, that is all."

These incidents worried Tatiana. Things were not as

they used to be in her parents' house. She believed the worst of her parent's behavior was past. Now it seemed even worse than before.

She sighed and kept sorting through the letters. They were getting hundreds of letters each day. The largest pile was of people wishing 'the great Tolstoy' quick recovery and many years of health.

She looked at Alexandra, who was simultaneously sifting through the sack of letters. The height of the pile of the 'Feel better letters' was so tall they started two other piles as well. In a notebook, each of them wrote of any notable people wishing health to their father. There were letters from many important figures. These letters were mostly brief and cordial, without real content, and they knew their father would only care to hear the names.

But among the many letters Tatiana found several ones which she knew her father would like.

After nearly three hours of sorting through letters, Tatiana followed Alexandra, both holding relevant piles of letters to their father's bedroom.

Alexandra turned around, whispering, "He is sleeping!"

Their father then groaned, "No I'm not."

Alexandra and Tatiana entered the room and sat down on stools near their father's bed.

Tolstoy whispered, "Close the door!"

Alexandra closed the door.

Their father sighed, "I was not sleeping. I was just pretending to be sleeping in case 'you know who' decides to peek in."

The daughters nodded in understanding. Tatiana began, "Papa, there are many letters today. We'll try not to disturb you for too long."

Her father grimaced, "Tanya, I would like for the two of you to disturb me the whole day!"

Tatiana smiled and looked at her notebook, "Greetings, Papa, and wishes of quick recovery, from Prince Kropotkin, Maxim Gorky, the Buddhist priest Soyen Shaku, George Bernard Shaw, Petr Verigin of the Doukhobors in Canada—"

Tolstoy shook his head, "Look at them all coming out of their holes! Thinking I am about to die, and everyone suddenly remembers me!"

The following hour passed in reading letters to their father.

"Papa," Alexandra said, "there is a letter, as well as a book, from one Hindu from London, following a correspondence between the two of you…?"

Tatiana took the letter from her sister and had a quick glance at it, "Papa, it is from the man who published your *Letter to a Hindu.*"

"Oh, that is good news." He looked at Alexandra, "Show me the book."

Alexandra handed him the book. He looked at it. On the blue cover it stated:

"M. K. Gandhi: An Indian Patriot in South Africa

By Rev. J. J. Doke"

"Interesting," Tolstoy mumbled. He looked at Tatiana, "What does the letter say?"

Tatiana handed Alexandra the letter and motioned, 'You read, I am tired.'

Alexandra nodded and read out loud,

> "Dear Sir:
>
> I beg to tender my thanks for your letter in connection with the letter addressed to a Hindu, and with the matters that I dealt with in my letter to you.
>
> Having heard about your failing health I refrained in order to save you the trouble, from sending an acknowledgment, knowing that a written expression of my thanks was a superfluous formality, but Mr. Aylmer Maude, whom I have now been able to meet thanks to your kindness"—

"Oh," Tolstoy mumbled, "that is good." He smiled at his daughters, "Now the poor Hindu won't be lonely in London."

Alexandra nodded and continued reading,

> "...but Mr. Aylmer Maude, whom I have now been able to meet thanks to your kindness, reassured me that you were keeping very good health indeed and that unfailingly and regularly attended to your correspondence every day.
>
> It was very gladsome news to me, and it encourages me to write to you further about matters which are, I know, of the greatest importance according to your teaching."

Tolstoy hummed, listening as he flipped through the pages of the blue book in his hand, "Go on, Alexandra."

Alexandra looked at the letter and read,

> "I beg to send you herewith a copy of a book written by a friend—an Englishman, who is at present in South Africa, in connection with my life, insofar as it has a bearing on the struggle with which I am so connected, and to which my life is dedicated. As I am very anxious to engage your active interest and sympathy I thought that it would not be considered by you as out of the way for me to send you the book."

Tolstoy mumbled, "No! Not at all."

Alexandra continued reading:

> "In my opinion, this struggle of the Indians in the Transvaal Colony is the greatest of modern times, inasmuch as it has been idealized both as to the goal as also the *methods* adopted to reach the goal. I am not aware of a struggle, in which the participators are not to derive any *personal* advantage at the end of it, and in which fifty-percent of the persons affected have undergone great suffering and trial for the sake of a principle."

Tolstoy hummed, "Interesting. Interesting...." He looked at his daughters and nodded, "The Hindus are proving to have a strong backbone!"

Tatiana nodded and looked at Alexandra for her to speed up. Alexandra kept reading:

> "It has not been possible for me to advertise the

struggle as much as I should like. You command, possibly, the widest public today—"

Tatiana shook her head, "Here it comes, Papa, asking you for favors...."

Tolstoy shrugged his shoulders and gestured with his fingers for Alexandra to continue.

> "You command, possibly, the widest public today. If you are satisfied as to the facts you will find set forth in Mr. Doke's book, and if you consider that the conclusions I have arrived at are justified by the facts, may I ask you to use your influence in any manner you think fit to popularize the movement? If it succeeds, it will be not only a triumph of religion, love and truth over irreligion, hatred and falsehood, but it is highly likely to serve as an example to the millions in India and to people in other parts of the world who may be down-trodden, and will certainly go a great way towards breaking up the party of violence, at least in India."

Tolstoy hummed to himself.

Alexandra continued:

> "If we hold out to the end, as I think we would, I entertain not the slightest doubt as to the ultimate success; and your encouragement in the way suggested by you can only strengthen us in our resolve."

Tolstoy nodded to himself, "Very well. Very well...."

Tatiana motioned for her sister to hasten up.

Alexandra shrugged her shoulders and read quickly,

> "My attempts to amend the situation have

yielded no fruits here in London. I shall therefore return to South Africa this week, and invite imprisonment."

Tolstoy shook his head disapprovingly, "Sheer stupidity! These imbecile Brits are bringing their own demise!"

Alexandra kept reading:

"I may add that my son has happily joined me in this struggle, and is now undergoing imprisonment with hard labor for six months."

Tolstoy tut-tutted, and Alexandra kept reading,

"If you would be so good as to reply to this letter, may I ask you to address your reply to me at Johannesburg...."

She added, "He gives the address," and then continued reading:

"Hoping that this will find you in good health, I remain,

Your obedient servant,

M. K. Gandhi"

Tatiana asked, her pen in hand, "Papa, shall I respond to him 'Thank you for your kind wishes and best of luck in your struggle'?"

Tolstoy looked at the window, "No, Tanya, something kinder, warmer."

"I can extend and lengthen it Papa."

Tolstoy sighed and looked at the window. It was snowing outside.

He then took a deep breath and looked at his daughters, smiling, tired, "Give the letter to me. I shall respond to it myself."

"Papa," Tanya said, "I can…."

But Tolstoy extended his hand to receive the letter.

Tatiana shrugged her shoulders and nodded to Alexandra. Alexandra handed him the letter.

Tolstoy thanked her and sighed, "I shall now take a rest."

They nodded and got up.

As they exited the room, Tatiana saw her mother walking, incidentally, away from the room, down the hallway, humming to herself while looking at the paintings on the wall.

Tatiana sighed. She walked to her room. Her father would be alright. He was not in any danger anymore. She could not do anything more for her parents. She missed her husband. Tomorrow she should leave. She now had to take care of her own life.

ROME,
DECEMBER 1931

Tatiana poured them more tea. Gandhi was sitting in front of her, speaking vivaciously. It was getting dark outside. She was wondering how long would Gandhi stay. She did not want to cause him any trouble.

"When I left London," Gandhi said, "I was a different man, you see?"

"How so?" Tatiana asked.

Gandhi nodded. "A few months earlier I arrived in London, frightened at the task, feeling confused, worried about the assassination of Sir Wiley. I was uncertain of the method I was choosing for my community...."

He sighed. "But when I left London I was a new man. I had gained the support of the world's greatest thinker! He had even arranged for me to meet his English translator, and blessed my struggle. I felt invincible."

Tatiana smiled.

"It was a ten-day journey to return to South Africa on the steamer. I felt like it was carrying me"—he paused and looked at her sheepishly—"do you know that feeling when you are on a boat or a train, and you can sense the passage of time? You can sense the change? As if the book of your life is turning to a new page?"

Tatiana nodded slowly. "When I took Anya with me and left Russia a few years ago, it felt that way to me. As if it was a moment of time, a *defining* moment in time."

"Exactly!" Gandhi exclaimed. "That is how it was for me. As the ship made its way, I sat in my room and worked like a madman!"

Tatiana laughed.

"Whenever I would go on the deck to catch a breath of fresh air, I would imagine your father blowing wind in my sail, so to speak."

Tatiana smiled, wanting to hear more.

Gandhi's eyes became moist, "Having an actual *letter* from your father, a letter of *support*, addressed to *me*, it... *intoxicated* me. I felt like it was no longer an *option* for me to retrace, to give up—I felt *compelled* to continue— obligated really."

Tatiana nodded.

Gandhi chuckled, "In those ten days I wrote more than I wrote in any other period of my life." He shook his head and sighed, his eyes moist as he murmured, "I felt your father's trust in me. And I did not want to disappoint him."

Gandhi wearing a turban, age 37, 1906.

ONBOARD THE *"KILDONAN CASTLE"* STEAMER
THE ATLANTIC OCEAN, NOVEMBER 1909

The steam ship *"Kildonan Castle"* sailed rapidly from the port of London through the English Channel. It was a bitter cold day, and it was raining heavily. All passengers, apart from the crew, spent two days hidden amongst the ship's seven floors.

The first floor near the deck contained the first-class rooms. The following two floors below were second class, and the last four floors were dedicated to third class.

On the ship's bottom floor, in a tiny room with a small round window, sat a Hindu man of 40-year-old, who worked at a frantic pace. There was no heating in the third class rooms. However, the engine rooms across the corridor brought plenty of heat. And constant noise.

But the constant hum from the engine rooms helped Gandhi concentrate. He folded the bed up, and brought the pull-down desk down. There he sat and worked. His goal was to translate the 20-page-essay by his great teacher into his mother tongue, Guajarati.

That evening he skipped dinner, continuing to work on the translation. What could have taken him three or four days in ordinary times, now took him less than a day and a half. He left the room only to go to the lavatory, skipping breakfast as well. At lunch the following day he rushed to the dining room to bring a few fruits and vegetables to his room.

By the second day in the late afternoon the translation was done.

Gandhi folded up the desk and brought down the narrow bed. He lay on it, his whole body aching from sitting at the small fold-up desk. But he also felt an enormous sense of vitality. Translating the document, pausing and pondering each and every word, made him feel *closer* to his teacher. As if they were one. As if he could feel the breath of his old teacher behind his shoulder, encouraging him, supporting him.

Tossing from side to side, unable to nap, Gandhi eventually got out of the bed, folded it up and brought the desk down. He sat by the desk, opened a new page in his notebook and wrote the title:

"Introduction to 'A Letter to a Hindu.'"

He closed his eyes. First, he thought, he should explain what this letter *is*. He wrote:

"The letter printed below is a translation of Leo Tolstoy's letter written in Russian in reply to a letter from the Editor of the magazine '*Free Hindustan.*' After having passed from hand to hand, Tolstoy's letter at last came into my possession through a friend who asked me, as one much interested in Tolstoy's writings, whether I thought it worth publishing. I at once replied in the affirmative, and told him I should translate it myself into Guajarati and induce others to translate and publish it in various Indian vernaculars.

The letter as received by me was a type-written copy. It was therefore referred to the author, who confirmed it as his, and kindly granted me permission to print it. To me, as a humble follower of that great teacher whom I have long looked upon as one of my guides, it is a matter of honor to be connected with the publication of his letter."

Gandhi looked at the two paragraphs. It was a sufficient beginning. He took a deep breath. Now he had to speak about the *content* of the letter. This was where he needed to be cautious.

He wanted to state the *truth*, but at the same time not to upset the British censorship. He had heard from acquaintances that the British government often prohibited the publication and distribution of writings of 'seditious quality.' He did not want this important essay to fall into this category because of an unwise introduction.

And yet, if he ignored the important message of the essay, it would do a *disservice* to the reader. He knew very well that many readers would judge whether to invest the time to read the long essay based on its introduction.

He sighed and wrote,

> "It is a mere statement of fact to say that every Indian, whether he owns up to it or not, has national aspirations. But there are as many opinions as to the exact meaning of that aspiration as there are Indian nationalists, and more especially as to the methods to be used to attain the end."

He paused. Now was the time to state clearly that violence was *not* the solution. This, he thought, would appease the British censorship. He wrote:

> "One of the accepted and 'time-honored' methods to attain this end is that of violence. The assassination of Sir Curzon Wylie was an illustration of that method in its worst and most detestable form.
>
> Tolstoy's life has been devoted to replacing the method of violence for removing tyranny or securing reform by the method of non-resistance to evil. He would meet hatred expressed in violence by love expressed in self-suffering."

It was important for Gandhi to also explain that this attitude by Tolstoy applies to *all* the problems that trouble mankind. So often was Gandhi confronted with the question: "Would Tolstoy *really* recommend non-violence for the just struggle of the Indian people?"

The answer, Gandhi knew, was a bold 'yes.' And he wanted to set that clear from the very beginning. He wrote:

> "Tolstoy admits of no exception to whittle down this great and divine law of love. He applies it to all the problems that trouble mankind."

Now, he knew, he had to give an example of what could go wrong, if the Indian nation *choose* to take the violent path, like so many other nations. He remembered his night at the *India House*. He nodded to himself and wrote:

> "When a man like Tolstoy, one of the clearest thinkers in the western world, one of the greatest writers, one who as a soldier has known what violence is and what it can do, condemns Japan for having blindly followed the law of modern science, falsely so-called, and fears for that country 'the greatest calamities', it is for us to pause and consider whether, in our impatience of English rule, we do not want to replace one evil by another and a worse."

He sighed. He hoped the readers could read his position in between the lines. Yes, he was *against* the British occupation. But no, he was not supporting violence, which he knew could lead to nothing else but more violence in the future. He dreaded to think of it.

He continued writing, trying to be as clear and remote, while feeling a great emotional intensity, being on the verge of tears:

> "India, which is the nursery of the great faiths of the world, will cease to be India, whatever else she may become, when she goes through the process of "civilization" in the shape of reproduction on that sacred soil of gun factories, armies and the likes.

> If we do not want the English in India we must
> be willing to *pay the price*. Tolstoy indicates it:
> 'Do not resist evil, but also do not yourselves
> *participate* in evil: do not participate in the
> collection of taxes, and in the violent deeds of
> the law courts and—most importantly—the
> violence of armies and soldiers. Do that, and no
> one in the world will be able to enslave you.' So
> declares passionately the sage of Yasnaya
> Polyana."

As he wrote that, his eyes became moist. There was
so much wisdom in Tolstoy's essay to be shared with
his people. Incredible wisdom. He wanted everyone to
read it.

Countless times he heard his own people—his own
family even—speaking of the British 'enslaving' the
Indian people. And yet, Tolstoy was the first to say out
loud what Gandhi had often felt: that the 'enslavement'
had to be *accepted* by his own people first. He often felt
that every Hindu, deep in their hearts, secretly, had an
inherent *doubt* as to the possibility of an Indian home
rule, or of an Indian-led state.

He nodded his head incessantly as he wrote:

> "Who can question the truth of what Tolstoy
> says in the following: 'A commercial company,
> the British East India Company, had enslaved
> over two hundred years ago a nation
> comprising *two hundred million*. Tell this to a
> man free from superstition and he will fail to
> grasp what these words mean!'

> Tolstoy goes on to write, 'What does it mean
> that thirty thousand people, not athletes, but
> rather weak and ordinary people, have enslaved

two hundred million of vigorous, clever, capable, freedom-loving people? Do not the figures make it clear that not the English, but the Indians, have enslaved themselves?'"

Gandhi felt his soul shaking by this truth. There was so much power in stating it clearly, simply, for what it *was*. For each one British person there were dozens of Indians—five dozen—who could easily oppose the one British had they *wanted* to, and at once end their 'enslavement.' No one could make a Hindu *feel* inferior unless he or she *already* feels inferior in his or her own heart.

Gandhi nodded to himself. Someone finally said it— Tolstoy had the courage to state it clearly. The 'sickness' was now diagnosed. But so was the remedy. Non-cooperation with the government. Gandhi's hand shook as he felt the gravity of the words. He could *see* clearly. There *will* be a time when India will be free. But first, Indians must free *themselves*.

He sighed and brought the preface into conclusion:

> "One need not accept all that Tolstoy says to realize the *central truth* of his indictment of the present system. There is no doubt that there is nothing *new* in what Tolstoy preaches. But"—

Gandhi paused, wishing to conclude his introduction with force. He would write succinct sentences. Short. Powerful. He tightened his fist and wrote:

> "But his presentation of the old truth is refreshingly forceful. His logic is unassailable. And above all he endeavors to practice what he preaches. He preaches to convince. He is sincere and in earnest. He commands attention."

246

Triumphantly, Gandhi signed his initials and put the pen down. It was dinnertime. He had not properly eaten since the day before. Relieved, exhausted and pleased, he walked to the dining room, feeling that he had earned that day's meal.

In the dining room he piled cauliflower, potatoes and rice on his plate and sat down near one of the long tables.

He had expected his mind to give him rest while eating. But his mind was racing. He could imagine the typical responses from people to the essay. "This may be true in *Russia*. But the British only understand force!"

Gandhi shook his head disapprovingly as he ate, 'What then,' he thought, 'more violence? How exactly do you think that violence could bring our freedom?'

"Well," a voice in his mind responded, "first we shall assassinate a few Englishmen and strike terror; then, a few men among us, who have been trained in armed combat, will fight openly. We may have to lose some people, at the most a quarter of a million men, but we shall regain our land!"

Gandhi sighed and responded in his mind, 'But do you not *tremble* to think of freeing India by *assassinations*? Also, you know very well that those who will eventually rise to power through *these* methods will eventually turn the same methods toward their own people! They will turn to murder their own people! This is not the kind of India that I want!'

He kept eating, unable to ignore the voice in his head, "But don't you think that the goal of making India free is a worthwhile goal?"

'Yes, worthwhile and a good goal indeed,' Gandhi responded to himself.

"So cannot this goal justify the means?" the voice pestered him, "Why should we not obtain our goal—which is worthwhile and good as you just stated yourself—by any means necessary?"

Gandhi smiled to himself. 'Your reasoning is plausible. My old belief used to be that there is no connection between the *means* and the *end*. But through that mistake even good men who have considered themselves God-loving have committed grievous crimes.'

The voice was not convinced. "Are you saying that the no violence at *all* can ever be applied?"

'Let us look at that,' Gandhi responded to himself as he took another bite of food. 'The *means* may be likened to a seed, and the *end* to a tree; and there is just the same inviolable connection between the means and the end as there is between the seed and the tree. Think: if anyone were to say, 'I want to worship God; it does not matter that I do so by means of worshiping Satan,' that person would be set down as an ignorant fool, would he not? It is the same in wishing to attain freedom for India and cease the violence practiced by the British by the very same means of violence. We shall then reap exactly as we sow.'

"But," the voice responded, "this is not the work of Satan. This *is* the work of God. It is self-defense only! Shall I think of the means when I have to deal with a *thief* in my own house?"

'Well—' Gandhi tried to respond, but the voice

interrupted him.

"Is it not my duty to drive the thief out of the house in *any* possible way?"

Gandhi sighed to himself. He looked around the room at the people eating. He thought that possibly through looking at them he could give his mind a rest. He was tired. He did not sleep for a day and a half.

"Answer me!" the voice in his mind begged, "Is it not my duty to drive the thief out of the house in any possible way?"

'Not in any possibly way,' Gandhi responded in his mind. 'First, let us identify who the thief is. You would agree with me that different thieves would require a different response, no?'

"No. Thieves are thieves!"

Gandhi took the last bite from his food, savoring the taste. He answered to himself, 'If the thieve is my *father*? I shall then use one kind of means; if it is an *acquaintance* I shall use another; and in the case of a perfect *stranger* I shall use a third. Also, if the thief is a *weakling*, the means will be different from those to be adopted for dealing with an *equal* in physical strength; and if the thief is *armed*, I shall simply remain quiet, wouldn't you? Thus we have a variety of means between the father and the armed man.'

"You are over-complicating the issue," the voice responded. "The simple way of looking at it is that the British are thieves that have invaded our land. That is all! And, given your example, the British are not my father nor an acquaintance, they *are* a perfect stranger, and an armed-one too!"

Gandhi rose from his seat, and took two apples, putting them in his jacket's pockets. He decided not to return to the room just yet, but to go upstairs to the deck. As he climbed the spiral staircase, he heard the voice in his head again: "Answer to me! Are not the British the stranger thief, coming fully armed to steal all of my valuables?"

Gandhi sighed, 'Let us say that this well-armed thief has *already* stolen your valuables, alright?'

"Alright. That is indeed the case, the British *have* already stolen our resources and land for two hundred years!"

"Indeed. But let us refer back to the thief. He came to your village, broke into your house and took your valuables. Naturally, you are filled with anger; you want to *punish* that rogue! If not for your own sake—for you yourself had already had your own belongings taken— then for the good of your neighbors and your village.'

'Now,' Gandhi continued the response, climbing the last floor, 'in response you have collected a number of armed men, you want to take the thief's house in a neighboring village by assault; he is duly informed of it and runs away; he too is incensed. He collects his brother robbers, and sends you a defiant message that he will commit robbery in broad daylight. You then arm your neighbors, and so the battle grows; the robbers increase in numbers; and so do you and your neighbors.'

Gandhi reached the deck, and enjoyed the cool air. He looked at the sky. The moon was full and bright, and the sky was filled with endless stars. He took a deep breath in, and was disturbed to suddenly hear the voice inside again: "But at least this way we can return the peace to my village! Should we ignore the thief and continue to live in terror?"

Gandhi shook his head. 'You wish to return the 'peace' back to the village. But can you see that through your own response and your own methods you have stolen the peace from yourself? Through wanting to take revenge upon the thief you have disturbed your *own* peace! You are now in perpetual fear of being robbed and assaulted! And more and more is at stake as everyone in your village is now involved. You invest in buying arms and in training to fight. You have further stolen peace from your own life.'

The voice in Gandhi's head was quiet.

Gandhi was pleased that he was able to silence the voice. But then he heard the reply, "What do you suggest then?"

Gandhi was annoyed to hear the voice again. He was exhausted from having worked for nearly two days without proper rest. He walked the deck. There were no people on the deck. He passed by the captain's cabin and heard two men laughing. One of them, a sailor, came out and looked at Gandhi.

Gandhi looked away. In the distance he saw dim lights.

The sailor leaned against the railing and looked into the distant lights. "Lisbon," he said to Gandhi, "Portugal."

"Already?" Gandhi asked.

"Indeed." The sailor said. He reached his hand to Gandhi. "I'm Lawrence."

"And I'm Mohandas," Gandhi said. He then followed up by introducing himself the way he always would to Europeans, "Mohandas Gandhi, a lawyer, Johannesburg."

"Lawrence," the sailor followed, "a sailor. The world."

Gandhi chuckled. He nodded and said, "Allow me to correct myself. Mohandas. A fellow traveler. The world."

They smiled to one another.

The man from inside the cabin called, "Lawrence! I need you here!"

Lawrence tipped his hat at Gandhi and hurried back into the captain's cabin.

Gandhi smiled to himself. He looked at the lights of the city in the distance, illuminating the darkness. Then he heard the voice in his head again, "Answer me! What do you suggest then? Should I have just let the thief be? Should I have sat in quiet and let him steal all my valuables?"

Gandhi sighed, closed his eyes and shook his head. 'No. Well... *yes*. At first at least."

"Explain!"

Gandhi walked away from the captain's cabin, striding slowly toward the back of the deck. 'Well, at first, do let him steal your valuables. But do not harbor hatred against him. Consider this armed thief an ignorant brother; intend to reason with him at a suitable opportunity. Remember that he is, after all, a fellow man. You do not know what prompted him to steal.

You, therefore, decide that when you can, you will destroy the man's *motive* for stealing.'

"How can I do *that?!* And besides, through all your kind reasoning, he may come to steal again!"

'Very well. Let him steal again! But this time, instead of being angry with him, take pity on him. Think that this stealing habit must be a disease with him. You therefore keep your doors and windows open, and you place your valuables in the living room, laid on the table, with a kind note. The thief comes, sees that, and is confused. To him, all this is new and bewildering.'

"But he nevertheless would take all the valuables!"

Gandhi arrived at the back of the ship and turned around. He wanted the voice in his head to go away. What was he supposed to do with all of this inner chatter? He leaned against the railing, trying to calm his mind by looking at the dark sea below. He could see the moon flickering on the waves, and hoped for this sight to sooth his soul. Instead, he heard the voice again, "But that damned thief would take all my valuables again!"

'Let us say that he did,' Gandhi responded. 'But, now, something had begun to stir in him! His mind is now agitated!'

"Agitated?"

'Yes! Never before did he come into a house in which the owners, whom he had stolen from before, left their valuables to him as *gifts*, along with a kind note! This stirs something in his *soul*. It is the spark of the greatest force in the universe, the force of love!'

"The force of *love?*"

'Yes.'

"And how exactly is this '*force of love*' going to bring me my belongings back?!"

Gandhi found himself talking out loud, 'Patience!'

He looked around the deck and thought to himself, 'Am I going mad?'

"Answer me!" the voice in his head demanded.

'The thief,' Gandhi responded, somewhat puzzled at what was happening to him, 'having been agitated by your act of kindness, goes to your village in daylight and inquires about you. He comes to learn about your broad and loving heart. This upsets him further. It is one thing for him to steal from *villains*, but to steal from the meek makes him feel troubled... He then repents, comes to meet you, begs your pardon, returns you your things, and leaves off the stealing habit altogether! He becomes your friend, and you help him find an honorable employment.'

"This is very unlikely! It is a made up story!"

'What do you suggest instead, then? The other method of you attacking the thief and arming yourself and your neighbors would only bring to an escalation of violence, to you being deprived of any peace, and for no triumph for either of you, nor you nor the thief. Instead, you can choose love. And through love you can change his heart.'

"But surely not all thieves would respond this way! Some will take advantage of my kindness!"

'True, not all thieves would respond this way. But some will. And at least you would know that you have chosen the path of love, the path of truth, the path of God.'

"But what does it matter if I choose love, while others choose the wrong path?"

'I only wish to show you that fair means *alone* can produce fair ends. And in the majority of cases the force of love and pity is infinitely *stronger* and more efficient than the force of arms in achieving the response you wish for.'

"I see what you are arguing. But how can that be used *practically* against the British?"

Gandhi sighed and walked to the front of the ship. He wished to quiet his mind. What good would all these thoughts have? At home, oftentimes he would roll in bed from side to side, being troubled with a difficult problem. Kasturba would sometime kick him out of bed, whispering, "Go! Write your thoughts down and then come back and sleep without tossing around like a madman!"

Gandhi smiled to himself.

But what good was writing these thoughts down? What would he do with all of them? Publish them in his magazine? Surely he could not publish this odd dialogue. No.

"Answer me!" the voice hassled him again, "How can that 'force of love' of yours be used *practically* against the British?"

'Simply,' Gandhi answered, looking at the dark sea filling the horizon, 'we tell the British: 'If you do not concede our just demands, we shall *no longer* be your petitioners. We shall no longer be your clients. We shall

255

no longer be your suitors. You can govern us only so long as we *remain* the governed; we shall no longer have any dealings with you. Think: why do the British want to remain in India? It is not because of our pretty eyes!'

"Of course not," the voice answered, "it is because of trade! We make them rich! We pay for their clothes from Britain, for their jewelries, and they take our money and further exploit our resources!"

Gandhi continued walking, looking at the deck, seeing the lacquered wooden floor reflecting the white moon. He thought, 'If the British want India for trade, remove trade from the equation.'

"What do you mean 'remove the trade from the equation'?"

'We shall stop buying, trading, dealing. But—' he said, raising his finger in the air and then quickly taking it down, looking around him in embarrassment, 'But we must stop trading with them not out of anger, but out of kindness. We must resist them with love.'

"Resist with *love*?"

'Exactly. You can call this power *love-force*, or, more popularly—but less accurately—'passive resistance.' But this resistance must be done actively, not passively. And when it is carried with love, this force is *indestructible*. The force of arms is powerless when matched against the force of love!'

Gandhi stopped walking, waiting for the voice to reappear. He smiled to himself, feeling triumphant. 'Here', he thought, 'with pure reasoning I have won over the voice in my head!'

Then, quietly, the voice asked back, "But is there any

historical evidence as to the *success* of what you have called *love-force?*"

Gandhi took a deep breath. He did not wish to continue this conversation. This was tiring for him! He had hoped to quiet his mind, but instead, his mind only became more and more aroused.

"Answer me!" the voice demanded.

Gandhi wanted to whine, 'Why? Why can't you leave me alone?'

Then a new voice appeared in his head. It was a voice of an old man, "Stop whining!"

Gandhi's eyes widened.

"Stop whining," the old hoarse voice said again. "When I am pestered with thoughts I write them down, and before I know it, I have a new book written!"

Gandhi shivered. This was a quote by Tolstoy he had read in an article.

His hands shook. He clung to the railing.

"Stop fearing!" the hoarse voice said, "Sit down and write this book and stop complaining!"

'But,' Gandhi found himself responding, 'I have never written a *book*. I have only written articles and essays. I don't know how to write a book!'

"How old are you?" the old voice asked.

Gandhi swallowed, 'I am forty-years-old.'

"I was forty-one when I first published *War and Peace.*"

Gandhi's heart yelped, 'Tolstoy? Is that you?!'

"Who did you think I was, Queen Elizabeth?"

Gandhi looked around the deck. He must be going crazy. He shook his head and walked away from the railing. He must get some sleep, and quickly.

"Stop running away!" the old voice said.

Gandhi stopped in his tracks. He looked around him. The voice in his head sounded crisp and clear. It spoke authoritatively, "There is a book inside you, and you must give birth to it at once!"

Overwhelmed, Gandhi thought, 'But I have never written a book before!'

"You have said that already! You do not wish to waste my time, do you?"

'Oh no! No!'

"Sit down and write that book then."

Gandhi gulped, 'But others can write it better than me. Who am I? I am not qualified!'

"You, young man, want to see a change in your motherland? In the world?"

'Yes,' Gandhi answered, 'Of course!'

"Then you must *be* that change. You must be the change you wish to see!"

Gandhi waited for more instructions. But the voice said nothing. Instead, he heard the other voice "You have yet to answer my question: is there any *historical* evidence as to the success of what you have called *love-force*?"

Gandhi shrugged his shoulders, 'It depends how you

define 'historical.'"

"Well how do you define it?"

Gandhi walked quickly toward the spiral stairway. Quotes by Tolstoy, Ruskin, and Rousseau appeared before him. He began running down the staircase, before all the information disappeared. He should explain what history *is*, and how it is merely the recording of disturbances to peace, and never of peace itself. And he should also explain about the nature of armed struggle, yes! And what *true* Indian home-rule would look like. And how the young generation should help educate the older generation in the force of love. And how the older generation *must* pass down to the younger generation its old ways that are now beginning to disappear due to the quick industrialization. And he should explain about the reform needed in education, yes, education! It would be the way to bring India out of its desperate state.

He ran down the staircase, nearly bumping into an older couple, before arriving at the bottom floor, running into his room, opening his notebook and writing in his mother tongue, Gujarati:

> Reader: "Is there any historical evidence as to the success of nonviolent resistance, otherwise known as love-force?"

> Author: "History, as we know it, is a record of the wars of the world, and so there is a proverb among Englishmen that a nation which has no history, that is, no wars, is a happy nation. How kings became enemies of one another, how they murdered one another, is found accurately recorded in history, and if this were all that had

happened in the world, the world would have ended long ago."

Reader: "How so?"

Author: "The fact that there are so many men still alive in the world today shows that the world is based not on the force of arms but on the force of love! Therefore, the greatest and most unimpeachable evidence of the success of this force is to be found in the fact that, *in spite* of the wars of the world, it still lives on."

Reader: "You mean that the existence of wars does not defy the 'law of love'?"

Author: "Little quarrels of millions of families in their daily lives disappear *due* to the exercise of this force. Hundreds of nations live in peace. History does not take note of this fact. History is really a record of every *interruption* of the smooth working of the force of love.

Reader: "Can you give an example of that 'force' in action?"

Author: "Of course, it is all around us. Two brothers quarrel; one of them repents and reawakens the love that was lying dormant in his brother; the two again begin to live in peace; history does not record that, true?"

Reader: "True."

Author: "But if the two brothers, through the intervention of solicitors or some other reason take up arms or go to law, their doings would be *immediately* noticed in the press, they would be the talk of their neighbors and would probably be remembered in 'history.' And what is true of families and communities is true of nations also."

Gandhi wrote furiously. One page turned into two, and two into four. He wrote and wrote, the dialogue clear to him in his mind as the sun in a bright South African day. He wrote at a speed he had never written before.

When his first notebook was filled, he took his only other one. Within four hours he had finished that one too. He had no more paper, and the sun was beginning to rise. The dark sky in the window was turning brighter by the minute. He folded the desk, brought down the bed, and lay down smiling, soon falling asleep.

Gandhi woke up a few hours later. Through the small rounded window, the sun looked bright. He got up and immediately heard the voice in his head, asking him about how could education alter the fate of India.

'Wait', Gandhi begged, 'First I need to go to the lavatory. Then I need to get more paper.'

"Well hurry already!"

Gandhi hurried. After visiting the lavatory, he ran upstairs, finding the climb up to be quite an exercise. The little shop of the ship near the first class dining room had no notebooks for sale, mostly cigarettes and liquor.

"No notebooks?" Gandhi cried.

The young vendor shrugged his shoulders, "You can perhaps ask at the captain's cabin, they might have some."

Gandhi thanked the young man and hurried to the deck. He ran across the deck to the captain's cabin and peeked in. He saw the sailor from the night before sitting by a map.

"Excuse me, sailor Lawrence?" Gandhi said quietly.

"Mohandas!" the sailor called.

Gandhi thanked God in his heart for the acquaintance. "Could you perhaps help me?"

"In which way?"

Gandhi smiled, "Do you by chance happen to have some paper?"

"Sure," Lawrence said and opened a drawer, handing a bunch of papers to Gandhi, "Will that do?"

Gandhi took the papers gratefully, "I sure hope so! Thank you very kindly!"

He ran downstairs, the voice in his mind appearing again, "And how do you suppose that India, mostly analphabetic, can learn of your 'love-force'? And what *kind* of education do you offer? Is *British* education necessary for obtaining home-rule? And how does that fit with your concept of self-reliance?"

He ran downstairs and answered all the questions. Soon the pages were piling up. He numbered them, thirteen pages, twenty-seven pages. Day turned into night. Gandhi wrote through all the paper and went and asked for more.

Lawrence look bewildered. "Are you a writer or something?"

Gandhi hesitated, "I am not sure!"

Down in his room, the new blank sheets of paper were soon filled too, and the numbers went to from seventy-four to ninety-three. By the time the boat passed Western Sahara he had finished a hundred pages. Three days later, passing by Côte d'Ivoire there were one-hundred and seventy-five pages. And when ten days were over, and the ship reached Cape Town, the book was complete, with 276 pages, with the stationary of the *"Kildonan Castle Steam Ship"* appearing at the top of each page.

At the last day of the voyage Gandhi took another page, wrote on it "Appendices" and then wrote "Some Authorities." Below he wrote:

> "The following books are recommended for perusal to follow up the study of the foregoing:
>
> "The Kingdom of God is Within You"—Tolstoy.
>
> "What is Art?"—Tolstoy.
>
> "Slavery of Our Times"—Tolstoy.
>
> "The First Step"—Tolstoy.
>
> "How Shall We Escape"—Tolstoy.
>
> "A Letter to a Hindu"—Tolstoy.

He followed the list by two books by Ruskin, two by Thoreau, one by Plato, and ten other books by various other authors. 'This will do,' he thought, 'it could give the necessary foundation for any Indian seeking personal advancement.'

He finally took one last sheet of paper, and placed it on top of the large pile of pages, writing in large print letters,

"INDIAN HOME RULE"

And below he added:

"By M. K. Gandhi"

Then he added below, in the tradition of the great manifestos he had read through, including some by Tolstoy:

"No Rights Reserved: May Be Reproduced Without Permission. November 1909."

He stared at the handwritten cover page in amazement. He had not slept much these past ten days. He had not eaten much either. But he was the happiest he had ever been.

He could not believe it. He had just completed a book. In his mind he heard a hoarse old voice, "Well done, young man. Well done."

APPENDICES:

Some Authorities.

Testimonies by Eminent Men.

APPENDICES.

Some Authorities.

The following books are recommended for perusal
to follow up the study of the foregoing :—

" The Kingdom of God is Within You."—*Tolstoy.*

" What is Art ?"—*Tolstoy.*

" The Slavery of Our Times."—*Tolstoy.*

" The First Step."—*Tolstoy.*

" How Shall we Escape ?"—*Tolstoy.*

" Letter to a Hindoo."—*Tolstoy.*

" The White Slaves of England."—*Sherard.*

" Civilisation, Its Cause and Cure."—*Carpenter.*

" The Fallacy of Speed."—*Taylor.*

" A New Crusade."—*Blount.*

" On the Duty of Civil Disobedience."—*Thoreau.*

" Life Without Principle."—*Thoreau.*

" Unto This Last."—*Ruskin.*

A page from Gandhi's Indian Home Rule, 1910, refering to
several of Tolstoy's books.

Leo and Sophia Tolstoy, c. 1905.

SUKHOTIN ESTATE, OREL, RUSSIA FEBRUARY 1910

Tatiana was reading a book when she heard the doorbell. Olga, the old maid, passed through the living room, walking toward the entrance door. Tatiana said, "Oh, I'll get it."

Olga looked at her and bowed, returning to the kitchen.

Tatiana walked to the entrance, but then turned around and hid her book under the pillow. She did not want whoever was at the door to see her reading such a cheap romance. Not *her*, not the daughter of Tolstoy.

She walked back to the door. The bell rang again. She hurried to it, not wanting it to wake five-year-old Anya, who was napping in her room.

She opened the door and gasped. Alexandra stood there, holding a small valise.

Alexandra snapped. "It's freezing. Aren't you going to let me in?"

Tatiana moved aside, flustered. "Of course! I was just shocked to see you—"

"…Unannounced?" Alexandra said as she walked in. It was warm inside. She took her shoes off and put on a pair of house slippers, enjoying the warm fur inside.

Tatiana stared at her, "You must be cold. I'll have one of the maids prepare some tea for us. Are you hungry?"

"Aren't you interested to know why I came?"

"Well," Tatiana said, looking at her 26-year-old sister, "I was assuming you will tell me—"

"It's Mama. She is unbearable! She pesters me, swears at me and calls me 'Papa's puppy!' Last night," Alexandra's eyes watered, "she entered my room and made a mess, looking everywhere!"

"Looking for what?"

"For these," Alexandra pulled a pile of journals wrapped with a black lace out of the valise.

Tatiana recognized them immediately, "Papa's journals?"

Alexandra nodded, walked into the living room and sank unto the large sofa, "She constantly looks for them, like a madwoman. I hid them under my mattress. You would not believe how unbearable she has become…"

Alexandra continued to speak about how 'intolerable' their mother had become. Tatiana took a deep breath.

Up until now she managed to stay out of the craziness at her parents' home. And now the craziness was spilling into her own home, into her safe haven. She looked at her sister, lying on the sofa, her cheeks red as she continued talking, "...and she listens in on *all* of our meetings, pretending to just pass by! It's pathetic! Papa threatened he'd go away and leave her. And she threatened that she would commit suicide if he would. It's unbearable, I cannot stand her—"

At that moment Anya ran into the living room. Nadya followed her, "I'm sorry, I tried to keep her sleeping, but she heard the noise...."

Tatiana smiled. "It is fine, Nadya." She hugged Anya.

Alexandra exclaimed, "Anyushka, aren't you going to say hello to your aunty?"

Anya walked to her and kissed her on the cheek.

Tatiana turned to Nadya, "Nadya, would you please bring us some tea and cookies?"

The nanny nodded, bowed, and exited the room.

Alexandra sighed, "It's unbearable, Tanya—"

Tatiana interrupted her, whispering, "I don't want Anya to hear these things."

"Why not?" Alexandra exclaimed, "She should know it all! Anya, your grand mama is crazy! And so is your grand papa and your entire lousy family!"

"Alexandra!" Tatiana exclaimed. She looked at her daughter and said calmly, "Go and ask Nadya for some paper and pencils, and you can come draw here."

Anya nodded and ran to the kitchen.

Tatiana looked at her sister. "Alexandra, you must get a grip on yourself! Just because Mama and Papa have their problems it does not mean that you should too—"

"I am trying, Tanya! Believe me! But it is unbearable to live there! Papa is upset all the time! He claims Mama has taken some of his letters."

"Letters?"

"There were some letters which he cannot find, one from that Hindu in South Africa, one from Bernard Shaw and a few others. He cannot find them, and he shouts at her to bring them back. She says she has nothing to do with it, and that he had misplaced them himself."

"She is probably right."

"I know. But he is correct about her meddling with his things, she comes in and looks for the diaries, or for his correspondence with Chertkov or who knows what—"

"But you should stay out of it, Alexandra!"

"I know, but I can't. She is following me everywhere, and does not give me a moment—"

At that moment, there was a knock at the door. Alexandra's eyes widened. Tatiana stood up and went to the door. She opened it and was stunned to see her mother wearing a large fur coat.

"Aren't you going to let me come in, Tanya?" Sophia exclaimed.

"Of course Mama!" Tatiana moved and cleared the way for her mother.

Sophia walked inside. "Where are they?"

Tatiana looked at her, "Where are who?"

"The diaries! Do not think me a fool." She walked into the house with her boots still on. She glanced at the living room, seeing Alexandra lying on the sofa. "Where are they Alexandra! I know they are here!"

Alexandra put her hand on her forehead. "Mama! Leave me *alone*!"

"Aha!" Sophia noticed the diaries on the table, ran toward them and grabbed them, hugging them to her chest, "Here you are! My diaries!"

Tatiana tried calming everyone down, "Mama, come and sit with us. We were just about to have tea—"

"You were just about to conspire against me!" Sophia said, "You, too, Tatiana? I was expecting more from you!"

Little Anya, having heard the voice, came running into the living room, "Grand Mama!"

"Anyushka!" Sophia exclaimed, leaning down to hug her granddaughter.

Nadya entered the room and quietly placed the teapot and the two teacups. She looked at Tatiana and murmured, "I will bring another cup."

Tatiana nodded.

Alexandra buried her face in her hands. "Mama! How did you know where I was?!"

"The porter told me. At least someone is still loyal to me in the household!"

"That good-for-nothing Abrasha!" Alexandra exclaimed, "I'll kill him!"

Little Anya began crying in Sophia's arms.

Tatiana whispered, "Alexandra! Don't talk this way!"

Alexandra looked to the ceiling, "Pardon me."

"Shhhh…" Sophia whispered to her grand daughter. "It is okay Anya, aunt Alexandra does not know what she's saying."

Anya sobbed, "Grand mama! She said you were crazy…."

Sophia glared at Alexandra.

Alexandra sat up. "No I did not! Anya!"

At that moment Nadya and Olga came quietly into the room, Nadya bringing an additional teacup and cookies, and Olga placing paper and pencils for Anya on the oak card table. Nadya poured tea into all three cups as quickly as she could.

When the two maids left, Sophia muttered. "Alexandra, don't poison my own granddaughter with your—"

Tatiana could bear it no more. "Mama! Enough!" she looked at Alexandra, "You too! The two of you, when visiting *me* and *my* household will have to *behave* or else I will throw you out!"

They both said nothing. Little Anya wiped her tears and went to the papers and pencils.

"Now," Tatiana said, as if speaking to toddlers, "we shall *all* have a *pleasant* cup of tea like *civilized* people."

Sophia muttered, "I'm taking the journals with me!"

Alexandra jumped, "No you're not. I promised Papa!"

"Enough!" Tatiana shouted.

She took the pile of diaries and placed them in the vase cabinet. "We shall talk about the diaries later, in private," she looked at her mother and widened her eyes. "Now," she said as she sat down on the sofa, taking a deep breath and then exhaling it, "Anya, bring grand mama proper house slippers."

"Yes, Mama," Anya said and ran into the entrance hall.

Alexandra sat up and took a cup of tea. She did not dare to look at her mother. Sophia, too, did not look her way, and raised her chin with pride as she took a cup of tea and a small cookie.

Tatiana nodded slowly at them. "How pleasant for the two of you to come and visit me! If I am not mistaken, it has been since Anya's birth five years ago, that the two of you have been here."

The two nodded quietly.

Tatiana smiled and looked at Alexandra. "At least, the events in Yasnaya Polyana make you want to visit your forgotten sister," she turned and looked at her mother, "and daughter."

Anya returned running into the living room, bringing her grand mother house slippers. Sophia mumbled, "Thank you Anyushka. At least someone cares for me here."

"Now," Tatiana continued, "all topics that have to

do with Papa, the family or the estate are off limits. *For once* we shall talk like a proper family. Recently I have taken to oil-painting."

Sophia and Alexandra both looked at their teacups.

Tatiana continued, "I have always liked drawing, but never really liked meddling with oils, the brushes and all that mess. But now, thanks to a tutor named Isaac, I am advancing rapidly."

Sophia sighed. "When are you coming to visit us next?"

Tatiana hesitated whether to answer the question or not.

"Answer me," Sophia pleaded, "for God's sake! I'm your mother!"

"In Easter. Both Anya and I are excited about—"

"Easter?!" Sophia exclaimed, "That is in two months!"

Tatiana feigned a smile. "Mama, at this rate, it may be the Easter of next year."

Alexandra chuckled.

Sophia pouted her lips.

They all sat there in silence. The only sound was of Anya, drawing with the pencils.

From left to right: Alexandra, Tatiana, Sophia and Masha
Tolstoy, c. 1900.

Gandhi in South Africa, c.1900.

PHOENIX SETTLEMENT, NATAL COLONY, SOUTH AFRICA, MARCH 1910

Gandhi sighed at the letter. It was the ninth letter with similar news. All was clear now. His book was banned. That was it.

He tried to remain calm, but he felt the anger building in him. He punched the desk with his fist, muttering, "Why? Why?!"

Kasturba hurried into the room. "Mohan? Are you okay?"

Gandhi buried his face in his hands, his elbows on the desk, "They've banned my book! Now it is official!"

"How do you know for certain?"

"I know! Because this is now the *ninth* letter. I sent the book to nine different people, and they all either did not receive it, or received the envelope *without* the book." He sighed and read to her, "Gokhale wrote to me:

> "Dear Mohandas,
>
> I'm afraid your book did not arrive with the envelope you sent me. I did a little research, concerned, and was led to a friend of a friend who works at the Censorship Department. He told me he had seen the name of the book, 'India Home Rule' in the recent list. I am sorry. You might want to write to the Censorship Department for a re-examination. But I have heard such process takes over a year. Do not lose hope.
>
> Yours,
>
> Gokhale."

Gandhi shook his head, moaning, and leaned against the back of the chair, "Stupid! The stupid, imbecile, ignorant British!"

Standing near her husband, Kasturba put her hand on his shoulder. She was alarmed to see him that way. Usually worse things did not affect him this way. She whispered, "It's only a book, Mohan…."

"'*Only a book*'?! It summarizes my life's work! Let me tell you, the people who are saying the British only understand brute power are correct! Let there be a few more assassinations."

"Mohan!"

"What? The British do not understand what I'm offering!" he placed his hand on his brown book, printed in Guajarati of which he worked for two months from morning to evening. "They do not understand that what I'm offering is a thousand times better than what they would receive if they would ban its contents from spreading!"

He leaned his head on his wife's waist.

She stroked his head. A few months ago, when he returned from London, she was so happy for him. He was ecstatic. He edited and laid out the book for print at the speed of light, with the help of their sons and the others in the commune. It was an exciting time.

It shifted his attention away from the harsh reality. In the Transvaal Colony up north, a few hours train ride away, his fellow men were being harassed more than ever before. Their own son had been in jail for five months now.

Some of the people released from jail needed to recuperate and be nourished back to health. But they were afraid to exit the Transvaal and go to rest at the Phoenix Settlement in the Natal Colony. They were scared that when they returned to the Transvaal they would be arrested again crossing the border.

Now all this reality was crushing her husband. And adding to this the censorship on his book in India—that was too much to bear.

She kept stroking his hair. "Haven't you told me many years ago of another author who was banned from publishing a book in his own country? Who was that?"

"I don't remember," Gandhi mumbled, his eyes closed, losing himself in his wife's gentle strokes.

"Of course you do. Was that Ruskin?"

"No, he was always hailed in Britain."

"Was it Tolstoy?"

"No, it wasn't. The Czar's regime is afraid of him."

Kasturba strained her memory. "Mohan, which book were you reading when we moved to South Africa? It was that *'Kingdom of God'*, wasn't it?"

Gandhi nodded.

"Yes," Kasturba said with more confidence, "You told me yourself, once, that that book was banned in its own country."

Gandhi looked at her suddenly. "Wait, I think you are right."

"I'm *always* right," Kasturba smiled.

"No, I think you are *right!*" Gandhi exclaimed, "It *was* banned at first in Russia! This is why Tolstoy printed it in Germany!"

"So you should do the same," Kasturba murmured.

Gandhi sighed, "But my book is in Gujarati!"

Kasturba smiled, "I know of a lawyer who claims to be an excellent translator from Gujarati to English. He even publicizes it in his own newspaper."

Gandhi grabbed her and tickled her, "Stop pestering me!"

"You stop pestering me!" Kasturba laughed.

He looked at her with his sad eyes.

She looked at him and gently caressed his face, "Translate it, Mohan."

He closed his eyes. He had hoped for someone in

India to publish it. He wanted it to be read in his *own* country. Should he write to the Censorship Department?

Kasturba gently placed her finger under his chin and lifted his face, "Translate it I say!"

A month later the book was published in English, after Gandhi, Herman, Gandhi's sons and fellow pacifists at the farm all worked on it together. First they translated it, then prepared it for the printing press, then bound it together with a brown cover.

Gandhi was extremely agitated. His son, Harilal, who was supposed to be released from jail, had his stay extended due to "disobedience" and "incitement of cellmates."

Gandhi was worried about his son's well-being, as no visits to the jail were allowed. Gandhi sent a clergymen friend to visit him, and he came back reporting that Harilal was not well.

There was also one little personal matter which had worried him.

"Tolstoy has not written back," he told Kasturba one night in bed.

Kasturba was quiet. "He must be busy," she said.

"Busy?" Gandhi murmured, "It has been five months!"

"He might have misplaced the letter."

Gandhi sighed. "I telegrammed the hotel in

London."

"You did? Why?"

"I thought that perhaps he had misaddressed his letter and sent it to the address from which I sent it. But they replied that they did not receive any letter for me."

Kasturba hesitated. She sensed the anxiety in her husband's voice.

Gandhi moaned, "I think it is because I was too presumptuous."

"Presumptuous? How so?"

"I asked him to publicize our struggle, given the publicity he commends. It might have been too much for me to ask in my second letter to him. I shouldn't have done it."

"Nonsense. This struggle is important to you. Of course you should have! I tell you, he must have simply misplaced it."

"I disappointed him in asking for this favor," Gandhi sighed.

Kasturba was quiet. "You should write to him again."

"Write to him again? What for? He did not reply to my last letter!"

"You should send him your new book. He would be pleased to—"

"No, that was my other mistake. I shouldn't have sent him my biography. It was too… self-promoting. It must have disgusted him."

"Mohan! Now you are imagining!"

Gandhi shrugged his shoulders and stared at the ceiling.

Kasturba shook her head, "You should write to him again. He must have misplaced the letter."

"I will not."

"Mohan!"

"I will not and that's the end of it!" Gandhi said. "I'm tired, let's go to sleep."

Gandhi turned around and wrapped himself in the blanket.

Kasturba laid there, wondering what could make her husband more at ease. She should convince him, she told herself. She knew how much another letter from Tolstoy could mean. She had seen how her husband had framed the letter from Tolstoy and hung it over his desk. She would convince him. But how?

Kasturba Gandhi, age 61, c. 1930.

Tolstoy family, 1903. From left to right, standing: Ilya, Lev, Alexandra and Sergey; sitting: Michael, Tatiana, Sophia, Tolstoy, Masha and Andrey.

YASNAYA POLYANA, RUSSIA, APRIL 1910

It was emotional for Tatiana to come back home for Easter. Spring was here, and the smell of the birch trees excited her nostrils, fresh and damp, reminding her of the smell of leather drying in the sun. It reminded her of her childhood.

As the carriage arrived at the gate, she smiled at Old Abrasha, who helped her, the nanny Nadya, and little Anya descend the carriage. Sukhotin was to come the following day.

Sophia looked extremely cheerful when seeing them. Anya kissed her grand mama obediently, as her mother taught her, with the special blessing for Easter, "Christ has Risen!"

Sophia's eyes watered, "Indeed, He has risen!" and she kissed her granddaughter three times.

Then she proceeded to kiss Tatiana in the traditional

Easter way, three times.

Tolstoy came downstairs, "Stop kissing this way, 'Christ has risen', ridiculous!"

"Hello Papa!" Tatiana exclaimed.

"Hello, hello," Tolstoy said as little Anya came to hug him. He tried lifting her up and his face tightened with pain. Instead he straightened, patted Anya on the head and said to Tatiana, "So glad you have *finally* come to see your parents before they tear each other apart!"

Tatiana kissed her father on the cheek, "I don't suppose you would be interested in joining Mama, Anya and I at the Easter service? We thought of going to the old church we used to go to when I was young—"

"I'd rather refrain from all of this pagan nonsense."

"So I thought," Tatiana said and looked at her mother, "but you shall come, right, Mama?"

Sophia hesitated, not wanting to be away from her husband, "Let us see. There is a lot of time until the evening."

In the evening, the three of them took the carriage to Tula. Alexandra decided to stay behind at the estate. Tatiana decided to be cheerful.

They visited the old church and little Anya was enchanted by the prayers and songs. After the Hallelujah blessing, they ate some bread and dates. Tatiana even allowed her to drink a little wine.

Then some of the priests remained in the church,

and Tatiana led the three of them to rest outside for the rest of the evening until midnight. Sophia was complaining about Alexandra deciding not to come. But Tatiana would hear none of it.

Sophia persisted, "If your sister Masha was here, she would have made Alexandra come too."

The memory of her late sister pained Tatiana. They walked the old streets of Tula for some time, and eventually returned to the church.

When they returned to the church it was very crowded. They sat down on one of the benches. Anya was tired and rested in her mother's lap.

They sang the old songs. Tatiana enjoyed singing the old songs. She glanced at her mother, singing them too. She thought that her mother was better off taking some distance from Tolstoy. Though her eyes were sad, she seemed comforted by the church service.

Then the ushers passed around candles for everyone. Anya sat up, excited.

All the lanterns in the church were then extinguished, and the only light remaining was the dim light from the 'unsleeping flame' on the altar. All waited in silence in the darkness, apart from a few babies and children who cried.

Then the priests entered in a procession from the doors into the church with the head priest holding one torch, lighting anew the unsleeping flame. The priest exclaimed, "Come receive the light from the light that is never overtaken by night. Come and glorify Christ, who has risen from the dead!"

Tatiana sent Anya with her candle to light it from the

Paschal liturgical candlestick. Tatiana watched her carefully as she joined the line with the other children, lighting her candle from the large Paschal candlestick, and then carefully bringing the lit candle with her.

Anya excitedly lit the candles of her mother and grandmother. Tatiana looked at her candle's flame. The scents of the incense, one in the altar and the other near the Paschal candlestick, filled the church and reminded Tatiana of times when her whole family, her older brother Sergey and all her little siblings, used to come to church on Easter. Their father included.

But that was years ago. Before her father turned his back to the Eastern Orthodox Church. Before he was excommunicated. Before the quarrels between her parents became so bitter.

Tatiana's eyes watered. She held her mother's hand, feeble and wrinkled, and squeezed it. Her mother nodded, tears in her eyes, and squeezed Tatiana's hand back.

Tatiana woke up late the following day. They returned very late from church, around three in the morning. She heard her mother going around the house and giving orders to the maids.

Tatiana got up and had breakfast in the dining hall. Anya was studying her Greek alphabet with Nadya in the adjacent drawing room.

The lunch was going to be in the large veranda on the bottom floor, like in the good old days.

Before noon Sukhotin arrived. Tatiana's brothers also arrived. Sergey came with his wife and five children; Lev came with his wife and six children, including the baby twins; Ilya came with his wife and eight children; Andrey came with his second wife and three children. Michael came with his wife and seven children. Tatiana glowed, seeing the family reuniting. Alexandra played with the children.

Their father, however, was not in the best of moods. He frowned at the lavish meal, muttered that this food should be given to the serfs who made it, and sat at the end of the table with a disapproving look. At first he seemed to enjoy the grandchildren but soon was tired of them.

Eventually his new assistant, a young man called Bulgakov, came and whispered to him, "The two Japanese visitors from yesterday are here."

Tolstoy got up heavily and excused himself, "I'm sorry, but I have some visitors from Japan that I must see. I was unable to meet them yesterday, and so I feel obliged to see them today."

Andrey, who sat next to Sophia, said to the table, half whispering, but loud enough for Tolstoy to hear, "Are these visitors more important than family?"

Silence followed. Alexandra jumped in, "It is important for Papa to be cordial to visitors, especially from Japan following the Russian-Japanese War."

Tolstoy moaned and left the veranda with Bulgakov.

Tatiana was relieved. At least her mother did not say anything, and there was no fight between her parents in front of the grandchildren.

After they ate cheese *Paskha* dishes, sweet *Kulich* bread, and sweet Easter cakes, the family retired upstairs. The children went outside to play with colorful Easter eggs.

A few hours later the brothers departed with their families, and the yard became quiet again. Tatiana looked at the empty yard. After the festivities and sounds of laughter of all her nephews and nieces, it was sad for her to see the yard empty again.

In the evening Anya came running to her mother and father, who were reposing in Tatiana's old room. "Mama! Mama!"

Tatiana was alarmed, "What is it, Anya?"

"It's Grand Papa! He is crying!"

Tatiana got up at once and looked at Sukhotin, "Play with her. I will be right back."

Sukhotin smiled at her. "We'll be here."

Tatiana proceeded to her father's study.

Tolstoy was sitting near the desk, with two oil lanterns lighting the room.

"Papa," Tatiana whispered, "is everything alright?"

"More than alright, Tanya," her father sniffled, "more than alright…. Finally, someone is truly applying my work!"

Tatiana did not understand, "Are you talking about the Japanese?"

"No! That meeting was rubbish! I'm talking about this," he said and pointed at a little brown book. He took a letter that he had shoved in between the pages of the book and handed it to his daughter.

Tatiana read the letter quickly:

"Johannesburg, 4th April 1910.

To Count Leo Tolstoy,

Yasnaya Polyana, Russia.

Dear Sir,

You will recollect my having carried on correspondence with you whilst I was temporarily in London. As a humble follower of yours, I send you herewith a booklet which I have written. It is my own translation of a Gujarati writing. Curiously enough, the original writing has been confiscated by the Government of India. I, therefore hastened the above publication of the translation.

I am most anxious not to worry you, but, if your health permits it and if you can find the time to go through the booklet, needless to say I shall value very highly your criticism of the writing.

I am sending also a few copies of your *A Letter to a Hindu*, which you kindly authorized me to publish. It has been translated into Gujarati also.

I am,

Your obedient servant,

M. K. Gandhi"

Tatiana looked at her father, "He sent you a book?"

"Not just a book, Tanya, a whole plan as to how to liberate India based on my approach!"

Tatiana was not sure why her father was being so melodramatic. Many people have sent her father letters and books regarding his nonviolent resistance methods. She looked at her father, "And I understand the book is good?"

"Not good. Very good!" her father shook his head, "Instead of a long and boring treatise, he has written it as a Socratic dialogue! It is quite refreshing. Here," he said, "Listen to this."

He then read a short passage from the book, which unfortunately did not move Tatiana at all. But she did enjoy seeing her 81-year-old father responding so enthusiastically to something. "Papa, it sounds very interesting."

"Interesting?! It is riveting! If the Indians follow what he argues here, then they will attain their freedom in a wholly nonviolent way!"

Tatiana sighed. This was a subject she was less enchanted by, mostly due to its unlikely nature.

"Oh, Tanya! Stop being such a small believer!" her father said, seeing her reaction. "It can work! This method can work!"

"But, Papa," Tatiana searched for words, wishing not to offend him, but at the same time to point at the ridiculous notion he argued, "you do not *really* believe that the British will just *leave* India? They've been there hundreds of years! Is it not the greatest asset of their Empire? And you assume they will leave willingly?"

Her father shook his head. "Tanya, Tanya.... Of

course they will leave. Of course! Once the Hindus and the Muslims in India unite, and together choose not to cooperate with the British, then it will be inevitable. The British *will want* to leave!"

Tatiana grimaced. She wanted to agree with her father, but she had learned to be more critical of his thoughts over the years. If it were up to him, there would be no organized religion, no private property, no industry and even—according to his recent books criticizing the very field which brought him world renown—no art.

She struggled to find the appropriate words. She knew her father could be extremely sensitive, especially around these subjects. She said, "I am glad that you are pleased, Papa."

"This book makes me feel, Tanyushka, like it all"—his voice broke—"like it all was not for *nothing*. Imagine," his eyes became moist, "if a great nation such as India manages to reject violence and harness the force of love, and shows the entire world what could be done through nonviolence," he breathed heavily, "then the whole world could learn! This can change the entire world! Rather than one violent revolution replacing a violent regime with another, regimes could instead surrender to love. The Negros of America could use that, and those of South Africa, and every people on the earth could use this against dictators and unjust regimes. South America could abolish its silly armies and wars, and the whole world could follow suit. There could be a better future, Tanya!"

Tatiana smiled, happy to see him happy. She thought that her father being delusional and happy was better than him being realistic and grumpy. "Good, Papa," she said, "I am glad."

She turned to leave the room as her father said, "Tanya, could you please help me find something?"

She turned around. "What?"

"His other letter," Tolstoy said, "I believe it was in a book about him, a blue-covered book by one Doke I believe…."

Tatiana turned around, "Where did you put it?"

"Had I known I wouldn't have asked you!"

Tatiana breathed in.

Tolstoy mumbled, his voice hoarse, "I looked everywhere, and so did Alexandra and the new fellow Bulgakov. But you—you *know* how to find things. Do you remember when I lost a whole chapter of *Anna Karenina*?"

Tatiana smiled, "And I found it on a high shelf in the pantry?"

Tolstoy laughed, "You remember that? You were only sixteen…."

"Eighteen, Papa. I was eighteen. Now, where do you think you put it?"

Tolstoy waved his hands around, "I don't know!"

"Alright, Papa. Keep reading. I'll look."

Her father gave her an appreciative look, his bottom lip placed atop his upper lip, and then continued to read the brown book.

Tatiana looked around the long shelf, quickly passing

her eyes on the titles. She looked in between large books, verifying the book wasn't hiding in between larger ones.

She then proceeded to the three piles of books at the corner of the room on the small table. She noted that the room was a mess. Back when she was in charge everything used to be in its place and there were no such piles.

She quickly looked through the books, ready to find the book at any moment. But to no avail. She then moved to the drawers of the desk, gently moving her father. There was a mess in the drawers, with some letters and papers, and even a few smaller books— mostly religious texts—but that specific book was not there.

She sighed, "It is a biography, correct?"

"Yes," her father said, lifting his head from the book. "Do not worry, Tanya, it is fine. It is not important."

"Just one more minute," Tatiana said, looking around. She walked into the adjacent bedroom. Apart from the bed, a nightstand and a small bench, there was nothing else in the bare room. She opened the drawers of the nightstand. There was a pile of papers there, but no book. She then reached to the back of the drawer, and she saw it. The blue book stated clearly on the cover:

M. K. Gandhi: An Indian Patriot in South Africa'

By J. J. Doke.

She said nothing. Alexandra would have shouted, 'I found it!' and so would her mother. But Tatiana walked quietly to her father's study, placed the book silently on her father's desk, and waited.

Tolstoy lifted his eyes from his book, looked at Tatiana, saw her smiling, and then noticed the book in front of him. "Tanya! You found it!"

She grinned.

"Where was it?"

"Deep inside the drawer, near your bed."

"Aha!" he grabbed the book, "Now I have something to last me for a day or two." He looked at Tatiana with appreciation. "Tanya, Tanya... Why would you not move back with us? Your presence in the house makes me calmer. And your mother does not act mad when you are here."

Tatiana smiled. "Papa, I have my own life. I have a husband to take care of."

Tolstoy's eyes twinkled. "Well, mistakes from the past cannot be erased."

"You are impossible Papa!" Tatiana retorted, smiling back. She leaned against his desk wanting to stay longer. Her father was in an unusually good mood. "Papa," she said hesitantly, "do you know you can always come and visit us?"

Tolstoy looked at her. His eyes reminded her the eyes of a child. "Tanya, that is very kind, but what would you do with a broken old cartwheel like me...."

Tatiana smiled, "Papa, I am serious. You can come and rest in our estate. Little Anya would love to spend more time with you. And Olga is a great cook. It could clear your mind when things become too intense here. I am sure Mama would not protest."

Tolstoy sighed and glanced at his daughter, examining her eyes. She seemed sincere. "Tanyushka. That is an idea. Thank you for not forgetting your old Papa."

Tatiana smiled, nodded, and walked to the door.

Her father opened the book again.

She looked at him for a long moment, appreciating his thick white eyebrows, his wrinkled forehead, his unruly beard and his curious eyes, devouring the book. She was happy for him.

She left the room quietly, as she used to do when she was a child, without disturbing him, without him noticing.

Leo Tolstoy and daughter Tatiana, 1895.

Tatyana Tolstoy-Sukhotin, age 82, 1946.

ROME,
DECEMBER 1931

Tatiana smiled to herself. "My father," she said to Gandhi, "was very moved by your writing."

Gandhi froze for a short moment, "You are being very kind to me, Tatiana."

"No," Tatiana said, "I do mean it. He was very moved by your writing. He thought it was…" she looked for the right words, "interesting, and thought-provoking, well written."

Gandhi seemed hesitant. "He did write to me that he 'appreciated' the book, but he had never praised it—"

"But he *did* praise it."

Gandhi smiled and shyly looked down, "You see, Tatiana, I do not wish to deceive myself. For me, for Gandhi, there was only one Tolstoy. But for Tolstoy, I am sure that there were countless Gandhis."

Tatiana shook her head and got up. She had to show him. She went to her desk in the corner of the room, and pulled out a folder from the shelf above it.

Gandhi looked at her curiously as she opened the drawer and put on white gloves.

"You see, Mohandas," she said, opening a brown bag with several notebooks, "when I say that he was fond of your writing, I do mean it. You see, my father was a very reticent man—"

"But," Gandhi insisted, "he did not write anything about my writing. He must have seen some flaws in it, and I assure you, the book was not—"

"Here," Tatiana said, pulling one of her father's journals from the last year of his life. She flipped through the pages until she found what she was looking for. "Come and see for yourself."

Gandhi walked to the desk.

"You see, this is the whole entry from that day, April 19th, only a few lines."

Gandhi looked at the Russian writing, cursive, beautiful handwriting. He looked at Tatiana and whispered, "Is this the *original?*"

Tatiana pouted her lips, "Let's just say that some of the journals currently in Yasnaya Polyana are reproductions."

Gandhi's eyes widened as he looked at the journal, "Well what does it say?"

Tatiana cleared her throat.

> "Just today two Japanese came: primitive people in an ecstasy of enthusiasm over European civilization. On the other hand, I received a book

and a letter from the Hindu."

Tatiana looked at Gandhi, "That is you."

Gandhi gulped and nodded.

Tatiana continued,

> "The book expresses understanding of all the shortcomings of European civilization, even its utter worthlessness."

Gandhi's murmured, "He wrote that? About my book?"

Tatiana nodded. She flipped to the next page, "Here, too, the following day he mentions you:

> "Still alive. Got up rather late. Walked through the young fir trees. The ants interested me. Made a few notes. Corrected the proofs of two booklets. Not bad. Went riding. Received a few interesting letters. In the evening I read Gandhi on civilization. Very good."

Gandhi gasped, "Really? He wrote that? Where does it say that?"

Tatiana smiled and pointed to the exact line, "You see here, here is your name in Russian, G-A-N-D-I. We write it without the *H*."

Gandhi nodded slowly. "Could you read it to me again?"

Tatiana smiled,

> "In the evening I read Gandhi on civilization. Very good."

Gandhi mumbled, "'Very good'?"

Tatiana beamed, "Yes. And he didn't *have* to write it, you understand? This is his diary. Many authors wrote to him and sent him their books, and he *never* mentioned them in his diary. And for my father there was a big difference between 'not bad', and 'good' and 'very good'," she grinned, seeing Gandhi's expression, "and you received the highest acknowledgement, 'Very good.'"

Gandhi nodded his head slowly, speechless.

Tatiana flipped to the next page. She skimmed through the entry. "Here, too, he mentions you, April 21st 1910:

> "Got up late in a very bad mood. A peasant came about the land. I behaved badly towards him. Then a lady came with her daughters. I talked to her as best I could. Read a book about Gandhi. A very important one. I must write to him. Then some guests came. Not very interesting. Not very serious, not profound. In the evening I read about suicides. It left a very strong impression on me."

Tatiana looked at Gandhi.

He nodded, his eyes moist, "He wrote 'A book about Gandhi', that must have been the biography I sent him."

"Yes," Tatiana said, "he first read the book you wrote, and then he wanted to read more about you. My father rarely read books sent to him, let alone biographies, which quite frankly always disgusted him."

"I see," Gandhi mumbled.

Tatiana noticed he had tears in his eyes. She smiled.

"It's just," Gandhi murmured, "that I did not receive this impression from his letter. I mean," he hesitated, not wanting to hurt Tatiana's feelings—after all, it was her *father* that Gandhi was talking about—"your father did write that the book *interested* him, but he wrote such a short letter as a response, I was not sure if he was just being cordial.…"

Tatiana nodded, "My father had a unique ability to abstain from praise." She placed the journal on the desk and walked to the couch, "I think you have now officially become a part of the family. He loved us all, but unless you read his diaries, you would not *know* it."

Gandhi sat in the couch in front of her. He was speechless. "He wrote '*very good*', correct?"

Tatiana smiled, "Yes."

"Very good," Gandhi said again. "I wish I had known it then."

Gandhi with Hermann Kallenbach, secretary Sonja Schlesin and others after his jail term in 1913

Herman Kallenbach, c. 1910.

PHOENIX SETTLEMENT, NATAL COLONY, SOUTH AFRICA, JUNE 1910

Herman sat across Gandhi and leaned forward. "I think we must buy it."

Gandhi shook his head. It was a big commitment.

The idea had been on his mind for a while now. The small Phoenix Settlement was crowded with nonviolent resistors seeking rehabilitation after long incursions. They also sought the mental support that would come through the evening gatherings that Gandhi led, reading together important texts, speaking about the importance of choosing love over fear and hatred.

But Gandhi knew very well, each time he took the one-day train ride to the Transvaal Colony, that the real struggle was happening there, not in the Natal Colony where the small Phoenix Settlement was located on a farm. The real struggle was in the Transvaal Colony in the north.

It was in the Transvaal that the prosecution took place. General Smuts had now strengthened his resolve to crush the Indian campaign. Some Indians were not even taken to jail, but deported back to India. Their only sin was not carrying the degrading pass, which only Asiatics had to carry at all times.

Gandhi sensed that spirits were low in the Transvaal. Many families whose fathers were in jail as part of the nonviolent campaign were in dire circumstances.

Herman awoke Gandhi from his thoughts, "What say you, Mohandas?"

"I don't know," Gandhi said grimly. "I agree that we must have a place in the center of the Transvaal. And I am happy it is not too far away from a train station, as you said—"

"And more so," Herman said excitedly, "it is a large piece of land. True, it only has one dilapidated house on it right now, but the property has nearly a thousand fruit-bearing trees! And two water wells! It can serve as our headquarters. It can be like the Phoenix Settlement, but bigger, and in a better location. And we can keep both."

Gandhi shook his head, "Herman, you do not know the financial situation of the community. All the money we have collected have nearly run out. And I cannot see how we could collect the money to buy this land." He sighed, "I agree with you that it is indeed the best thing to do, as I am afraid for the continuity of our struggle. I have seen some of the most ardent nonviolent resistors beginning to fail and complain."

Herman put his hand on Gandhi's shoulder, "I thought about it myself. I have the money to buy that land."

Gandhi's eyes widened. "I will not let you do this!"

Herman spoke softly, "Listen, I can pay with my own money for the land and have it as my own, and as long as the campaign lasts, I can put it at the disposal of the Indian community and whoever participates in our struggle."

Gandhi looked at his friend with disbelief. "Herman, you are not even a Hindu, what makes you—"

"Mohandas, do you remember Tolstoy's book *'A Confession'?* I gave it to you back—"

"Of course I remember! *'A Confession'* is one of his best ones."

"Well, I went through the same stages that Tolstoy describes that he went through. I was at first ignorant. Do you remember when we met, seventeen years ago, when you first came to South Africa, how I used to drink and smoke—"

Gandhi smiled, "And chase women!"

Herman nodded, "That too. But that kind of hedonistic life led me to nothing but self-disgust."

Gandhi looked at Herman with empathy.

"I even," Herman hesitated, "I even considered suicide."

"Really? Herman! I did not know!"

Herman nodded, "And the only thing that saved me was understanding I am here for *others*. I am here to give to others, to help, to lend a hand. This is what brought my life meaning and purpose."

Gandhi nodded.

"Please," Herman said, "allow me to give my life more meaning. What else do you want me to do with the money? Spend it on meaningless possessions or let it collect dust in the bank? I want to help."

Gandhi's eyes watered, "Herman. I don't know what to say...."

"Say nothing. Give this farm your blessing, and come help me build it."

"I will, Herman. We all will. This is what I've been praying for."

Herman smiled. "I have a name for the farm, too."

"A name?" Gandhi looked at Herman, "Tell me!"

A month later Gandhi and his family moved to the new farm. Soon they were joined by a few more volunteers, many of who were families of nonviolent resistors sitting in jail, or some of the nonviolent resistors themselves. Herman prepared large wooden sign which could be seen from the main road:

"Tolstoy Farm"

Soon Gandhi began implementing the ideals which he believed in: communal living, farming, self-reliance and free education. He became the head teacher for the dozens of children. Each morning the bell rang at six. Everyone would clean the rooms and the toilets. Then they ate a shared breakfast in the gathering room. Everyone, including the children, was assigned a task for the morning, either in the orchards, cleaning or construction.

The midday meal was served at one p.m. School commenced then, lasting until the evening meal at five thirty. At seven in the evening all the residents would assemble in the gathering room, review the day's events, share any difficulties, offer solutions and read together. All meetings ended with readings from books on religion and the singing of hymns led by Gandhi himself.

As weeks progressed they were able to assemble two more large wooden houses. Gandhi noticed how the general morale was growing. He was pleased. Once every two weeks he would go back to the Phoenix Settlement, review the newspapers articles and the operation of the printing press, and see that everything functions well at the flourmill and at the oil press.

But most of the time Gandhi spent with his family, Herman, and other volunteers and nonviolent resistors in the Tolstoy Farm. They soon established a sandal-making workshop and a sewing workshop.

Gandhi loved the farm being self-reliant, and one of his most joyful moments was when he finished his first pair of sandals. He wore them proudly, walking through the farm, greeting everyone and boasting of his new sandals, "Handmade!"

In an evening gathering two weeks later Gandhi

presented the second pair he made and asked the congregation: "Who do you think I shall give my new pair of sandals to?"

Some laughed. The children yelled, "Me! Me!"

Some suggested it was to be given to Kasturba. But Gandhi responded, "No, she deserves better than these!"

Kasturba shook her head and smiled. Everyone laughed. Yet the people pressed, "Well to whom then?"

"I must offer it to my greatest friend, who has been building my moral fiber, and strengthening my belief in the force of love. This great friend has been doing this for four years now!"

The children clapped, "Herman, Herman!"

Herman smiled and shook his head.

Gandhi laughed, "Not Herman, he already made his own sandals, far better than mine!"

"Who then?" everyone pressured Gandhi, "Tell already!"

Gandhi enjoyed the curiosity. "Well, who do you think is this friend of mine? Who had helped me the most with my journey of choosing the force of love?"

There were many guesses, but none of them was correct.

"I shall send these sandals," Gandhi said finally, articulating each word, "to the Colonial Secretary himself, of course, General Smuts!"

Some burst into laughter, some shook their head disapprovingly.

Gandhi raised his finger in the air and said, "For we shall always offer to others the kindness we wish to receive ourselves!"

The following day Gandhi sat in his small office going through the mail. Suddenly he jumped up, ran across the farm, and shouted, "Kasturba! Where is Kasturba?!"

One of the women said, "She's in the sewing workshop today."

Gandhi thanked her and ran to the sewing workshop, "Kasturba! An urgent matter!"

The three women and the two men all looked at Kasturba and Gandhi curiously. Kasturba looked unimpressed, "I'm sewing new trousers, what is more important—"

"It's Tolstoy!" Gandhi exclaimed, "he wrote *back*!"

Kasturba seized paddling the sewing machine, and so did the others.

Gandhi looked at her sheepishly, "Do you not want to go out for a moment and I'll read it to you?"

Kasturba smiled, "You yourself have said that in our commune there should be no secrets."

Gandhi gulped, looked at the others and said, "Very well. You are right." He looked at the letter, his hand shaking, and then at his wife and the other five members of the farm, "Friends, this is an important day! Our sage writes:

"Dear friend,"

314

Kasturba interrupted him, "So he calls you 'friend'?"

Gandhi looked at her, unable to hide his grin.

Kasturba looked at his and nodded slowly, knowingly.

"Dear friend," Gandhi continued,

> "I have just received your letter and your book, "Indian Home Rule." I read your book with great interest because I think the question you treat in it: the passive resistance—is a question of the greatest importance, not only for India but for the whole humanity."

Gandhi's voice trembled. One of the man said, "That's quite a statement. For the whole humanity!"

Gandhi nodded, "Yes! And also 'a question of the greatest importance'!"

Kasturba smiled, "Go on!"

Gandhi nodded,

> "I could not find your former letter, but came across your biography by J. Doke, which too interested me much and gave me the possibility to know and understand you better."

Kasturba clapped her hands together, "What did I tell you?! He misplaced your letter! This is why he had not written back!"

Gandhi smiled and nodded at her.

Kasturba pointed at Gandhi, "I told you so!"

Gandhi laughed. He looked at the letter and continued reading,

> "I am not quite well at present and therefore abstain from writing to you all what I have to say about your book and all your work, which I appreciate very much, but I will do it as soon as I am better.

> Your friend and brother,

> Leo Tolstoy."

The men and women clapped, but Kasturba shook her head, "Too short! I expect a longer one next time!"

Gandhi reprimanded her, "He wrote he is not feeling well!"

Kasturba leaned against the back of her chair with pleasure, "Read the last paragraph again."

Gandhi read it again,

> "I am not quite well at present and therefore abstain from writing to you all what I have to say about your book and all your work, which I appreciate very much—"

Kasturba repeated, "'Which I appreciate *very much!*"

Gandhi smiled.

Kasturba said, "And how did he sign it?"

Gandhi looked at the letter, and suddenly felt a rush of emotion, his eyes watering, "He wrote…. 'Your friend and brother'!"

Kasturba wobbled her head, as if tasting something good, "'Your friend *and* brother!"

Gandhi laughed. He looked around the room, "Now, friends, do not let me disturb your work," he looked at his wife, "I just wanted to share this with you." He

316

bowed gently and said, "I must find Herman now!"

One of the men said, "He's in the apple grove."

Gandhi nodded in appreciation, smiled at Kasturba, and quickly exited the sewing workshop. They all watched him through the window as he ran past the two houses and into the orchards. Kasturba shook her head and looked at the other women, "It was me who told him to write to him!"

Tolstoy Farm, June 1912, from left to right: Herman Kallenbach, Gandhi, unknown, Kasturba Gandhi, unknown, Sonia Schlesin.

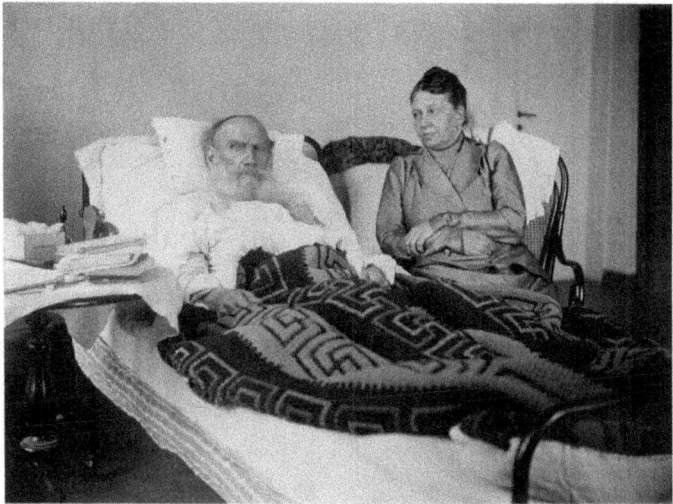

Leo and Sophia Tolstoy, c. 1903.

OREL TRAIN STATION, OREL, RUSSIA SEPTEMBER 1910

Tatiana waited patiently on the platform. The train from the Tula district was slowing down and finally halted at the station.

Tatiana nodded to Vadim, a servant from her estate, "My mother should be on this one."

Vadim nodded, ready to take the suitcase and drive the two ladies back to the Sukhotin estate.

People descended from the train. Tatiana looked carefully to spot her mother.

Then she saw her. Sophia Tolstoy disembarked from the train, seeming upset. Behind her Natasha, the maid, carried two suitcases.

"Mama!" Tatiana called and headed toward her mother.

Sophia was far from cordial. "Why did you take him

from me, Tanya!"

Tanya gulped. No. She would not fall into a fight. She would be smarter than that. "How nice to see you Mama!"

"Take me to Papa! I cannot believe he has left this way! How long does he intend to stay with you?"

Tatiana gestured for Vadim to take the luggage from Natasha. He took the two suitcases and quickly led the two countesses and the maid through the train station.

Tatiana smiled to her mother as they followed the servant. "How was your ride, Mama?"

"You are ignoring my questions! I cannot believe that you have become like your disobedient sister. You have *all* sided with him!"

Tatiana took a deep breath in. She offered her arm to her mother. Sophia hesitated for a brief moment, but then wrapped her arm in her daughter's arm. She spoke a little quieter, "I am telling you, Tanya, I will not let him fool you! He has been *impossible*. I swear to you that he and that bastard Chertkov intend on taking *all* of the money away from the family. He has signed a new will, I tell you—"

"Mama, did you notice, on your train ride, the round bales of wheat in the fields? I thought you would enjoy the view."

Sophia groaned, "I was too preoccupied with thoughts about your father and his insults."

"Do you remember, Mama, how we used to take the train to Moscow in the summers, and would count the bales we'd see from the train?"

Sophia mumbled something incomprehensible.

"And do you remember, Mama, how you would explain to us about chamomile flowers and how to differentiate them from regular daisies?"

Sophia's tight expression soften a little, "Well, everyone should know *that*."

They walked around the many people. Tatiana smiled and said cheerfully, "I remember how you used to explain to us *not* to look at the flower on *top*, as daisies are very similar to chamomile. But you said we must look at the leaves *below*—if they are regular leaves than it is a daisy, and if the leaves are hairy and bushy, then it is a chamomile!"

Sophia sighed, "Masha always loved identifying flowers."

Tatiana pursed her lips. She knew the subject of her late sister could further aggravate her mother. "Mama," she said, "would it not be nice to have some chamomile tea later today? I much rather have flowery teas than regular Russian Caravan, which is a little too smoky for me, especially in the summer, would you not agree?"

Sophia sighed again. They followed Vadim out of the station and Vadim opened the carriage door. Tatiana offered to help her mother up, but Sophia pulled her arm away, "I may be old, Tanya, but I'm not dead!"

Tatiana nodded and smiled cordially. She climbed after her mother, and Natasha then climbed up as well. Tatiana sat down near Sophia, and Natasha sat across from them. The horses neighed as Vadim began driving them to the estate.

They drove through the town, "Mama," Tatiana said,

"would you be interested in visiting Sukhotin in the assembly house? He would be so glad to see you—"

"I want to see your father. Your husband shall return in the evening, would he not?"

Tatiana nodded.

"Then I will see him then."

Tatiana looked through the window at the houses of the town. Soon the houses gave way to large fields with many bright sunflowers. "Isn't it beautiful out here, Mama?"

Sophia sighed and nodded.

"They will harvest them very soon, Mama, and also the corn. There is a large field near our house. I remember last year, one week the corn fields were taller than me, and then the following week there was no evidence of the tall corn except for corn stubbles, and you could see from our estate all the way to the Orel."

Sophia looked at her daughter, "Has Chertkov come here?"

Tatiana hesitated. She knew her mother was watching her face closely. "Only once, but most of the time Papa writes—"

"I am telling you, Tanya, that man will ruin your father!"

Tatiana took a deep breath and smiled, "You would enjoy our piano, Mama. It was tuned last week, the sound is bright and clear as a crystal! It will be so wonderful to hear you play again."

"We haven't adjusted our pianos for some time now.

No one plays."

"I told Anya of your talent, Mama. She would adore you playing for her!"

"We'll see."

As Tatiana expected, her parents began quarrelling a few minutes after her mother had arrived. Tatiana took Anya by the hand, "Let us let the grandparents talk, and you and I shall have a walk in the field."

Five-year-old Anya resisted, wanting to stay where the obvious excitement was. But Tatiana lifted her daughter up and quickly left the house. Her parents' shouting could be heard outside as well. She walked quickly, nearly running, Anya in her arms, to the little woods near the entrance to the estate. The shouting was less prevalent there, and they could hear birds chirping.

Anya looked at her mother, "Mama, are you crying?"

Tatiana hurried to wipe her eyes, "No, Anya! Of course not!"

Anya nodded and kept looking at her mother.

"Come," Tatiana said, "let us pick some flowers. We'll make a beautiful small bouquet to give Grand Mama. She would like that."

The following morning Tatiana helped her father with letters. Her mother had brought with her the letters

Tolstoy had received to Yasnaya Polyana. Tatiana went over the letters with her regular efficiency. She was delighted to see that one of the letters was from the Hindu from South Africa. She quickly read it, making sure that there was nothing there that would aggravate her father. When she saw it was all good, she put it on top of the 'important pile.'

Later, when she was telling her father about the letters, Tatiana said, "Papa, there is a letter here from the Hindu, the one from South Africa—"

"Gandhi?" her father asked, his eyes lighting up.

"Yes, Papa. He has sent a short letter, but there is also another letter from a friend of his, as well as some folded newspapers."

Her father leaned back against the couch, "Please, Tanya, read it to me."

Tatiana nodded. It was a quiet morning, and the birds were chirping outside. Her mother and was in the living room reading a book. Tatiana hoped that the calm atmosphere in her household would help her parents.

Her father looked at her in anticipation, resting on the couch, a thin blanket thrown on his legs.

Tatiana coughed gently and read:

"M. K. GANDHI,

Attorney, Johannesburg,

15th August, 1910

To Count Leo Tolstoy,

Dear Sir,"

Her father interrupted her, "Why 'Sir'? Why all this formality?"

Tatiana shrugged her shoulders and kept reading,

> "I am much obliged to you for your encouraging and cordial letter of last May. I very much value your general approval of my booklet, *Indian Home Rule*. If you have the time, I shall look forward to your detailed criticism of the work which you have been so good as to promise in your letter."

Tolstoy mumbled, "Oh yes. I do hope I shall get to it one day."

Tatiana nodded. She did not like the fatal undertone in her father's words, but decided to ignore it. She continued reading:

> "My friend, Mr. Herman Kallenbach has written to you in the attached letter about the *'Tolstoy Farm.'* Herman and I have been friends for many years. I may state that he has gone through most of the experiences that you have so graphically described in your work *My Confession*."

Tolstoy chuckled, "Yes? He *too* drank himself unconscious, gambled off his house, considered suicide and drowned himself in the breasts of whores?"

"Papa!" Tatiana scolded him. She looked toward the closed door, hoping none of the servants were nearby, "Please, Papa, behave!"

Tolstoy chuckled, and motioned with his fingers for her to continue. Tatiana shook her head disapprovingly and continued reading, a tiny smile on her face.

> "No writing has so deeply touched my friend Herman as yours did; and, as a spur to further effort in living up to the ideals held before the world by you, he has taken the liberty, after consultation with me, of naming his farm after you."

Tolstoy snorted, "Another 'Tolstoy Farm' sprouting yet again!"

Tatiana nodded. There were by now dozens of farms around the world bearing her father's name, led by various communes. But none of this had impressed her father. She took a deep breath and continued,

> "Of his generous action in giving the use of the farm for passive resisters, the numbers of the magazine 'Indian Opinion' I am sending herewith will give you full information."

Tolstoy motioned to Tatiana, "Let me have a look at these papers."

Tatiana nodded and gave him the three issues of the 'Indian Opinion.' Her father looked through them with interest. He sighed. He then looked at her.

She waited for his glance and promptly continued reading,

> "I should not have burdened you with these details but for the fact of your taking a personal interest in the passive resistance struggle that is going on in the Transvaal Colony.
>
> I remain,
>
> Your faithful servant,
>
> M. K. Gandhi."

Tatiana finished reading and looked at her father.

Tolstoy hummed to himself, "Mmm, very well. Very well *indeed*. So those brothers keep up their struggle, they have not given up yet! That is good. This will teach the English who really are the English *gentlemen* here, and who are the brute *savages!*"

Tatiana nodded. She noted to herself that this was the first full sentence her father had articulated since arriving in her home. Since he arrived he was mostly sad, recluse and non-talkative. She had worriedly read his diary at night, and did not like what she saw there. He mentioned death.

But now he finally seemed joyful again. Tatiana looked at him smiling. She wondered whether it was indeed the letter from the Hindu that engaged him, or perhaps—could it be?—the arrival of her mother yesterday.

'Interesting', she thought to herself, 'it may well be that *he* needs her no less than *she* needs him.'

"What are you thinking?" her father asked her suddenly.

"Oh nothing, Papa."

"Don't fool me Tanya! I may be old but I'm not dead yet!"

Tatiana smiled, "Mama just said the same thing yesterday."

Her father shook his head and looked out the window, looking insulted.

"Papa," Tatiana asked quietly, "do you love Mama?"

Tolstoy glanced at Tatiana, and then sighed and looked at the bright morning outside. "I do, Tanya," he said finally, "I do. Very much. This is a part of the problem."

"Why is it a *problem*, Papa?"

Her father sighed and waved his hand dismissively. Then, after a moment, he said, "She told me yesterday she wants me to come back to Yasnaya."

"You don't have to go if you don't want to, Papa."

Tolstoy sighed. "September is always a sensitive for your Mama."

Tatiana nodded. September 23rd was her parents' wedding anniversary. In the past few years her mother threw lavish parties in the estate to celebrate the anniversary. It seemed that the more Tolstoy had *avoided* his wife, the grander and elaborate these parties became.

Tatiana looked at her old father. Suddenly he looked like a sad little child. She felt pity for him. "Papa," she said quietly, "you don't have to return if you don't want to."

Tolstoy took a deep breath, "I know, Tanyushka. But, at least I have until the twenty-third...." He sighed. "The twenty-third... Have I ever told you how we were married in the Royal Church of Our Lady?"

Tatiana hesitated. She did not want to say 'yes' and to upset him. He had told her the story many times. But he was now 82-years-old, she did not want to upset him. "No, Papa," she said, "do tell me!"

Her father smiled. She noticed his eyes. They, too, had become older. They were still vibrant, and his glare was still fiery, but his eyes had become a little waterier. A thin layer of misty gloss had begun to cover his eyes in recent years. It made him look as if he was always on the verge of tears.

"She was so intelligent," Tolstoy spoke, as if from a dream, "your Mama… she was so thought-provoking, so *feisty!* I remember writing in my diary, 'I am in love. I am in love as I did not think was possible to *be* in love! I am a madman!'"

Tatiana laughed.

"I was!" Tolstoy looked at her, "I really was! I would visit her family's house *daily*, not missing a day! Finally, I got the courage and wrote her a marriage proposal."

Tatiana smiled to herself. Even in her father's *romance* he found it easier to *write* rather than to *speak* of his emotions.

"Oh Tanyushka, I was so happy when she agreed! There was no happier person than me in the entire world!"

Tatiana looked at his hand as he wiped a tear from his eye.

"Papa? Are you crying?"

"No!" he exclaimed. He composed himself, pulling his chin backwards. "It's just that she was so… so *charming!* And she used to write, and write well!"

Tatiana nodded, her father had said it before, but she personally found it hard to believe. She had *read* her mother's writings. She did not find them appealing at all.

"No Tanya!" her father insisted, "She was very good!

330

She was young, only eighteen! And she wrote well! Simple, yes, but in a truthful and honest tone!"

Tatiana shrugged her shoulders. Her father must have been very much under the influence of *love* to find her mother's writing appealing.

Her father sighed, "And so we got married, and a new carriage waited for us outside the church, with six horses!" he shook his head disapprovingly, "What an unnecessary extravaganzance…. Then the postilion, an old man—he had died long ago—took us all the way to Yasnaya."

He shook his head and closed his eyes. "She was wonderful. She took care of the household, quickly learned all the details of the estate. And then you, children, came. One after another. And she never complained. Never once. I was always the grumbler. She was impeccable."

Tatiana nodded. She had wondered countless of times what was it that *changed?* What had happened to the relationship that both her parents so often admitted was 'wonderful' in its outset?

"It is not *her*, Tanya," her father said quietly, his voice nearly unheard, "it is *me*. If *I* would go back to being the Leo Tolstoy which I *used* to be, the Leo Tolstoy that she *married*, in a day your mother would stop being this nerve-racked and would become all smiley and pleased, like the princess she always was. 'Countess Tolstoy'! How she loved that title."

He sighed, his eyes watering again, "But I nowadays bring her nothing but misery! Sometimes I think," he bit his lips, "that when I'm gone, she would be the happiest."

"Papa!"

"No, Tanya, listen to me!" he looked at her, his eyes glaring, "I mean it! You girls were always on my side. Only the boys see your mother for what she is. Do listen to me! Your mother is wonderful."

"I know that, Papa."

"No you don't! Do you know how often," he wiped a tear from his eye, "how often she would feed you all day, take care of you, teach you music and drawing and what not, listen to your quarrels and make peace between all of you, and then at night would copy my writings into legible form? You have no idea how she would help me with the characters, shedding light on things that sounded unnatural. She would say, 'No, Leo, Natasha would not speak that way!' Or, 'this sentence sounds too *conceited*, Leo, too *simplistic*...'"

Tolstoy shook his head, "No, she always knew what needed to be fixed. And she was right."

Tatiana looked at her father. She remembered him speaking fondly of her mother before. But she could not recall him ever being *that* warm.

Somehow this worried her. She knew she was supposed to be pleased with her father's memories, and that his fond memories should make her feel happy. But there was *something* in her father's *tone* that worried her. This brought her back to what she read in his diaries. Leaving. Death.

"Tanya?" her father probed, "You look sad!"

She closed her eyes tightly, stopping herself from

crying, "It's nothing Papa...."

"Tanya!"

Tatiana looked at her hands. She felt her father looking at her. She wanted to speak to him. She wanted to really *speak* to him. About her fear of him dying. And what would her mother do.

She also wanted to speak to him about little Anya. And about Sukhotin's work. About how her husband was trying to balance the difficult task of collecting taxes from the people—which grew more difficult each year—while at the same time being the people's representative in the regional council. She wanted to speak to her father about her husband's affection to her. About his tenderness. About how he never yells at her, and always praises her. About how he adores her.

She wanted her father to *approve* of her marriage. Now, eleven years after she had done what he threatened would be "the worst decision of your life!" she longed to hear him saying, "Tanya, you were right."

She wanted him to be *happy* for her. To *compliment* her on how she was a good parent to Anya. How she had raised a responsible young girl, who everyone finds adorable. She wanted to tell her father about the daily lessons she was giving her five-year-old daughter, who was now able to read both Russian and Latin, and was slowly progressing with the Greek alphabet. She wanted her father to be *proud* of the responsible mother she had become.

She wanted her father to compliment her. To notice how humane, she was to the serfs in the estate, calling each of them by name, and not accepting them ever calling her "The Governor's wife," "Countess" or "Madam," but always demanding them to simply call her "Tatiana." Her father would approve of that, would he not?

She wanted to say so much. But, alas, she said nothing. She felt all the words—and the subsequent tears—being pushed down. She was a champion at that.

Her father said nothing. And neither did she.

Finally, she got up. "Papa, you should probably rest a little."

"Yes, Tanya," her father murmured, and stared at the window.

She adjusted the blanket that had fallen from his legs when he spoke excitedly a few minutes earlier.

He nodded to her in appreciation and closed his eyes.

She left the room quietly, opening the door handle with both hands as not to make any noise, and then quietly closing it behind her.

Her mother was sitting in the sofa down the large hallway, reading a book. "How is he?" she asked Tatiana.

"He is fine. He is now taking a rest."

"Has he said anything about me?"

Tatiana found herself saying—without even noticing or stopping to think—"No, Mama."

Her mother nodded forlornly, and looked down at her book.

Tatiana walked away. She suddenly felt a rush of emotions. She hurried to Anya's room and became worried when she did not see her, "Anya?! Where is Anya!" she shouted.

Olga came out of the kitchen, with Natasha picking out of the kitchen as well. Olga said, "It is her time now for playing, she is outside with Nadya!"

"Of course," Tatiana said and hurried outside. She opened the large door and the light outside blinded her for a moment. She then spotted Anya and Nadya sitting with some books on a blanket, near the woods, and hurried toward them. Her walk soon turned into running, her dress flying around her. "Anya!" she called.

Anya and Nadya looked at her.

"Anya!" Tatiana called again, panting. She grabbed Anya in her arms, lifting her in the air, hugging her. "Anya! Anya!"

Nadya looked worried, "Is everything alright, Tatiana?"

Tatiana nodded, "Can I have a moment with my daughter?"

Nadya looked a little bewildered. But she quickly nodded, took the blanket and the books, and left, walking fast as to not disturb the countess.

Anya hugged her mother back, "Mama! Are you sad?"

"No!" Tatiana said, "No! I am… *happy*…. I *love* you, you know that Anya?"

Anya nodded, "And I love you, Mama."

Tatiana felt her heart pounding fast. She began crying. She kneeled down onto the blanket. Anya tried to wipe her mother's tears, "Don't cry Mama!"

Tatiana smiled, looking at her daughter through her tears, "I'll be a good mother, you hear me?"

Anya nodded slowly.

"You can *always* speak to me if you want, you understand?"

Anya nodded, "Don't cry Mama!"

Tatiana wiped her tears, "Come here," she grabbed Anya and hugged her, sat her down on her lap, looking at her daughter's little red shoes. She whispered into Anya's ear, "I love you Anya. Mama loves you!"

Two days later Tolstoy and Sophia had a big argument.

Tatiana heard her father saying terrible things, about leaving his mother and about his life with her becoming an intolerable jail. She heard her mother screaming, weeping, crying, "You are *murdering* me Leo Tolstoy! *Murdering* me!"

Tatiana asked Nadya to take Anya for a walk. Nadya did so immediately, more than willingly, and quickly left the house with Anya.

Tatiana went to the room she had given her father as his study. As she neared it she heard her parents, screaming and shouting ever so loudly. She opened the door wide and shouted, "Enough!" she yelled at both of them. "You are not allowed to speak this way in *my* house!"

To her surprise it was her father who yelled back, his hoarse voice as loud as he could muster, "No Tanya! Your mother needs to understand, for one and for all, that she will not control me!"

"It is you"—her mother interjected—"who is controlling me! Threatening me all the time, not willing to cooperate with the *little* that I ask!"

"Enough!" Tatiana screamed. She told her father, "To your bedroom! Right now!"

"But I've been writing a damned letter, and she interrupted me—"

"Papa! Right now!"

Tatiana looked at her mother, "And you, Mama, to your own room, right now!"

"I was looking to see if any letters were addressed to me—"

"Right now Mama! This moment!"

Her mother raised her chin, pulled her shoulders back, and began walking out when she suddenly burst into sobs and ran out of the room, covering her face in her hands.

Tatiana watched as her father shuffled to his bedroom. He closed his door. In the back of the house, she heard her mother slamming her door.

Tatiana sighed, falling on the couch, wanting to cry.

That evening Tolstoy did not come to dinner, and explained that he was sick. No, he said to Tatiana, he did not want to eat. No, not even if food was brought to his room.

Dinner was grim, with Sukhotin trying to converse with Sophia, to no avail.

At night, when everyone was sleeping, Tatiana got out of her bed. She took the small oil lantern from the side of her bed, lit it, and walked quietly to the room serving her father's study. She heard him snoring from the adjacent room.

She turned the oil lantern's nob to the bare minimum, casting a dim light across the room. She walked quietly to the desk. She saw a small pile of letters her father had written. She skimmed through them quickly. The first was to Chertkov:

> "I am attaching two letters which I have written. One in Russian, the brief one, you can send it as it is. The other, to a Hindu in the Transvaal, needs to be translated into English. I am too fatigued to write in English myself these days. Translate yourself or ask Bulgakov to do it, and return it back for review.
>
> Leo."

Tatiana quickly looked through the letters below, one, to a Russian pacifist, was one page. The other, addressed to the Hindu Gandhi, was three pages long. She looked at it quickly. Her father had not written such a long letter in the longest time.

She then quickly moved the letters and found her father's diary underneath them. She opened it, turned to the days she had missed, beginning three days before:

> "6 September. Sukhotin's Estate. I woke up sick, probably just senile-gangrene. It was nice, though, as it caused me not only unease, but also a rather pleasant feeling of death approaching."

Tatiana's heart sank.

> "In addition I felt overall fatigue. Good news from the Transvaal about the colony of passive resisters. I do not eat much. A lack of appetite. Sophia had arrived this morning. We spoke calmly, all is well."

Tatiana quickly flipped to the next page,

> "7 September. Sukhotin's Estate. My health was better today. Only my leg hurt. But altogether I am better. Took a walk in the park. Only wrote two letters, one to a Russian passive resistor, the other to the Hindu. Countess becoming irritable and more irritable. It's depressing. But I am holding on."

Tatiana's eyes shifted to the last entry from that day:

> "8 September. Sukhotin's Estate. I'm restless. Haven't written anything. Walked round the park and made a few notes. I can't yet go as far as doing what ought to be done calmly. Sophia and I had a painful talk about my departure. I stood up for my freedom. I'll go whenever I want to. I'm very sad, naturally, because I'm not well. I'm going to bed."

Tatiana felt her heart beating fast. She reread the entry:

"I can't yet go as far as doing what ought to be done calmly."

What did her father mean by "what ought to be done"? Was he going to commit suicide? No, it was not like him. So what, then? Leave? Where to? She reread the rest of the entry again,

"Sophia and I had a painful talk about my departure. I stood up for my freedom. I'll go whenever I want to. I'm very sad, naturally, because I'm not well. I'm going to bed."

Tatiana flipped quickly to the pages before, reading again,

"I woke up sick, probably just senile-gangrene. It was nice, though, as it caused not only unease, but also a rather pleasant feeling of death approaching."

She closed the journal quickly, feeling her chest rising and falling rapidly.

Suddenly she felt someone looking at her.

She looked at the door, and saw a figure there holding an oil lantern.

Her mother.

Tatiana wanted to say something, but was afraid to speak. Their eyes met in the darkness.

Sophia walked slowly into the room. She carried herself in a dignified manner. She approached the desk.

Tatiana made way to her mother. She wanted to say, 'No, Mama, do not read it.'

But she couldn't.

Her mother placed the lantern on the desk and opened the journal.

Tatiana stood there, frozen. She looked at her 66-year-old mother flipping through the pages quietly, nearing the lantern to the diary.

Tatiana decided to leave. She took her own lantern and left the room, glancing back at her mother. Her mother ignored her, reading.

Tatiana walked quietly down the large hallway. She quietly opened the door to her bedroom. Sukhotin was snoring. She did not want to close the door. She placed the lantern on her bed and turned the nob to the end. The light died away.

She sat in bed, propped against the pillow. She waited for her mother to return to her room. Finally, after many long minutes, her mother walked quietly across Tatiana's bedroom, opening the door to her room, then closing it quietly behind her.

Tatiana could not fall asleep that night. She feared what she knew was to come.

Leo and Sophia Tolstoy at their 34th wedding anniversary, September 23, 1896.

Members of the Tolstoy Farm, 1910.

TOLSTOY FARM,
TRANSVAAL COLONY, SOUTH AFRICA,
OCTOBER 1910

Gandhi looked through the letters that arrived at the farm. Then he saw it, the envelope with the red and yellow stamps from Russia, addressed to him, from "Leo Tolstoy, Yasnaya Polyana, Russia."

His heart beat faster. He opened the letter with his thin letter opener, afraid to harm it, but at the same time wanting to open it as quick as he could. He noticed the envelope was thicker than usual.

As he pulled the letter out of the envelope and unfolded it, he noticed to his delight there were three full pages. This time, unlike the previous letters, it was printed, not handwritten.

> "To Mr. Gandhi, Tolstoy Farm, Johannesburg District, Transvaal Colony, South Africa.
>
> From Leo Tolstoy, Sukhotin's Estate, Russia, 7th September 1910."

Gandhi shook his head disapprovingly at the date. The letter was written two and a half months earlier! What had taken it so long? Usually letters arrived in South Africa within a month at the most! He sighed and read:

> "I received your journal, 'Indian Opinion', and was glad to see what it says of those who renounce all resistance by force, and I immediately felt a wish to let you know what thoughts its perusal aroused in me.

> The longer I live—especially now when I clearly feel the approach of death—the more I feel moved to express what I feel more strongly about than anything else."

Gandhi's eyes stopped at that sentence, in between the long dashes, merely written as a passing note, "especially now when I clearly feel the approach of death."

Gandhi was alarmed. 'No,' he said in his heart, 'please, no. You have so much more to give.' He shook his head and kept reading, feeling a uneasy:

> "In my opinion what is of immense importance is namely what we call the renunciation of all opposition by force, which really simply means the doctrine of the law of love unperverted by sophistries.

> Love, or in other words, the striving of the human's souls towards unity—and the supportive behavior to one another that results therefrom—represents the highest and indeed the only law of life."

Gandhi marveled at the words. Only Tolstoy could

speak in such a strong and confident manner, calling things as they were. "Love… represents the highest and indeed the only law of life." Magnificent! He went on reading:

> "Each person knows and feels deep in the depths of his or her heart this very truth. We can see it most clearly in children. And this truth of love remains clear and bright until the child grows and becomes involved in the lying net of worldly thoughts.

> This law was announced by all the philosophies—Indian as well as Chinese, along with Jewish, Greek and Roman. Most clearly, I think, it was announced by Christ, who said explicitly that on it hang all the Law and the Prophets."

Gandhi nodded to himself. While he was not Christian, he admired Jesus, especially his Sermon on the Mount. He cherished Jesus' words: "Whoever slaps you on the right cheek let him do it again." What courage. What bravery.

He went on reading:

> "Jesus Christ, foreseeing the distortion that has hindered the recognition in the Law of Love, specifically indicated the danger of misinterpretation of the law, which happens when men interpret this law according to their worldly interests.

> This leads one astray, away from the law, into believing that they have a right to defend their interests by force or, as Christ expressed it, to repay blow by blow and recover stolen

property by force, etc."

'Yes!' Gandhi thought, 'True! All too true…'

He continued reading, enthralled:

> "Christ knew, as all reasonable men must do, that any employment of force is incompatible with love as the highest law of life, and that as soon as the use of force appears permissible— even in a single case—the law itself is immediately erased."

Gandhi had heard these thoughts expressed before in Tolstoy's books. But now there was a sense of weight to them. They were meant for *him*. Could it really be that Leo Tolstoy himself wrote these very words especially for him? Especially for Mohandas Gandhi?

> "The whole of Christian civilization, which is outwardly so splendid, has grown up on this strange and flagrant misunderstanding and contradiction, which is partly intentional but mostly unintended.
>
> Fundamentally the law of love can be no longer valid if defense by force is set up beside it. And once the law of love is not valid, then there remains no law except the right of might."

Gandhi nodded. So well put! This is what he himself had tried to explain in his 'Indian Home Rule', in the metaphor about the thief entering your home. The *truly* religious man, the *truly* god-loving man, will *never* attack back!

Gandhi sighed. This was such a difficult concept to explain to others. But he felt that Tolstoy *lived* this principle.

This principle, Gandhi knew, was better *exemplified* than *spoken about*. When one *shows* you true love, and is willing to even lose him or herself in submission to your wrongdoing, every person's heart is bound to open. Every person.

Gandhi took a deep breath and kept reading, feeling the excitement being built in him. Tonight he shall read this letter to the whole community in the evening gathering.

> "Christendom has lived in that state for 1,900 years. Certainly men have always let themselves be guided by force as the main principle of their social order. The difference between the Christian nations and all other nations is only that in Christianity the law of love has been more *clearly* and *definitely* given than in any other religion, and that its adherents solemnly *recognize* it."

Gandhi shook his head. Recognizing isn't enough. It must be *practiced*. He continued reading:

> "Yet despite this Christians deem the use of force to be permissible, and base their lives on violence. The life of the Christian nations therefore presents a contradiction between what they believe in—namely, love—and the principle on which their lives are built: force. While love should prescribe the law of conduct, it is the employment of force which leads instead."

Gandhi sighed. These were harsh allegations to blame Christians with. No wonder Tolstoy was excommunicated from the Church. He was able to see what most Christians and Europeans were not willing to see: the exploitation of the rest of the world through colonialism and wars. How was Tolstoy, there, in the snowy Russian landscape, able to understand all that, as if he were non-European? And how was he able to name things as they really were?

Gandhi continued reading:

> "This employment of brute force is recognized under various forms such as nation's armies, which are not only accepted as necessary, but are *esteemed*.
>
> In recent years, with the development of the spiritual life of Christianity, the contradiction between the loving *message* of Christianity and the *methods* employed by the Christian nations, have reached the utmost tension.
>
> The issue now is that we must choose one of two things: either to admit that we recognize no religious ethics at all and let our conduct be decided by the right of might or to demand that all our military institutions be abolished."

Gandhi sighed. Tolstoy had seen with his own eyes the effects of war. He saw the death of comrades in the frontline with his own eyes. He knew how futile wars could be. But Gandhi disagreed with Tolstoy on the exact method. Tolstoy had also argued at times for the abolition of the police and law courts. No, Gandhi thought. Rather than thinking on what should be *abolished*, the attention should shift to what should be *accomplished*. And the primary attention he had in his mind was education.

This is why Gandhi himself was the main teacher at the Tolstoy Farm. He believed that nonviolence and a life according to the law of love had to be *taught*. In regular schools most people learned of "history" or, as he saw it, the chronicles of wars. Instead, the children had to learn of the greatest expressions of love exhibited throughout history: of the cooperation, peace, and kindness that were more prevalent than the wars!

Gandhi kept reading eagerly:

> "This spring, at a scripture examination in a Moscow girl's school, the girls were examined on the Ten Commandments. They were first examined by their teacher and then by an archbishop who was present. They were especially questioned about the Sixth Commandment, 'Thou shalt not kill.'

> After the Commandments had been correctly recited the archbishop would often put a question, usually: 'Is it always and in every case forbidden by the law of God to kill?' And the unfortunate girls, misled by their instructor, would have to answer: 'Not always, for it is permissible in war and at executions.'

> When, however, this customary additional question—whether it is always a sin to kill—was put to one of these unfortunate creatures (what I am telling you is not an anecdote, but actually happened and was told me by an eyewitness) the girl blushed and answered decidedly and with emotion: 'It is always forbidden to kill!'

> Despite all the customary sophistries of the archbishop, she held steadfastly to it: that to kill is under *all* circumstances forbidden, even in the Old Testament, and that Christ has not only

> forbidden us to kill, but also forbidden us in general to do any harm to our neighbor. The archbishop, for all his majesty and verbal dexterity, was silenced, and victory remained with the girl."

Gandhi chuckled, 'Good girl', he thought.

He felt flattered that Tolstoy would take the time to share with him this story. He was curious as to why it was so important to the great sage to share it with him.

> "Yes, we may write in the papers of our progress in mastery of the air, of complicated diplomatic relations, of various discoveries, of all sorts of alliances, and of so-called works of art, and we can choose to ignore what that young girl said. But we cannot completely silence her, for every Christian feels the same, however vaguely he or she may do so.
>
> Socialism, Communism, Anarchism, the Salvation Army, the growth of crime, the fearfully rising number of suicides—are all indications of that inner contradiction which must and will be resolved."

Gandhi was a little taken aback by the tone, 'the growth of crime' and the 'fearfully rising number of suicides.' Tolstoy seemed to be indeed troubled.

He continued reading, shaking his head:

> "This inner contradiction between love and force must be resolved, and in such a manner that the law of love will be recognized and all reliance on force abandoned.
>
> Your work in the Transvaal, which to us seems to be at the end of the earth, is yet in the center

of our interest—"

Gandhi paused reading, and then slowly reread that last part, lavishing every word:

> "Your work in the Transvaal, which to us seems to be at the end of the earth, is yet in the center of our interest—and supplies the weightiest practical proof, in which the world can now share, and not only the Christian but all the peoples of the world can participate."

Gandhi smiled to himself, feeling immense pride.

He flipped to the last page, disappointed to see the end of the letter was approaching,

> "I think it will please you to hear that here in Russia, too, a similar movement is rapidly attracting attention, and refusals of military service increase year by year.
>
> However small as yet is the number of those who renounce all resistance by force in your camp in South Africa, and however small is the number in Russia of those who refuse military service—both of us can say: God is with us, and God is mightier than man.
>
> All governments and their armies are growing aware of the doubt people begin to find in militarism. This is true to your British government as much as to our Russian government. Naturally, our governments will oppose the people's calls for justice, more energetically than they would oppose any other 'hostile' activity. We in Russia have already began to experience this, as you in South Africa did too, as I could read in the articles in your

magazine."

Gandhi arrived at the last paragraph:

> "The armies and the governments which they support know from what direction the greatest danger threatens them, and are on guard with watchful eyes not merely to preserve their interests but actually to fight for their very existence.
>
> Yours etc.,
>
> Leo Tolstoy."

Gandhi put the letter down.

He was feeling a mixture of emotions. He was pleased, excited to read the letter. It was a long letter, and it stated Tolstoy's clear support of the struggle Gandhi led.

But he also felt something different in Tolstoy's writing. A sense of bitterness. It did not have the love flowing from its lines, like his *Letter to a Hindu* had two years earlier.

An unpleasant feeling creeped into Gandhi's heart. He felt that Tolstoy was in a dire situation. As if his wellbeing was on the line. Gandhi was worried for his teacher.

That evening Gandhi read Tolstoy's letter to the whole assembly. He hoped to hear Herman's opinion, but Herman was in Johannesburg, returning only at night with the last train.

The assembly was pleased with the letter from Tolstoy, showing clear support to their struggle.

Later that evening, Gandhi tried to dismiss the hard feeling he had. Tolstoy might have had a negative mood during that day. That's all.

But that evening Gandhi did not want to go to bed. He stayed in his small office, wanting to talk to Herman when he returned.

At eleven p.m. Gandhi saw from his window Herman returning to the farm. He quickly went outside, "Herman!"

Herman was surprised to see Gandhi awake. "What are you doing up, Mohandas?"

"Herman, I need to talk."

"What is it? What happened?"

"It's Tolstoy. I'm worried about him."

Gandhi and his wife Kasturba, 1914.

Tolstoy, 80-year-old, Yasnaya Polyana, 1908.

SUKHOTIN ESTATE
OREL, RUSSIA
OCTOBER 1910

It had been four weeks since Tolstoy returned to Yasnaya Polyana. Tatiana had a bad feeling. Her feelings were confirmed when she received a letter from her father.

"Yasnaya Polyana, 1910, October 12th,

Dear Tanya,

Here I finally write to you, dear Tanya. My consciousness torments me for not having done so until now as I promised. Are things good in your home? I hope all is well for you. As to us, we can unfortunately not report the same: things are still difficult. Every day brings with it more reproaches and tears. Yesterday and today were especially bad. Now it is midnight. Just now your mother had reproached me about the new will I had signed with the guidance of

Chertkov. I don't know how, but she somehow learnt of it. I was silent and did not respond, and so she eventually left me alone.

This morning I thought that I shall declare that I am leaving to visit you in your estate. But then I changed my mind.

Sad, isn't it? That you who love me must hope for me not to come.

All else is well. I cannot however boast of any writing of quality recently. Perhaps that is better. I have already ruined enough paper.

Of the visitors recently it was nice to see Mr. Nazhivin. I am waiting for Ivan Ivanovich to visit soon.

Just now Sophia interrupted me, demanding me to read to her an old excerpt from my diaries of the time I was in love with her. Again came the tears.

And now, again, she had come, again in tears, begging me please not to write to you about her.

Please send my greetings to Sukhotin, Anya, and your whole household.

Your father."

Tatiana stared at the letter. She sat down and wrote quickly, hoping to have the letter leave with the post office's last shipment at five.

She wrote the most loving of letters, urging her father to come and stay with her again. She wrote that Anya missed him terribly. And she encouraged him to ignore Sophia's mood.

She sent the letter and hoped for the best.

But as the days passed she had a grave and sick feeling in her stomach, which she tried unsuccessfully to ignore.

Then it came. At noon of October 28th there was a knock on the door. Tatiana jumped toward the door. She had an ominous feeling. She opened the door.

The deliveryman from the post office said, "A telegram! Mrs. Sukhotin?"

Olga, the maid, came to the door and looked at Tatiana.

"I am her," Tatiana said to the deliveryman and quickly signed the form. She opened the telegram anxiously:

"To: Tatiana Tolstoy-Sukhotin

From: Alexandra Tolstoy

Telegram:

Papa left early morning. Unknown destination. Mama is distraught. Come at once."

She looked at Olga. "I need to leave."

Olga asked, "Shall I get Anya ready?"

"No." Tatiana said with a heavy heart. "I need to go on my own."

Olga nodded.

"Please have Vadim prepare the carriage. I shall

hurry to the train station. I do not know for how long I shall be gone. Please tell Sukhotin."

Olga nodded and headed out to the stables.

Tatiana walked quickly to her bedroom, placing the suitcase on the bed and throwing a few dresses into it. Anya came quietly into the room. "Mama? Are you leaving?"

Tatiana looked at her. Nadya stood away in the hallway. Tatiana said to Nadya, "It is fine. She'll be with me for a moment."

Nadya nodded and stepped away walking toward the nursery room.

"Mama!" Anya repeated, "Are you leaving?"

Tatiana sighed heavily and kneeled down, "Yes darling. But I will be back soon."

"Where are you going to?"

"To Grand Mama," Tatiana said and then added quickly, "and to Grand Papa."

"Mama! Can I come with you?"

"Not this time," Tatiana said.

"Mama! I don't want you to go!"

Tatiana kissed her daughter on her forehead and thought, 'Me neither, Tanyushka.'

Within a few minutes the suitcase was packed, the two horses were mounted, and Tatiana drove away from the estate. It was snowing already. She hated November. She remembered rushing, four years earlier, to the train station when Masha was reported sick. It was November then too. And snowing as well.

Five hours later Natasha, the maid, opened the door to Tatiana. Natasha looked frightened.

Tatiana said nothing, running up the stairs into her mother's bedroom. Alexandra was there, as well as Tolstoy's assistant, Bulgakov. Her mother, sleeping, looked extremely pale.

Alexandra was relieved to see her older sister. She hugged her, her embrace a little too tight.

Tatiana whispered, "How is she?"

Alexandra's eyes widened, her voice trembling, "She threw herself into the pond!"

Tatiana looked at her sister's eyes. "What?!"

Bulgakov nodded sadly to Tatiana.

Tatiana hurried to her mother's bed, put her hand on her mother's forehead and was relieved to feel the skin was warm. What was her mother *thinking*? This was too much even for her mother! The pond was nearly frozen at this season. It could have killed her! She could have drowned!

Alexandra whispered, "Bulgakov saved her."

Tatiana looked at Bulgakov. He bowed his head gently, looking sad. Tatiana nodded to him in appreciation.

Alexandra whispered, "Papa left her a letter. She read it and then ran to the pond." She paused, "I telegrammed all the brothers."

"Good," Tatiana whispered. She then looked at her mother. She put her hand on her mother's hair, stroking the 66-year-old woman as if she was a child, "Mama? Mama, it's me, Tanya."

Slowly, Sophia opened her eyes, staring into space. She then turned her head toward Tatiana. "Tanyushka," she mumbled, "Tanyushka! He left. He left!"

"Shhh," Tatiana said, "I came for *you*. We are all with you."

Sophia closed her eyes and sighed. "But he isn't."

During the following hours the other brothers came. First Andrey came, then Ilya, and then Sergey and Michael. They all spoke quietly in the dining room. Andrey was extremely upset with their father. "He will kill her," he muttered, "he will absolutely kill her!"

Sergey, the eldest, was less moved, "Andrey, she would have killed him first. Mama would not die that easily."

Andrey had tears in his eyes, "Sergey, she nearly drowned!"

Sergey said nothing.

None of them knew where their father was. They had several ideas. Perhaps he headed to one of the Tolstoy communal farms. Perhaps one of his friends. Andrey was certain that he went to aunt Maria, living in a convent. "Don't worry," Sergey murmured, "the press will tell us in a day or two."

Tatiana did not know what to do.

That night she decided to sleep next to her mother in the large bed that many years ago used to be her parents, before her father moved to his own bedroom near his study.

As Tatiana came into bed with the small lantern at night she was pleased to see her mother snoring quietly. It was a good sign. Sophia refused food the whole day. But at least she was sleeping. Tatiana nodded to Natasha, who sat in the corner, that she could leave the room.

Natasha nodded, "Call me if you need me."

As Tatiana made place for herself in the large bed, she found a piece of paper under her elbow. She raised the paper to her eye-level and looked at it. It was her father's writing. Dated that very day, October 28th:

> "Dearest Sophia.
>
> My departure will distress you. I'm sorry about this, but please understand and believe that I couldn't do otherwise. I can't live any longer in these conditions of luxury in which I have been living, and I'm doing what old men of my age commonly do: leaving this worldly life in order to live the last days of my life in peace and solitude.
>
> Please understand this and do not come after me, even if you find out my whereabouts. Your coming would only make your position and mine worse and would not alter my decision.
>
> I thank you for your honorable 48 years of life

with me, and I ask you to forgive me for everything I am guilty of before you, as I, with all my heart, forgive you for what you may be guilty of before me.

I advise you to adjust to the new conditions of life you will face on my departure, and to bear me no ill will.

If you wish to write to me, tell Alexandra. She will know my whereabouts and send me anything I need; but she cannot tell you where I am, since I have made her promise to tell no one.

Yours,

Leo. October 28th, 5 a.m."

Tatiana bit her lip. She shook her head. Her father could have done better. The letter felt cruel. "I advise you to adjust to the new conditions of life you will face on my departure."

She felt the urge to cry. Often times in her life she felt more mature and grown-up than her two parents. Especially now, with the way her father carried his silly 'escape' and with her mother jumping into the lake. She felt as if she had no parents. No real adults in her life. She had to be her parents' parent.

In the middle of the night Tatiana heard something. She opened her eyes at once, hearing her mother opening the drawer of the nightstand. Tatiana saw her mother taking a small bottle in her hand and looking at it.

Tatiana looked at the small vial. The inscription said clearly, in capital letter, "OPIUM." She reached her hand at once and snatched it from her mother's hand.

Her mother screamed, "Give it to me! Tanya!"

Tatiana jumped out of bed, "Natasha! Sergey! Alexandra!"

The following hour Tatiana, Natasha, Alexandra and Sergey searched for anything Sophia could hurt herself with. They found a small penknife and removed it from the drawer. They took the oil lamps from the room. Sergey even locked the window with an old key he took from Old Abrasha the porter.

All along Sophia sobbed and sobbed. Finally, when the four of them finished securing the room, it was agreed that the maids would take shifts staying awake in a chair outside the door.

Tatiana climbed into bed, hugged her mother and stroke her head. Her mother sobbed in her arms. After a whole hour of sobs and outrage, Sophia finally cried herself to sleep in her eldest daughter's arms.

The following morning, while Natasha was with her mother, Tatiana went to the dining hall. Sergey and Alexandra shared last night's events with the other brothers. Sergey was determined that their mother needed more than warmth and comfort, but rather professional help. He convinced all of them that she needed a psychiatrist.

Andrey took on himself to telegram a friend of the

family, a doctor, from Moscow. An hour later Andrey returned saying the doctor promised to come promptly with two nurses.

In the afternoon Alexandra received a telegram from Chertkov. She took Tatiana aside. "I got a note where Papa is."

"Where?"

"He is staying at the convent, where Aunt Maria lives. I shall go to him."

Tatiana sighed, "Mama should not know where he is. She would want to go too."

Alexandra nodded.

Tatiana held her sister's hand. "I would like for you to bring him a letter from me. I will ask the others to write to him as well."

Alexandra agreed. "But do so quickly. I want to leave soon." She went to pack her suitcase, and included some bedding for her father. He would appreciate some familiar linen, she thought.

Meantime, in the dining hall, Tatiana asked her brothers to write letters to their father.

Andrey jumped, "Do we know where he is?"

Tatiana hesitated, "I do not."

"Then where are we going to send the letters to?"

Tatiana mumbled, "Alexandra said she knows."

Andrey went to Alexandra's room. He returned a few moments later, "Auntie's convent, I told you! He wants to live like a monk!"

Sergey whispered, "Mama should not hear you!"

Andrey looked exasperated, and sat down near the long table to write to his father.

Tatiana looked at her four brothers. This reminded her somehow of her childhood. They would all sit together and do their 'homework' that Papa had given each one to do. She was fourteen, Sergey fifteen, Ilya twelve, Lev was nine, Masha—dear Masha—must have been seven. Andrey was just born. Michael and Alexandra were yet to be born. They would sit this way. Concentrating. Sometimes Sergey would play the piano. Everything was perfect then.

She looked down at the empty paper in front of her. She wanted to write to her father, but did not know what to write to him. She noticed Andrey writing rapidly, a long letter. The others soon finished writing, but Andrey continued.

The other brothers then sealed their letters in envelopes and left them in front of Tatiana to give to Alexandra.

Andrey gave Tatiana his letter, opened, "Have a look," he said.

She read it quickly:

> "Dear Papa,
>
> Only the very best of feelings oblige me to say what I think about Mama's condition.
>
> Tanya, Sergey, Ilya, Michael and I have gathered here, and however much we consider the matter, we have been unable to think of any way but one of protecting Mama from herself,

though I think she will eventually kill herself no matter what we do."

Tatiana looked at Andrey worriedly. He looked back at her adamantly. She shook her head and kept reading:

"The only way to prevent it is to put her under constant supervision. Of course, she would never submit to it. The present situation is an impossible one, since we cannot abandon our own families and work to remain at our mother's side. I know you have finally decided not to return, but as a conscientious duty I must warn you that by this final decision you are killing our mother.

I know how heavy the burden has been for you during the last months, but I also know that Mama is mentally ill."

Tatiana felt a little uneasy to see the words written so clearly: "Mama is mentally ill." She kept on reading:

"I also know that living together has, in these late years, been rather unbearable for both of you. Had you summoned us to speak with Mama, so that you might not separate for an infinite period but instead find a way to calm down her nerves, we might not have experienced this dreadful suffering that we all now share."

Tatiana took a deep breath and went on quickly to read the last paragraph:

"As to what you said to me the previous time we met about the luxury surrounding you, it strikes me that since you have tolerated it up until now you might have sacrificed the last years of your life for the sake of your family and endure it just a little longer.

Yours,

Andrey."

Andrey looked at his older sister in anticipation. "Does it convey the message?"

Tatiana nodded slowly. "That it certainly does."

She closed her eyes. She was realizing how things were changing—how what had happened was indeed an earthquake, and not yet another fight between her parents. Was Andrey right in his sharp tone to her father?

Andrey signed his letter, put it into an envelope and placed it in front of Tatiana, heading to sit with his brothers in the drawing room.

Tatiana closed her eyes again, feeling overwhelmed. She should soon go to her mother and see how she was faring. Was she being willing to eat finally? Or at least willing to drink?

She suddenly missed Sukhotin, Anya, the servants and the estate. It hadn't even been two days. She did not know how long she was going to last like this. She felt exhausted already.

She suddenly felt a hand on her shoulder. Alexandra said, "I'm ready." Tatiana looked at her, her suitcase in hand, wearing her large fur coat.

"Wait," Tatiana said, "I need to finish my letter."

"Hurry then," Alexandra whispered.

Tatiana nodded. She wrote down:

"Dear precious Papa,

You have always suffered from a great deal of advice, and so I will not give you any.

Like everyone else, you have to act as best as you can and as you consider necessary. I shall never condemn you.

About Mama, I will only say that she is both pitiable and touching. She is unable to live otherwise than she does live, and probably she will never change fundamentally.

We all try to calm her, and I do hope this would help.

I have written quickly, for Alexandra is now leaving to take this letter to you. Forgive me for being brief.

Good bye, my friend,

Tanya."

She sealed the letter and gave it to Alexandra along with the others. They hugged. Alexandra went downstairs, not before having a short argument with Andrey, who wanted to come with her. Nevertheless, she left alone.

Tatiana rushed to her mother's room.

The days passed slowly. Tatiana was anxious to find out how her father was faring away from home. Was he still in the convent? She had a feeling that he had left. Finally, three days after Alexandra's departure, two letters arrived in the morning from their father. The first was for their mother. The second was addressed for Tatiana and Sergey. Tatiana opened it, her hand quivering:

"Optina Monastery, 1910, October 31

Dear Sergey and Tanya,

Thank you very much, kind friends—true friends—Sergey and Tanya, for your sympathy for my grief and for your letters. They both gave me special pleasure—brief, clear, and above all generous.

I cannot free myself from a sense of responsibility. However, I had not the strength to act otherwise.

I am also writing to Mama. She will show you the letter. I wrote after thinking it over carefully, the best I was able to write.

We are now leaving here, but we still do not yet know where we are heading. You can always reach me through Chertkov.

Good-bye, and thank you, sweet children. I am sorry for the fact that after all I am now the cause of suffering for you. Especially you, dear darling, Tanya.

That is all. I am in a hurry to leave, hoping to avoid what I fear the most—that your mother would find me. A meeting with her now would be terrible. Good-bye then.

Your father.

Optina Monastery, 4:00 A.M."

Tatiana fell unto the couch in the drawing room. She had terrible three days, with her mother not eating nor drinking. The doctor from Moscow said that she would need to be fed by force soon.

Tatiana stared at the letter again. Her eyes looked again at the words "Good-bye, and thank you, sweet children. I am sorry for the fact that after all I am now the cause of suffering for you. Especially you, dear darling, Tanya."

Her eyes welled-up as she felt the enormous pressure put on her. She held the other letter, addressed to her mother, in her hand.

Perhaps, she thought, Andrey was not being melodramatic when he wrote to their father that he was killing their mother. Perhaps he indeed was.

She was afraid that the letter in her hand would further put yet another nail in her mother's coffin.

At that moment Natasha the maid came to the dining room, "The Countess calls you, Tatiana."

Tatiana sighed, stood up, hid the letter to her mother inside the cabinet, and quickly went to her mother's bedroom.

Her mother looked terrible, faint and sickly, "Tanya!" she said and looked at Tatiana suspiciously, "Where is the letter?"

"The letter?" Tatiana tried to seem surprised.

"Tanya," her mother said slowly, her voice gruff, "do not think me a fool. I am not dead yet! Your father *must* have written to me. I heard the post had arrived. Give me my letter!"

Tatiana nodded obediently and left the room. She was distraught. She wished Alexandra were here so that she could speak to her. She passed by the room where Sergey was staying. "I need you, Sergey, and the others."

"Why?" Sergey asked, still waking up.

"Mama has received a letter from Papa."

"Well don't give it to her—"

"It's too late."

Walking to the dining room she took the letter from the cabinet, marveling at how her mother, who had now been fasting for nearly five days and most of the time in a state of delirium, was still in control of everything that happened around her.

She walked slowly to her mother's bedroom with the letter, as Sergey and Ilya were joining her. Soon behind them came Michael and Andrey.

Tatiana gave the letter to her mother.

Her mother sat up in her bed, and seemed rather alive. She was still extremely pale and gaunt-looking, but it looked as if a new wave of vitality had washed over her.

Tatiana stood not too far from her mother, while her brothers came and stood near the door.

Sophia read the letter, pursed lips.

She read quickly.

She then pulled her shoulders back and said, "I need a paper and a pen."

"Of course," Tatiana said. She walked quickly to her

father's study, two rooms away. The room was cold and had an eerie feeling. Tatiana quickly took a pen and some paper and closed the door behind her.

She gave the paper and pen to her mother and watched her writing quickly.

Tatiana glanced at the letter from her father, lying on the bed.

Sophia immediately caught her daughter looking and said, "Go ahead, read, I could not care less."

Tatiana remained standing, not wishing to take the letter in her hand. Nevertheless, she glanced at it.

"Dear Sophia,

Our meeting, as well as my return home, are currently completely impossible. For you it would be, as everyone warns me, highly detrimental. As for me, it would be terrible to experience your agitation, irritation, and overall excitement. All of this would only make my rather weak, sickly state, much worse. I advise you to come to terms with what had happened. Try to accept the new situation and, above all, attend to your health.

If you love me, or at least do not hate me, then you must put yourself in my position. If you would do that, not only will you not condemn me, but you will wish me best in finding rest, and possibly living some human life. Help me by controlling yourself, by not wishing for me to return at the time.

Your mood now and your suicide attempt, more than anything shows of your loss of control over yourself. This makes it ever more clear to me that I cannot comeback now.

You—no one else, me included—can relieve you of the suffering you experience and which you inflict on all those who are close to you. Try to direct all your strength toward pacifying your soul.

I have spent two days at the Optina Monastery, and am leaving now. I will post this letter on the way. I do not say where I am going, because I consider separation essential now both for you and for me. Do not think that I have left because I do not love you. I love and have compassion for you with all my soul, but I cannot do otherwise than I am doing.

To return to you while you are in such a state would be equivalent for me as to committing suicide. And I do not believe that I have a right to do that.

Farewell, dear Sophia. God help you. Life is no jesting matter, and we have no right to throw it away at our own will. Perhaps those months which we have left to live are more important than all the years lived before, and we must live them well.

Yours,

Leo."

Tatiana read the letter quickly, without flinching. Her mother, writing, looked up at her, "Not precisely all loving and gentle as he would like for all of you to think…."

She then looked at her sons, standing clumsily at the

door, awaiting a dramatic scene. "Why are you standing there? I am not going to jump from the window. Go away!"

Reluctantly, the sons left the room, though Andrey lingered near the door.

Sophia gave the short letter she had written to her daughter, "Send it to him."

Tatiana nodded, and took the letter with her. As she was about to leave the room, her mother said, "Oh and Tanya?"

"Yes Mama?"

"Do bring me some tea, Tanyushka. Russian Caravan. Make it strong."

"Yes Mama!" Tatiana said, suddenly tearing up, "Right away!"

Andrey entered the room to speak to his mother.

Tatiana went to Natasha and asked her to bring some tea, "Make it strong," she said, "Oh and try bringing her some food again. I think she might eat."

Natasha nodded and hurried to the kitchen.

Tatiana stood in the hallway and could not help not to open her mother's letter. She looked at it. It was unbelievably brief:

> "Leo,
>
> Do not think I shall try and come after you. I can barely move and I am sick. I also do not want to force anything on you; do what you think is best for you.
>
> Sophia."

Tatiana was riveted by her mother's response: without any excessive emotional outcry. She suddenly had a glimpse of hope that maybe—just maybe—everything would be better this way. She was pleased that her mother was not interested in madly running after her husband.

The hope for her mother letting go of Tolstoy shattered into pieces the following day when Sophia received a telegram from a newspaper reporter from the '*Russian Word*' notifying her:

> "Count Tolstoy sick, at Astapovo Train Station. Dire state."

Within minutes the whole house was on their feet. And the Countess, who had barely eaten for over five days, now seemed filled with zest. "We are leaving, right now!" she exclaimed, "Right now!"

Tatiana ran into the room, seeing the maids packing suitcases for her mother. The brothers were there too. Ilya was gone, as he had returned to his wife and children the evening before. But Sergey, Michael and Andrey remained. Tatiana, Sergey, and Michael tried to dissuade their mother, but she screamed at them with all her might, "What if your Papa would die without seeing me? What if I could save him?" she then barked at the maids, "Pack his pillow and his beddings! Quick!"

"But Mama," Sergey tried, "we do not know when the next train leaves, and it's cold—"

"You think of the *weather* when your Papa needs us?! Of the weather?! You should be ashamed of yourself

Sergey!"

Sergey stepped back, overwhelmed. Michael tried too, "Mama, Papa had asked *you*—I mean, *us*—not to come—"

"What does *he* know?" Sophia shouted as she put her coat on. "He might have been delirious! Or worse, Chertkov might have convinced him—he is not in his right mind!" she then barked at the two maids running around the room, "Pack three nightgowns for me, and my perfumes too!"

Tatiana felt helpless, "Mama, can we first sit and think about it?"

The glare her mother gave her silenced Tatiana at once; her mother's eyes, widened, her pierced mouth, her raised eyebrows—made Tatiana feel like a child again. She said nothing else.

Within less than an hour they were all at the train station in Tula and Andrey went to the ticket booth. Light snow was falling on the tracks. Tatiana looked at the snow, wanting to cry. She felt like everything was becoming worse, and that the worst had yet to come. She did not dare say a word to her mother. None of the children said anything.

Andrey returned from the ticket office and said, "The last train has left, Mama. There is only one to Moscow, in the other direction, and it is only in the evening."

Sophia pouted her lips, "Let me see for myself."

She walked determined to the ticket office, and asked to speak to the stationmaster.

Several minutes later she returned with a smile on her face and stood among her children, saying nothing. A few train operators went out to a train engine which stood in the station's workshop, and brought it out to the tracks, then adjoining to it one small train car behind it.

Alarmed, Sergey asked, "What is happening Mama?"

"I hired a private train."

"A private train?!" Sergey exploded. "How much did it cost?"

"Not more than your father's life, Sergey," Sophia said, "now be quiet."

Within a few minutes coal was loaded to the engine, and the party boarded the train car. The train left the Tula station heading South. Tatiana looked out the window, dreading what was to come.

From left to right: Michael Sukhotin, Tatiana, Anya, and Leo
Tolstoy. Sukhotin estate, 1910.

Tolstoy farm and surroundings, 1913.

TOLSTOY FARM,
TRANSVAAL COLONY, SOUTH AFRICA
NOVEMBER 1910

Gandhi looked at the morning newspaper. On the third page he saw it. A short article. His heart sank as he read the title:

> "Author Leo Tolstoy Runs Away from Home, Terminally Ill"

Gandhi went on reading, feeling his heart pounding:

> "The South African Star has received wired news regarding Count Leo Tolstoy, author of *War and Peace,* who is said to be terminally ill.
>
> Tolstoy, now 82-years-old, travelled by train away from his estate south of Moscow, allegedly following an irreparable argument with his wife, Countess Sophia Tolstoy. The destination of his flight was unknown; some estimated he was on direction to China. However, his health did not permit the Count to travel as far, and the

doctor accompanying him demanded they stop their journey and disembark the train at Astapovo, 300 kilometers south of Moscow. There Tolstoy was admitted to bed in the house of the train stationmaster, where he currently stays.

Additional doctors, summoned to Astapovo from Moscow, identified Tolstoy's illness as pneumonia, and reassured the press that the situation was reversible. However, a growing crowd of admirers currently gathers around the train station. The South African Star will continue to report on the matter, and wishes Count Tolstoy quick recovery."

Gandhi ran to find Herman, who was at the apple grove. Herman looked worried, "What happened?"

"Read this," Gandhi said.

Herman quickly read the short newspaper article. He looked at Gandhi. "It doesn't sound good."

"I know," Gandhi said and sighed. "At first I thought it might just be yet another newspaper hoax, but when I read that he had run away from his home...."

Herman took a deep breath in, leaning against one of the trees. "Too bad we cannot do anything."

Gandhi looked at Herman, his eyes shining, "There *is* something we can do."

Gandhi in South Africa, 1909.

Leo Tolstoy with granddaughter Tatiana (Anya), c.1908.

ASTAPOVO TRAIN STATION, LIPETSK DISTRICT, RUSSIA, NOVEMBER 1910

It was evening when the train slowed down as it approached the station. Tatiana looked through the train window and to her alarm saw a huge crowd, with several large cameras directed straight at the halting train.

As they all headed down, several magnesium flashes nearly blinded Tatiana. "Leave us alone!" she shouted through the crowd, trying to protect her mother walking behind her.

The reporters attacked them with questions, "Why did Count Tolstoy leave?"; "Countess—is it true you had a quarrel?"; "Is the Count dying?"; "Is it true the Count commanded a revolution from the Russian people?"; "Do you regret sending the Count off?"

These questions fired at Sophia with Tatiana trying

to shelter her, nearly made Tatiana faint. The brothers followed behind. Tatiana thought that they should have been leading in the front. She wanted to run back to the train and head back to Yasnaya—No, better yet—to her *own* home, to her *own* husband and daughter.

But she had to help her mother. Seconds later, as they approached the house of the train stationmaster, followed by the reporters. Chertkov came out of the door of the house. Sophia, seeing him, stepped forward and shouted, "I want to see my husband!"

Chertkov replied stiffly, "The Count has refused to see you, Countess."

Tatiana saw Alexandra coming from behind Chertkov.

Sophia was flustered, "Does Leo know I'm here? Did you tell him I was *here?* Surely he would want to see me had he known I had come!"

Chertkov repeated, "The Count has instructed me not to let you in."

"That cannot be true!" Sophia shouted.

Tatiana embraced herself, looking at Sergey behind her. He said nothing. She hated the embarrassing situation, especially as they were surrounded by reporters.

Sophia screamed, "He is my husband! What does it mean that he does not want to see me?! Alexandra!" she looked at her daughter, "Is it true?"

Alexandra nodded.

To add to the havoc, the reporters were recording the whole humiliating argument. The sound of the film wheel sickened Tatiana. She held her mother's hand, whispering, "Mama, let us go, we'll visit Papa later—"

But Sophia wouldn't have it. She screamed, "You murderers! You are murdering my husband! Let me see him at once! At once!"

Tatiana and Sergey had to pull their mother away, in front of the reporters and the cameras. They did not know, however, where to take her. The only structure was the house they were now denied entry to. Sergey looked at Tatiana, "Where to?"

Her mother fighting her in her arms, Tatiana muttered to Sergey, "Back to the train!"

Tatiana did not want to see her father. Not yet. She stayed with her mother in the train car. They closed all the curtains, trying to get some privacy from the reporters. The brothers came and left, going back and forth. It was cold outside. Sophia cried and hallowed on Tatiana's lap.

Finally, Sophia said, "If he does not want to see me, at least bring him his pillow. He so likes his pillow!"

She and Natasha the maid unpacked one of the suitcases to bring the pillow out. "Tanya," Sophia begged, "At least give him his pillow!"

Tatiana, reluctantly, acquiesced. She went outside the train, walked through the few reporters who stayed awake during the night. She saw Sergey and Andrey speaking outside. "Give the pillow to Papa. Mama begged," she said dryly. They said nothing, but took the pillow.

An hour later Andrey came running to the train, "Tanya, Papa wants to see you."

Sophia jumped, "What about me? Does he not want to see me?"

Andrey did not respond.

Tatiana got up. She was exhausted, as well as nervous to see her father. She wanted to see him, but in a different setting. At Yasnaya. Or at her own home. But not now, not like this. As she walked to the train's door her mother grabbed her hand, "Tanya, just tell him I'm here! That's all Tanyushka! Tell him I'm here and that I would like to see him. I'll make no scene, Tanyushka, I promise!"

Tatiana nodded as she left her mother, feeling her mother's eyes on her as she crossed the railways tracks and was admitted into the train stationmaster's house. She ignored the four reporters who attacked her with questions.

Andrey joined her. Inside it was warm, which made her pleased, at least her father was warm. Sergey met her in the entrance hall, whispering, "Not a word about Mama being here. Papa is very sick. We do not want him to get overly excited."

Tatiana sighed. Ilya came to her as well, "Tanya, not a word about Mama."

She nodded.

They admitted her into the room. It was dim inside, only two oil lamps burning in the room. Her father was laying on a small bed at the center of the room. She saw

Alexandra sitting next to him. And she noticed Chertkov standing aside. As she neared her father she was alarmed to see just how bad he looked. He looked gaunt, frail. She could tell at once he was not well at all.

She had seen him sick before. Many times she attended to him while he was sick. But now he looked so frail. So old... So thin!

She walked to him. Alexandra gave her chair to her sister and whispered, "I'll be right back."

Tatiana nodded and sat down. She was glad to see he was resting on the large white pillow from home. She reached for her father's hand. He was warm, that was good. She stroked his wrinkled hand, the hand which had produced so many words in his lifetime.

She saw her father's lips moving, his eyes closed still closed, "Tanya? Is that you?"

Tears welled in her eyes. "It is me, Papa," Tatiana said. She noticed Chertkov coming closer, and Sergey too, both watching her carefully. She felt the pressure from them not to tell her father anything about her mother. But could she really not say anything?

Her father turned his face to her slowly and opened his eyes. They looked red. "Thank you for coming, Tanyushka."

"Of course, Papa," Tatiana mumbled, "How are you feeling?"

Her father tried to shake his head, "Not well. How is your mother?"

She hesitated. "She is well, Papa."

"Well? Where is she?"

Chertkov moved closer to the bed and looked at Tatiana. She closed her eyes and whispered, "She's at home."

Tolstoy mumbled, "At home? That is so strange. How is she doing?"

"She is doing well, Papa," Tatiana forced herself to say, "Do not worry about her."

"But how does she feel?" her father insisted, "Is she eating at all?"

Tatiana nodded.

"Well, isn't she going to come here?"

Sergey put his hands on his sister's shoulder.

Tatiana bit her lips.

"Answer to me Tanya!"

"It is not important, Papa—"

"Not important?! What can be more important than that?!"

Tatiana felt tears streaming down her cheeks. Chertkov said, "It seems like the Count should be resting now, no, Doctor?"

Tatiana suddenly noticed Dr. Makovitsky, standing all along near the wall by the entrance to the room, in the shadow. He walked closer, "Certainly, the Count must rest."

Tolstoy looked at Tatiana, "Tanya! Tell me! Where is your mother?"

Tatiana could not stand the pressure. Tears began flowing down her cheeks as she mumbled, "I cannot do this" and ran out of the room, exiting the stationmaster's small house, running into the cold night, past the doctors outside and past the reporters, sobbing and sobbing. She cried for the impossible situation she was put in. She cried for her father. She cried for her mother. And she cried, too, for herself.

Leo Tolstoy with grandchildren Sonia and Ilya, 1909.

Countryside near Tolstoy farm, 1913.

TOLSTOY FARM,
TRANSVAAL COLONY, SOUTH AFRICA
NOVEMBER 1910

Gandhi looked at the assembly. "There isn't much we can do. We are not there to be with Tolstoy, to help alleviate his pain. We cannot be with the family. But there is one thing we can do."

Everyone looked at Gandhi. The atmosphere was intense. The whole farm was named after this one sage, living somewhere in the other side of the world. They often read his writings in the evenings, followed by interpretations by Gandhi. Even the children read some of Tolstoy's stories for children. He was their spiritual benefactor. And now he was in 'dire state' according to the newspapers.

"The one thing we *can* do," Gandhi continued, "is pray. While many of us with European education might scoff at the idea, allow me to expand on that."

Gandhi looked around the room, marveling at how even the children were quiet and attentive. "As a child," Gandhi said, "I was taught to disdain prayer. My education doubted everything that was not physical, anything that was not to be seen. I thought that prayer is an old woman's idle amusement. However," he paused and looked intently at the room, "properly understood and applied, prayer is the most potent instrument of action."

Some of the elder people in the assembly nodded. Gandhi continued. "I had also thought that prayer could be divisive. I, a Hindu, may pray in a different way than you," he looked at one of the three Muslim-Indian families, "as you may invoke the name of Allah. And you," he looked at Herman and at the other Jewish couple, Henry and Milli Polak, "may invoke the name of Jehovah, while you," he looked at Mr. Coates and Mr. Baker, "may pray with the name of Jesus Christ on your lips. However, prayer, in its original meaning, never divides. It always unites."

Some of the people nodded. Gandhi was encouraged. Up until then they would sometime chant some old hymns, but they had never held a gathering with the intention of praying for a cause. This was an experiment.

"What is divisive is the *words* one may use, the *name* one may give God. Oftentimes people focus on the words so much that they forget the heart." He looked at Kasturba. She smiled at him. "The heart," Gandhi continued, "is the most important part of the prayer. It is better in prayer to have a heart without words than words without a heart."

Many people nodded.

"I am a Hindu," Gandhi said, "but I do not wish to convert any of you."

People smiled. Gandhi continued, "What I offer is that each one of us would pray along to his or her faith. The power of this congregation is great when we join together in prayer, each according to his or her own faith and tradition. After a few minutes, I will teach you an old mantra, and we can all recite it together, if you do not find that offensive to your own heritage. Is that agreeable by everyone?"

People nodded. Gandhi looked around the room making sure that everyone was in agreement. He then closed his eyes, "We therefore wish to pray for the quick recovery of our spiritual founder, the Count Leo Tolstoy." He then remained silent.

The assembly prayed. Herman, who was a non-practicing Jew, pulled out a traditional Jewish head-cup, and prayed nodding back and forth. The Muslim families prayed as well, nodding their heads, playing with a string of prayer bids. The two Christians held hands together. Kasturba recited mantras.

His eyes closed, Gandhi repeated in his heart, 'Please, God, the divine power, bring our teacher rapid recovery.'

Finally, after a few minutes, Gandhi opened his eyes. He was moved to tears as he saw all the people, including the children, praying in their hearts.

"Thank you," he mumbled a short time later, "thank you." The room was quiet, and Gandhi enjoyed the unique feeling in the air. He was at peace. "Now I would like to teach you an old Mantra my mother used to recite. She called it," Gandhi smiled, "'The death-conquering mantra' which helps get rid of diseases, ailments, injuries and accidents, and helps prolong one's life."

Gandhi took a deep breath and closed his eyes, "*Aum tryambakam,* Oh God, *yajamahe sugandhim,* we worship your sweet fragrant, *pushti vardhanam,* you who strengthens and restores health." He went on to teach this part several times, and then the second part of the mantra, meaning "Liberate our loved one from the bounds of death."

The assembly chanted the mantra again and again, "*Aum tryambakam, yajamahe sugandhim, pushti vardhanam.*" Gandhi remembered his late mother. As he led the chanting, he opened his eyes for an instant and saw Kasturba nodding at him in approval.

Tolstoy farm, c.1910. Gandhi and Herman Kallenbach sitting in the center.

Crowds outside Tolstoy's room, Astapovo train station, .1910.

ASTAPOVO TRAIN STATION, LIPETSK DISTRICT, RUSSIA, NOVEMBER 1910

The days passed at the train station. For a while it seemed as if Tolstoy's health was stabilizing. He spoke more clearly, and tried to dictate some writing to Alexandra. But then his state worsened again.

Tatiana spent much of the time in the train car with her mother. But Sophia, sensing the end of her husband's life might be near, managed to leave the train and head to the stationmaster's house, yelling at the new doctors there, "My husband may be dying in there! I lived with him 48 years and now you tell me I cannot see him?!"

Tatiana, Sergey, and Andrey rushed to take her away from the door. They grabbed her arms and carried her across the tracks to the train car.

One of the new doctors from Moscow brought with him a new bed for the patient, *digitalin* and two oxygen balloons. But his prognosis was not good. After taking

Tolstoy's pulse and conferring with the other doctors present, his prediction was that at any moment the Count's heart might give up.

That night Alexandra wished to rest for a few hours in the train car, and Tatiana replaced her at her father's side. Tolstoy had been in a state of delirium the whole day. Then, waking up after several hours of half-sleep half-awareness, he turned to Tatiana and murmured, "Tanya... Much has befallen on your mother...."

Tatiana, who had longed for her father summoning her mother to his bedside, said eagerly, "Do you want to see *Mama*? Do you want to see *Sophia*?"

Her father sighed and closed his eyes.

Chertkov came to her, looking at her with a severe, intimidating look. She ignored him, "Papa? Tell me, do you want to see *Mama*?"

But her father turned his head away from her and closed his eyes. Chertkov looked at her disapprovingly and moved back to the back of the room, where he had set a small desk for himself.

A few hours later Alexandra came back. Tolstoy woke up from the sound of the door. His sight must have been blurry, as he shouted at Alexandra as she entered the room, "Masha! Is that you?!"

Tatiana tried to calm her father down, but he sat upright with a mighty force, "My beloved Masha! You came to me!"

Alexandra came near the bed and said quietly, "Papa, it is *me*, Alexandra."

Tolstoy looked helpless. He sank back onto the

pillow, "I am very tired," he murmured and closed his eyes, "Do not torment me anymore!"

Night turned into day. Tatiana spent most of the time near her father's bed. The brothers spent much time in the room as well, quietly speaking, but mostly avoiding talking. Each one was lost in his own thoughts.

Their father continued being in a state of delirium. In the afternoon, he awoke and said, "Tanya? Tanya I want to dictate you something."

Tanya nodded, and began writing down. But her father said nothing and fell asleep again. An hour later he woke up again and said, "I tell you: seek! Never cease seeking!"

He then fell asleep again.

A few hours later he opened his eyes widely. His eyes stared straight at Tatiana. She thought that he might be getting better, and exclaimed, "Papa, you are looking better!"

The brothers joined her and Alexandra near the bedside. Tolstoy stared at them all, "The problem with you is that... you are always looking at Leo Tolstoy! There are many people in the world beside Leo Tolstoy but you are looking at this one only!"

He then closed his eyes.

Tatiana was disappointed to see he was sleeping again. He had slept most of the time now.

The hours passed, and by the evening Tatiana was alarmed to feel her father's hands getting cold. His ears began turning blue, and his nose, too, began having a sickly color. "Doctor!" she called.

Dr. Makovitsky hurried to the bed. He measured Tolstoy's pulse and muttered, "It is getting weaker."

He summoned the other doctors, and they administered together a camphor injection.

Tatiana rushed to Sergey at the entrance hall. "We must let Mama see him!"

Sergey looked at her, tired, "But Papa had asked *not* to see her, Tanya."

"Then why did he *repeatedly* ask me about her all the time? And Sergey," she began weeping, "he is *dying*. Papa is dying! He can die at any moment"—she said through her tears—"You will never forgive yourself for not letting Mama see him! We all could never forgive ourselves!"

She could see that Sergey was moved by her words.

Chertkov, however, would not hear of it. He argued with Tatiana quietly in the entrance hall, "You must respect his will."

Tatiana burst at Chertkov with anger, "He is *my* father, and *I* know his will without him even opening his mouth!"

He smiled at her, his body blocking her from exiting the house. "Calm down, Tatiana."

She looked at him, shaking her head, "You calm down! If you will not admit my mother right now, I will go to the press and say *exactly* what I think about your behavior!"

Chertkov looked at her for a long moment. "I thought you were different than your mother. I was wrong."

She glared at him, "Let me through!"

Reluctantly, he moved aside.

Tatiana hurried to the street car. The reporters, who set up several tents across the railway, sensed that something was happening, and were following her. She climbed into the train car and awoke her mother, who was seated there with her eyes closed. "Mama! Let us go!"

Sophia jumped at once, not asking questions. She followed her daughter. They walked arm in arm across the railway. The reporters asked, "Is the Count dying? What do the doctors say?"

They ignored the rude reporters. Tatiana knocked on the door forcefully. She heard Andrey shouting inside, and then the door opened. Tatiana walked inside with her mother. They turned to the main room. Sophia saw her husband and ran to him, ignoring Chertkov and the doctors, and fell unto the bed, grabbing Tolstoy's hands in hers, "Forgive me!" she cried, "Forgive me Leo! Forgive me!"

Tatiana rushed to her, "Mama, calm down!"

Sophia looked at her like a child, unaware of everyone in the room looking at her. She nodded slowly, but still grabbed to her husband's hands.

Chertkov shook his head disapprovingly. He looked at Tatiana. She glared back at him.

Before sunrise Count Leo Tolstoy breathed his last breaths.

Tatiana held her mother's hand. Sophia, strangely enough, did not cry. She seemed calm. It was Tatiana who cried, then joined by Alexandra, who came to hold her mother's hand.

They hugged there, crying. The brothers stood still near the bed. Sophia stroke Alexandra's head. Tatiana leaned her head against her mother, weeping.

That day they spent time near their father, murmuring as if not to wake him.

By the afternoon a coffin was brought to the station: a large, mahogany coffin, with gold trimmings. Tatiana and Alexandra held their mother's arms on both sides, as they followed the coffin carried by all the brothers out of the trainmaster's house and unto the train.

There were immense crowds outside. They all murmured as the coffin passed by, parting the gathering, and as it was brought unto the train many people cried. Sophia, along with her daughters, then climbed the train. The people then began singing 'Eternal Memory,' an old hymn that Tolstoy was known to admire. One woman shouted, "God be with you, Countess Tolstoy!"

Sophia was touched by these words.

Tatiana and Alexandra sat next to their mother's side. The train left the station, and slowly drove through the countryside. The news had spread quickly, and in every station a crowd of hundreds, sometimes thousands of people, gathered, waving at the slow-passing train. Tatiana could not stop weeping. She thought that though her father shunned the admiration and scuffed at it his entire life, he would have nevertheless appreciated this last respect.

The following day they left the house with the coffin, among thousands of people who came from all parts of Russia, and from all walks of life. Judge by their clothing, many of them were poor peasants and serfs. Tatiana could not find it less fitting. Her father loved these simple people.

Sukhotin, who had come in the morning, walked along her, holding her hand.

The coffin was carried by the sons and a few other friends of the family to the middle of the forest where Tolstoy used to take his daily walks. The family was followed by the huge crowd.

There was no priest presiding over the funeral. The Church insisted that since Leo Tolstoy had been excommunicated, the funeral could not be a Christian one.

While at first Tatiana found this to be irritating and condescending on the part of the Church, she then thought that her father would have preferred it that way.

She stood there, near her mother, Alexandra standing on her mother's other side. Sergey and the other brothers, along with several serfs, dug a deep hole in the ground. It was cold outside, but at least it was not snowing.

Finally, several minutes later, the casket was lowered

down slowly, men holding it from all sides.

Tatiana stopped herself from crying. She was awed by her mother, who stood erect, dignified, not shedding a tear. Tatiana planned to support her mother, with Alexandra and her stopping their mother from losing her sanity. But now, instead, it seemed as if it was their mother, supporting them.

Everyone stood in silence near the casket laid in the ground. Where usual speeches would have been given, the family chose to follow Tolstoy's request of not having any ceremony.

The great crowd stood there in silence. The wind was cold and Tatiana grabbed more firmly to her mother's arm, protecting her mother from the harsh November wind.

Suddenly, someone began talking. Tatiana looked with anger at the direction of the gruff voice. But then her heart softened at once as she saw it was none but Old Abrasha speaking, exclaiming, "Count Tolstoy was a great man! A dear man! What a kind heart! With his heart he had changed our lives! He had showed us what true love was! Rest in peace, Count Tolstoy!"

People shouted, "Rest in peace, Count Tolstoy! Rest in peace!"

Tatiana heard her little sister crying on their mother's arms. Her sobs brought Tatiana to tears as well.

Finally, Sophia nodded at Sergey.

Sergey then took the shovel and gently threw the first clump of dirt on the casket. It was when Tatiana saw the dirt piling on her father's coffin that her tears turned into howling. She looked at her brothers casting earth unto the coffin. She felt her mother's hand squeezing her hand with warmth. Sukhotin, standing behind her, put his hand on her shoulder.

Slowly, shovel after shovel, the casket disappeared under the dirt, under the soil which swallowed her father.

Yet it seemed as if people refused to leave the graveside. No one moved, no one walked away. Tatiana's tears subsided, and so did Alexandra's. Tatiana looked at her husband. His eyes were moist.

Everyone remained standing there. The cold wind suddenly turned into thin snow. At first it was just a fluff. Slowly, the snow thickened.

Sophia nodded to her children, and slowly turned around to face the trail back to the house. As she did, everyone began turning, hundreds of people beginning to face the other way, until slowly the procession headed away from the grave. One of the serfs began singing, "*In a blessed sleep, grant O Lord, eternal rest unto Thy departed servant!*" Everyone joined him in singing, "*And make, O Lord, his memory eternal! Eternal! Eternal!*"

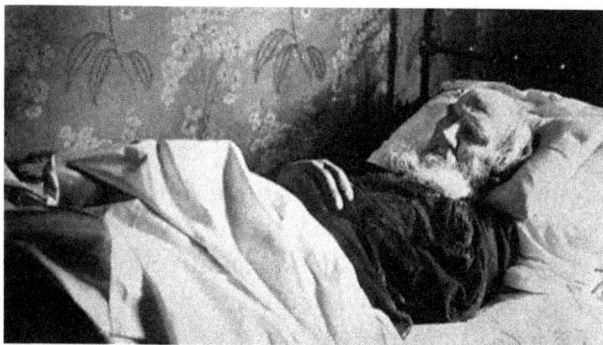

Leo Tolstoy on his deathbed, 1910.

Crowds at Leo Tolstoy's funeral, November 20th 1910.

ROME,
DECEMBER 1931

Tatiana looked at Gandhi with a sad smile.

Gandhi nodded slowly. His eyes were moist.

Finally, Gandhi said, "It must have been difficult."

Tatiana nodded. She noticed an odd hum. A little like the sound of people. At first she brushed it off, thinking that the memory of the funeral in her head was blurring her good senses.

But then—no. There was a distinct sound.

She walked to the window. She moved the curtain and was alarmed to see a sea of people outside filling the street. Before she could understand what was happening, someone noticed her, and cameras flashed from the street below, trying to take her photograph. She quickly closed the curtain.

"What?" Gandhi asked, seeing her white face.

Tatiana looked for words. At that moment there was

a knock on the door.

Tatiana felt trapped. The sight of all the people brought her an alarming sense of unease.

The knock repeated. Gandhi looked at Tatiana.

Tatiana came to her senses and hurried to the door. She opened it. The two guards were there, with the lady who had come earlier with Gandhi. She looked very displeased.

Gandhi jumped from his couch and exclaimed, "Mirabehn! Is everything alright?"

"Mahatma," Mirabehn looked at him and then quickly lowered her gaze, "I am afraid that if we won't leave soon, we might be late. You had a tour arranged of the palace—"

"I told them I was not interested!"

"But, Mahatma—"

"The dinner is at eight isn't it?"

Mirabehn nodded, "But, there are crowds outside, and it is already a quarter to seven."

"Oh no worries," Gandhi smiled, "I asked the driver how far the Palace was, and he said twenty minutes. We will be there on time!"

Mirabehn nodded and looked down.

Tatiana, feeling a little pressured by the situation, turned to Gandhi, "Mr. Gandhi, it has indeed been my pleasure—"

"No," Gandhi insisted, "we have yet to conclude our meeting! Mirabehn, I am very punctual! This meeting is important to me. Thank you very kindly."

The two guards, who were certain that the lady who had come with Gandhi would be able to fetch him, looked disappointed. Gandhi nodded and firmly said again, "Thank you. Thank you!"

The guards and Mirabehn turned around and began descending the stairs.

Tatiana closed the door slowly. "Mr. Gandhi—Mohandas—I do appreciate your kindness, but I sincerely do not wish to cause any trouble—"

Gandhi took her hand—which surprised Tatiana—as he said, "Tatiana, please, spare me the cordiality. This meeting with you is the most restful moment I have had in a while."

Tatiana smiled. She nodded.

Gandhi walked back to the couch. "Where were we?"

Tatiana sat down.

"Indeed," Gandhi said, "Your father's burial. How terrible."

Tatiana nodded. "We all die sooner or later."

Gandhi took a deep breath, "But your father's death came all too soon."

Tatiana appreciated that comment. Though her father was indeed old, the loss she and the family felt was immense indeed.

Gandhi hesitated, "Could you tell me how your mother was following your father's death? She must have been distraught."

"Well, I had always imagined that would indeed be the case. And yet," Tatiana smiled, "my mother, oddly enough, was not as distraught as you might think. She had a sense of peace to her, as if all her life were dedicated to the support of her husband, to his life's work, and when he was gone... she felt a sense of completion. Of accomplishment, really."

Gandhi's eyes widened in wonderment. "Really?"

Tatiana nodded, "She lived for another happy nine years. If you ask me, I think these were her best years. She was surrounded by us and by the grandchildren, and dedicated her time to my father's library, to publishing collections of his works, to publishing his unpublished works and his letters to her.... She was so happy, so kind, she became very gentle, not worried at all."

Gandhi nodded with empathy, "How pleasing it is for me to hear!"

Tatiana continued, "She became a different person. No anxiety, no distress." Tatiana's eyes became moist. She took a deep breath, "She and my young sister, Alexandra, became great friends... she simply turned out be a different person."

Tatiana suddenly began tearing. "I'm sorry," she said as she wiped her tears.

"Do not be," Gandhi murmured.

Tatiana sniffled, "She... I was so happy for her. She deserved the rest she had longed for. She won our respect. Many people came to her to interview her about my father. And she felt accomplished, satisfied. When she died she was a happy person. I would like to—"she paused for a moment—"I would like to die that way."

Gandhi closed his eyes and smiled.

Tatiana was quiet. "And how did you receive my father's death?"

Gandhi chuckled, "Oh, I was a wreck!"

They both laughed.

"I guess I had always thought," Gandhi said sheepishly, "that your father would never die. Otherwise I would have written to him earlier, had I had the courage. I assumed he would live forever. I know it sounds silly—"

"Not at all. I, too, had thought of him as eternal in some way."

Gandhi's eyes shone, "That is exactly what I wrote about him."

Tatiana looked at him questioning, "Wrote about him?"

У приготовленной могилы. 78.

Mourners at Tolstoy's grave following the burial. November 20th 1910.

Kasturba Gandhi and four sons, Harilal, Manilal, Ramdas and Devdas, c. 1902.

TOLSTOY FARM, TRANSVAAL COLONY, SOUTH AFRICA, NOVEMBER 1910

It was on the night of the 20th of November when Gandhi received the evening newspaper. He stared at the headline in the front page:

"Tolstoy Is Dead; Long Fight Over"

The headline did not shock him. He had had a heavy feeling throughout the previous few days, ever since reading of Tolstoy's condition.

He continued to read the article:

"ASTAPOVO, Russia, Sunday, Nov. 20—Count Tolstoy died at 6:05 this morning.

Countess Tolstoy was admitted to the sickroom earlier. Tolstoy suffered several attacks of heart failure during the night. During the early morning hours, they followed each other in rapid succession. Between the first and second attack the members of the family were admitted to the bedside.

The novelist's condition after each attack was what the attending physicians called "deceptively encouraging." The patient slept for a little, seeming to breathe more comfortably than usual. Dr. Makovitsky, the family's doctor, did not hesitate to predict under ordinary mortal circumstances. Tolstoy, he said, was a splendid patient in mind and body, except for his heart.

When one of the heart attacks seized him, Tolstoy was surrounded by his family. He was 82-years-old in his death."

Below this article there was yet another bearing the title:

"A Novelist Who Gradually Became a Mystic: Who Was Leo Tolstoy?"

Gandhi went on reading:

"Tolstoy had long been prepared for, had even looked forward to, his end. Two and a half years ago, when his admirers in St. Petersburg organized a committee to arrange a fit celebration of his eightieth birthday, he wrote to the secretary of the committee begging that the preparations be stopped. He spoke of his approaching death and wrote that he could not bear to be the cause of still more fuss and trivial celebrations. The committee respected Tolstoy's desire and dissolved.

The story of the life of Leo Tolstoy has yet to be written, if it ever can be written; but in its essentials it is the story of other great men who, through an inner awakening, have turned from the world to find their salvation in the life of the spirit.

Count Leo Tolstoy was born on the ancestral estate of his family, Yasnaya Polyana, in the governmental district of Tula, Central Russia, 150 miles south of Moscow, on Sept. 9, 1828. His father was Count Nikolai Tolstoy, who was the companion and friend of Czar Peter the Great.

As a youth Tolstoy entered the University of Kazan, but before the close of his second year of study he left the university to begin a self-taught private regiment of study. That same year Tolstoy had entered the Russian Army and was appointed a subaltern of artillery. While in the army, bearing merely perfunctory duties, he began his long career as a novelist. He published in rapid succession his "Childhood and Youth," "An Attack," and "The Cossacks."

When the Crimean War began Tolstoy was anxious to see active service. Tolstoy went forward at a head of a battery and took an active part in the siege at Sevastopol, distinguishing himself by personal acts of bravery. He had first-hand experience with war which was most valuable to him in his later work as a novelist.

At the close of the war Tolstoy resigned his commission and went to St. Petersburg. But he soon became utterly disgusted with his life there. He described himself afterward in a passion of remorse as having been an adulterer, a liar, and a robber.

He signalized his return to his estate, Yasnaya Polyana, by freeing his serfs, by dressing himself in peasant costume, and by preaching the gospel of the simple life.

In 1862 Tolstoy met and courted his wife Sophia Behrs. At the time that he met her she was 18 years old. He was 34 years old and already by his own account, a jaded man of the world. They were married soon afterward and the Countess began her life of constant self-sacrifice by going to a little hut on the Polyana estate—all that was left after Tolstoy lost the greater part of the mansion in gambling. There she lived for many years in a lonely, deserted place, many miles from any town.

The Countess nursed each one of her thirteen children, and taught the children English, French, and German, gave them music lessons, made their clothes and her own. Each time, as soon as her husband commenced a book, she began revising it, translating it from Russian into French or German, copying it in her clear handwriting, so that the printers could read it, and attending to the publication of the book when it was completed.

With her help and constant inspiration Tolstoy wrote his great novels. "War and Peace," published in 1867, won him his great reputation as a novelist. Eight years later Tolstoy produced his celebrated "Anna Karenina," a study of the marriage question, worked out in the novel to a conclusion of terrible tragedy. This work provoked discussion throughout the civilized world.

Throughout this time Tolstoy also devoted much time to the education of the peasantry. In 1892, when a particularly severe famine prevailed in Russia, Tolstoy established a number of relief stations in Tula and Samara and published his volume "The Famine." In the course of the next two years he produced "The Kingdom of God Within Us," "Christ's Christianity," "My Religion," and "Patriotism and Christianity."

Early in 1900 Tolstoy published the novel "Resurrection," his last novel. The immediate object of its publication was to aid a community of pacifists to relocate outside of Russia.

The publication of "Resurrection" led to Tolstoy's excommunication from the Eastern Orthodox Church, which had previously manifested its displeasure at Tolstoy's open disbelief in its dogmas. Tolstoy replied to his excommunication by addressing an open letter to the Czar, in which he denounced both the State Church and governmental despotism in Russia.

The work done by Tolstoy during his last years is not quite so well known, but some of his admirers declare that in the end it will be these latter writings that will be regarded as his greatest productions. If this be the case there will be a curious similarity between his career and that of the late John Ruskin; during Ruskin's life, his early books on art were admired while his later works on political economy were laughed at. However today people are neglecting his art criticism and reading his philosophy.

Despite his advanced years, Tolstoy kept busily at his work. His home was a center for pilgrims from all over the world, including many South Africans and British visitors. He was 82 years old at his death. The South African Star expresses condolences to the family, and especially to Countess Sophia Tolstoy. The funeral is to take place tomorrow, November 21st, at the Yasnaya Polyana estate."

Gandhi sighed.

He took a deep breath.

He thought the article insufficient in describing who Tolstoy *was*. The two articles did not do justice to the hero that Leo Tolstoy was. Gandhi then took his notebook and began writing:

"Of the late Count Leo Tolstoy, I can only write with reverence. He was to me more than one of the greatest men of his age. I have endeavored, so far as possible, and so far as I understood it, to follow his teachings.

I firmly believe that, as time rolls on, his teaching will more and more permeate mankind."

Gandhi sighed. He went on writing:

"Though a devout Christian, he truly interpreted not only Christianity, but he likewise gave a realistic presentation on the substance underlying the great world religions, and he has shown as no other teacher how present-day civilization, based as it is on brute force, is a negation of the divinity in man, and how, before man can realize his manhood, he must substitute brute force by love in all his actions."

Gandhi suddenly began to realize that Tolstoy was indeed gone. He looked at the long, three-page letter on his desk. He should publish this letter in the coming issue of the '*Indian Opinion.*'

He went on writing:

"Perhaps his letter to me, from September was one of the last, if not the last, writings from his pen. In it he almost foreshadowed his dissolution, and it must be a matter of great encouragement and melancholic satisfaction to Indian passive resisters that the sage of Yasnaya Polyana considered the Transvaal struggle to be one of worldwide importance."

Gandhi put the pen down and began crying. Like the time when he had arrived from his studies in London back to India, and had learned that his mother had died. He felt an orphan then. Now, too, he felt alone in the world.

He cried through the whole night.

The following day Gandhi showed Herman the short article he had written. Herman was emotional and murmured, "This would have pleased Tolstoy."

Gandhi spoke quietly, "I surely hope so. I also hope that he would have been pleased by all of this," he gestured at the farm through the window, "this is his legacy. This way he will never die."

Herman was quiet. "These are powerful words," he said finally, "you should add them to the article."

"What words?"

"That Tolstoy had not died. That he is still with us through his legacy."

Gandhi nodded.

That night, Gandhi labored on the article, and added to it:

> "The end of Tolstoy's bodily life has but put the final touch to the work of humanity that he, in his own inimitable manner, inaugurated. Tolstoy is not dead; he lives through the lives of his innumerable followers throughout the world."

Kasturba stood at the door to her husband's small office. "Mohan?"

Gandhi looked at her.

She came and hugged him, "Come to bed already."

He nodded and followed her. In bed, she laid her head on her husband's chest. "How are you feeling?"

He breathed in, "I think I am alright."

"Are you not sad?"

"No," Gandhi said quietly. He bit his lip, "I am inspired, Kasturba."

"Inspired?"

Gandhi nodded. "I think a life such as this, such as his, is a life worth living. Shedding such a light, first on

426

his own existence, then on his family, and then on his larger family of the world—that is a life I'd like to live. I think one could be happy to die this way."

Kasturba said nothing. She felt her husband's heartbeats.

Gandhi closed his eyes. He thought of Tolstoy. He sensed a weird sense of peace and calm. He felt that Tolstoy was well. All was well.

Supplement to INDIAN OPINION,
26th November, 1910.

THE LATE COUNT LEO TOLSTOY
મરહુમ મહાન નર લીઓ ટૉલસ્ટૉય.

Special issue of *The Indian Opinion*, November 26th, 1910,
featuring Leo Tolstoy.

Tatiana Tolstoy-Sukhotin and Leo Tolstoy, 1910.

ROME,
DECEMBER 1931

"I think," Gandhi murmured, "that you should be very proud of your father's legacy."

"I am," Tatiana said. "I certainly take pride in his life's work."

"Would you not say," Gandhi smiled, "that he was the kindest person that you had ever met?"

Tatiana wetted her lips. "Most kind," she said cordially, "very kind indeed."

Gandhi noticed an air of unease about her. He leaned forward and said, his eyes fixed on her, "May I ask why are you angry with him?"

Tatiana's face reddened, "Angry? Me?"

"Oh I don't mean any offense," Gandhi hurried to say, "it's just that…" he closed his eyes, "whenever you speak of him there is a feeling of respect but also a trace of anger, if I may say."

Tatiana got up from the couch at once. This was a little *abrasive* of Gandhi to say! He barely *knew* her. They had only met three hours earlier. How could he be so disrespectful!

She wanted to say something but could not find the appropriate words. The noise from the street below made her feel nervous. "My father," she finally mumbled, "was a *noble* man. I hold him in a great esteem."

"But," Gandhi spoke softly, "you *do* hold some resentment toward him—"

"Mr. Gandhi!" Tatiana said sharply, this time addressing him formally without correcting herself. "I'm afraid my relationship with my late father is a delicate subject—"

"Which is exactly why I am asking," Gandhi said. He folded his fingers together, "Mrs. Sukhotin, you and I may never meet again. We are both no longer young. I may never come again to Europe," he looked at her, "and I do not assume you plan to visit India, even though when you do, you'd be my honored guest."

Gandhi smiled. Tatiana did not.

Gandhi kept looking Tatiana in her eyes, "As we shall most likely *not* meet again, you can confide in me like a complete stranger. I do not mean to intrude. And, if you'd wish, I'd drop the subject altogether. But you seem to—"

"My father," Tatiana said loudly, nearly shouting, "was a very *complicated* man, Mr. Gandhi! He was indeed a kind person, especially in his correspondence, but he, like all of us, he had his flaws—"

"Most certainly," Gandhi murmured.

"—which I'm afraid you tend to gloss over," Tatiana said. "This is but natural, for you to ignore these flaws of character. I, and my siblings, know a *complex* father." She hesitated, worried of saying things she did not intend to say. "Nevertheless I most certainly respect him!"

Gandhi said nothing. He kept looking at her. His eyes were large and reassuring.

Tatiana looked at the clock, and then at the door. She wished someone would knock and bring this cordial meeting to an end.

She turned her gaze and saw his eyes looking at her. 'Clearly,' she thought to herself, 'his mannerism was *not* a European one. And his questioning could be so perturbing!'

She wished to change the subject, but thought of nothing to say. She wished to walk to the window, but then remembered the crowd outside. She noticed her desk at the corner of the room, with her father's diaries laying on it. She walked quickly to the desk, feeling Gandhi's eyes following her.

She put on the white gloves and pulled one of the diaries from 1899, the year she was married. She opened it, though she did not need to—she knew that specific entry by heart. Nevertheless, she found it and read out loud, her back to Gandhi:

> "Tanya has gone away—God knows why—with Sukhotin. It is pitiful and offensive of her. For seventy years my opinion of women has done

432

nothing but sink steadily, and yet it must go lower still!"

She kept reading out loud, pronouncing each word:

"The problem with women? One thing is sure! It is not solved by allowing women to run one's life, but by preventing them from destroying it!"

Tatiana turned to Gandhi, "You called my father 'loving.' This, in my eyes, is not very loving."

Gandhi said nothing. His hands clasped each other tightly.

Tatiana flipped to another page, and read out loud:

"Tanya's frivolity disturbs me; she has embarked upon a purely selfish love."

She sighed and looked at Gandhi, "This 'selfish love' was my *marriage*. To a man I loved *wholeheartedly*. To a man who treated me better than my father had ever treated my mother or anyone else, really. And to this great love my father calls "selfish." She looked down and read:

"I hope she will come back."

She closed the diaries and took off gloves, "You see, my father was very"—she searched for the right word but found none—"very complex."

Gandhi murmured, "But I am certain that he loved you very dearly."

His words stung her. She said succinctly, "He certainly found me *useful*."

Gandhi was taken aback by her comment. He thought to himself that what he saw was indeed anger.

Tatiana stared at Gandhi. "You see Mr. Gandhi, in his *writings*, my father was very sensitive. But more often than not, in his *personal* life, he was quite the contrary."

She hesitated whether to share with him anymore of her thoughts. After all, this was not *his* trouble. But she saw him looking back at her attentively. She noticed just how large his eyes were. She spoke, looking toward the window, "A year after my marriage I gave birth. It was a stillborn baby. My father said nothing. Nothing! Not 'I'm sorry Tanya,' or 'How are you faring Tanya?' Nothing. As if it did not happen."

Gandhi remained still. Only his fingers moved, ever so slowly, caressing one another.

"Then, a year later, I gave birth again. Nine long months of yet another pregnancy, and the doctors said the signs from the fetus were good. And yet," her voice broke, "she—the baby—was born dead as well."

Gandhi nodded.

"My father said nothing to me. Nothing! Years later I found him at least mentioning it in his diary. Mentioning!" she went to the diaries, this time not putting her gloves on, flipping quickly through the pages, and then found it. She cleared her throat and read:

> "Today I feel more awake, mostly because I have written. Tanya gave birth to a dead child again. She survived."

"Then," Tatiana said, her voice harsh, "he continues,

"I think I finished "On Religion" today...."

Her eyebrows raised, she looked at Gandhi, "I am

434

only reading this to you to explain to you that," her chin began quivering, "that he might not have been a *saint* in all his affairs!"

Gandhi nodded.

Silence followed.

Tatiana came back to the couch, but did not sit down. "I had yet another pregnancy. Yet another still born. You know what he told me?"

Gandhi shook his head.

"He told me, 'Good Tanya, this must be building your moral strength!'"

Gandhi grimaced, his face twisting in pain.

"Exactly!" Tatiana exclaimed, "This is all he could say, all the *empathy* he could show, to a person who dedicated most of her life to him and his work! To his very daughter! 'Good Tanya!'" her voice broke, "'This must be building your moral strength!'"

Gandhi nodded slowly.

Silence followed. Tatiana took a deep breath in and exhaled slowly.

Gandhi murmured, "And yet he loved you."

His comment infuriated her, "Why do you keep saying that? *Loved* me? My father's capability of loving was non-existent! He '*loved*' my mother too, and we all know what that led to."

Gandhi said nothing. He kept his gaze on Tatiana.

Tatiana sighed. She did not want to speak about it. These were things she had always tried to avoid thinking about. These were painful thoughts. "When I was 19 years old," she said suddenly, "my mother was pregnant. Yet again. My father had already begun with his gospel of 'Let's live like paupers.' He decided to give away most of our horses and leave but two. And he simply did that: without consulting my mother, he gave all of our horses away. When my mother found out she argued with him that he should have consulted with her…. They began fighting. It became dreadful."

Tatiana looked at Gandhi and sighed, "I was already used to their fights. Usually after a fight my father would lock himself in his study, and a few days later they would be talking again. But this time after the shouting my father mumbled, "I had enough! I had enough!" and he rushed to his room, took some cloths in a knapsack, and then announced that he was leaving and going to America. My mother was nine months pregnant."

Tatiana's eyes became moist, "She cried and hollowed, but he did not relent and exited the house. My mother ran after him, and I followed with Ilya. My older brother, Sergey, was away in university. It was me and Ilya, who was 17, who ran after her. She fell to the ground weeping, shouting my father's name, but he disappeared down the trail, leaving us. My mother suddenly began having contractions…"

Tatiana wiped her tears. She spoke quietly, "She did not want to come inside. But we called the midwife, and Ilya and I eventually were able to take her upstairs."

Tatiana's eyes shone as she looked at Gandhi. "Only several hours later, when she was already approaching labor with the midwife, did my father return."

She took a deep breath. "I don't know why I'm telling you this. I haven't told this to anyone."

Gandhi nodded. He asked quietly, "And the baby?"

Tatiana murmured, "Alexandra. She was born the following day, July 18th."

"Thank God," Gandhi mumbled.

Tatiana sighed, "All I am trying to tell you is that my father wasn't as spotless and pure as one might think."

Gandhi nodded, "Indeed, no one is perfect."

Tatiana shook her head slowly. Something in Gandhi's comment made her upset yet again. She was alarmed by her own reaction. Him saying 'no one is perfect' showed her yet again how blind he was to her father's shortcomings. "Yes," she said slowly, "no one is perfect, *true*. But my father—" she paused. "People often blamed my mother for not being kind to him. But I dare those who say that to try and live one week with Leo Tolstoy!"

Gandhi gulped.

"My father *was* a saint to many people. Surely the serfs in our estate saw him as one! But to his *own* family, he was nothing but *harsh*. Harsh is not a sufficient word—he was often *terrible*. He never gave me compliments. He never approved of my marriage, even though he had *eleven years* to see that I was happy, that my late husband treated me well. He never said, 'Tanya, you chose well' or, 'Tanya, you were wise.' No! Nothing!"

Gandhi looked at her without moving.

She walked around the room, restless, "He was

impossible. So often he was cold, distant... remote. He was so reticent—but he did not lack for words when he wished to criticize you! He would say, 'Tanya, how foolish you are!' or 'Tanya, you are such a disappointment to me!' He would say that! To my face!"

Gandhi's face twisted with pain.

"Yes! That was your grand Leo Tolstoy! I am not saying he wasn't a great author. He *was*. But let me assure you that he was far from *'perfect.'*"

She breathed in and composed herself, "I'm not sure why I am telling you all of this. I guess you must go. I am sorry if I have been too frank."

"Oh, not at all," Gandhi said. He looked at the clock, "I do think we have some more time."

Tatiana walked to the window, carefully moving aside the curtain a little, glancing at the street below. She saw hundreds of people standing, looking toward the entrance to her apartment building. They looked anxious. She was alarmed. She had never seen her street like that. "Many people are waiting for you," she murmured.

"Let them wait," Gandhi said quietly.

Tatiana left the window, the curtain falling back, "May I ask you why?"

"*Why?*"

"Why do you care? Why are you so eager to hear me? Why did you inquire about... this?"

Gandhi shrugged his shoulders. He wanted to say that he had been, for years now, interested in Tolstoy. He wanted to say that he had thought about meeting his eldest daughter for years. He wanted to say that he cared. That he felt a little—though it was senseless to think that—that he was a part of her family.

Tatiana looked at him, trying to guess what he was thinking. She sat down on the couch.

Gandhi finally opened his mouth and murmured, "I have read several biographies about your father. But I always seem to miss some details about his childhood."

"That is because he did not have a childhood," Tatiana smiled, "we always joked that my father was born an old man."

Gandhi nodded, but did not smile. "I understand that his mother died when he was a child."

"A toddler, really," Tatiana said, "he was two years old."

Gandhi nodded, "And his father died when he was nine years old?"

Tatiana nodded. She appreciated people who knew more than the basic facts about her father.

"So in many ways," Gandhi said quietly, "your father was an orphan."

"An orphan?" Tatiana asked, looking dismayed, "No! He was cared for by the family, his grandmother and his aunts."

"Yes," Gandhi nodded, "but he did not have a mother and a father. Forgive me about the terminology. I do not mean that he was an orphan on the *street*, but that he lost both his parents at a young age."

Tatiana nodded slowly, "In that sense he was."

Gandhi paused for a moment. "I could not find much information about his mother, your grandmother."

Tatiana shrugged her shoulders, "She was wonderful. My father could not remember much of her. He just said that she must have been the most loving person in the world."

Gandhi smiled and nodded his head. The nod continued for a long moment. "Was she?"

Tatiana frowned, "I beg your pardon?"

Gandhi leaned forward in his couch, "I can understand the romanticism that a child would create regarding his deceased mother. But was she indeed as loving?"

Tatiana looked offended, "I am not certain where you are headed, Mr. Gandhi."

"Mohandas," Gandhi corrected her quietly. "I have read somewhere—I am not sure if it was in Aylmer Maud's biography or in another—but I've read that your father's only memory was of his mother scolding him, when he cried, telling him that he should not cry... 'like a girl'?"

Tatiana's expression changed rapidly from surprise, to consent, to unease. "He *did* tell me that. But I never thought of it as anything—"

"When a child cries—do you have grandchildren, Tatiana?"

Tatiana smiled, "I have just become a grandmother in September, to a beautiful grandson."

Gandhi smiled, "Congratulations."

Tatiana smiled, "I assume that you have grandchildren?"

Gandhi laughed and motioned with his fingers, "I have ten of them! And the number is growing by the year!"

Tatiana smiled.

Gandhi took a deep breath, "Assuming your grandchild would cry, what shall you do?"

"Why of course I would embrace him and quiet him down."

Gandhi nodded. He said nothing else.

"But," Tatiana said after a moment, "my father always said great things about his mother!"

Gandhi said nothing.

"Are you saying," Tatiana continued, "that she was a terrible mother? I think that's quite an—"

"I did not say that," Gandhi said quietly.

Tatiana looked thoughtful, "Well, most likely, she was a *disciplinarian*. But *all* parents were that way in Czarist Russia."

Gandhi nodded. "Even if something is the norm, it does not make it correct, or pleasant. Does it?"

Tatiana became quiet. "I had always imagined her as the most loving of all people. Are you saying that this might not be the case?" she stood up, lost in thought. "Frankly, what could have my father remembered? He was only two years old."

Gandhi nodded. "And your father's father? Nikolay

was his name?"

Tatiana nodded.

"What do you know of him?" Gandhi asked quietly.

"Well," Tatiana sighed, not liking the direction of the conversation, "he was often gone on business trips. He then decided to move the family to Moscow, for the education of my father's older brothers."

Gandhi nodded. "What else do you know of him?

"He was a noble man," Tatiana said and then hesitated. "He did have a liking to alcohol, but most people back home had, and still do."

Gandhi nodded.

"Anyway," Tatiana continued, "he died when my father was nine years old."

"And who took care of your father afterwards?"

"Well, mostly his grandmother, my great grandmother." She became quiet for a moment, "But she, too, died a year later."

Gandhi took a deep breath, "Your poor father."

Tatiana hesitated. She had never before thought of her father as 'poor.' "But we must remember," she said, "that his lot was not like a Dickens novel. He was thrown to the street, but rather well taken care of."

Gandhi nodded. "I read somewhere that due to monetary issues, the brothers were then separated?"

Tatiana nodded slowly and squinted, looking at Gandhi carefully, wondering how come he knew so much. "It was costly to raise the children in Moscow," she explained, "so my father's older brothers remained there, while my father and the two other young siblings moved to Yasnaya Polyana."

Gandhi nodded.

"May I ask why are you so interested in my father's childhood?"

Gandhi hesitated. "You see, Mrs. Sukhotin—"

"Please, do call me Tatiana."

"You see, Tatiana. The picture that I have of your father is of a thoughtful young boy, who lost his mother at a tenderly young age. I see a sensitive boy—"

Tatiana spoke slowly, as if to herself, "He was sensitive. He cried a lot. His nickname was *'Lyova-Ryova'*, or 'Leo the howler.'"

Gandhi nodded. "Indeed, a sensitive boy, who lost his mother, and who had a distant father, who was prone to leave often. When he was home, he was prone to drink."

"But everyone did—"

"I understand that. But that does not necessarily give a feeling of security to a child, does it?"

Tatiana nodded reluctantly.

"And then, his father dies, at the tender age of nine. His grandmother takes over the household, but a year later she, too, dies. This, to me, sounds like a rather shaky life for a tender soul. If I were him, I would have found a way to somehow protect myself from the world."

Tatiana frowned, "Are you a follower of Freud?"

Gandhi smiled, "I have read some of his books. But I found 'psychoanalysis' unnecessarily complicated. I am only interested in the plain facts."

Tatiana nodded and looked at Gandhi inquisitively.

Gandhi continued, "What I hear, when I hear you talking of your father's childhood, is a boy who lost those who are dear to him one after another: his mother, his father, his grandmother, and soon his two older brothers who are to live apart from him."

Tatiana nodded. She thought of Gandhi's words.

"And," Gandhi continued quietly, "his vision of a mother, all warm and loving, seems to me like a fantasy of an abandoned boy. Especially if his only real recollection is of her scolding him."

Tatiana nodded slowly. She felt her heart beginning to pound. She suddenly remembered reading in her father's diaries about the maid, Mrs. Filippovna, who told him that his late mother used to be "self-possessed, reserved, and hot-tempered."

Could it be, Tatiana thought, that her father's memory of his mother was *invented?*

She looked at Gandhi. She felt uneasy. Her thoughts turned to her father's father. She did hear that he was often remote. Her father told her that his father, Nikolay, was rarely home. And when he was, he often preferred hunting. Her father also told her he was hard to talk to.

Tatiana's heart pounded fast. She got up from the couch, undecided where to go. She then sat down and took the teacup, sipping some of the cold tea in her cup. She didn't have the energy to prepare another pot of tea. She was confused. Overwhelmed. She looked at Gandhi, who seemed tranquil, sitting quietly in front of her.

Her thoughts unsettled her. Thinking of her father she always thought of the tall man, confident, admired, with an air of importance around him. She had *known* about his childhood, but never dedicated much thought to it.

Gandhi murmured, "I have found that whenever I am *resentful* at someone, it is useful for me to 'walk a mile in his shoes' so-to-speak."

Tatiana whispered, "I'm not resentful."

But she felt uneasy. "I am embarrassed to say that— but I had never thought of my father in these terms. Whenever he spoke of his mother he always cried. So I assumed they had had a wonderful relationship." She hesitated, "I was sometimes even jealous of their relationship. But... I feel stupid now. What could he have remembered? Nothing really...."

Gandhi nodded, a sad smile on his face.

Tatiana talked quietly, "My father always spoke matter-of-factly about his father's sudden death, and of his grandmother dying...."

Gandhi nodded.

Tatiana's eyes became moist. "I am sure he found it difficult. He was just a child. But he always spoke about in such an indifferent way...."

Gandhi nodded, "It must have been his way of coping."

Tatiana nodded. Her face twisted in pain, and she

began crying, quietly. Her posture wilted, her shoulders fell. She covered her face. All the thoughts about her stirred sentiments within her. She felt pity for him. And she was embarrassed of never having felt that before.

She looked at Gandhi, sitting in front of her, unflinching.

"I am sorry," she mumbled.

"Don't be." Gandhi said. "My father used to cry a lot. His tears taught me nothing but love."

Tatiana nodded. She thought of her remote father. So distant. So aloof. She remembered how once she had given birth to little Anya—a healthy child finally—her father cried. Not in front of her, but in front of Alexandra. Alexandra recalled to her sister how she was sitting in the study with their father, crying tears of joy after Anya was born.

Her father scolded her, saying, "Stop crying Alexandra!"

"But Papa," Alexandra mumbled through tears, "the baby survived! The baby survived!"

She then noticed tears running down her father's face.

It was only years later, after her father's death, that Alexandra told that to her older sister. And Tatiana found this incident so meaningful. Why? She felt that he *did* care for her. He *did* have emotions for her.

She bit her lip, feeling tears streaming down her cheeks. Another memory came. Her brother Lev, having to bury his child after he died from pneumonia. When Tatiana expressed her sincere condolences, Lev said matter-of-factly, "Father wrote us a short note of consolation."

Tatiana was pleased to hear that, and said, "Really? That is so kind of him!"

Lev then muttered, "Yes, but as always with Papa, it was philosophical. Cold. Lacking any heart."

Though she did not admit it to Lev then, Tatiana knew *exactly* what her young brother meant.

But now she began wondering. Could it be that her father was simply incapable of more? In a way he always had a tendency to detach himself—he even spoke of it. He once muttered to her, after Masha's death, "I shouldn't cry over her death. My mistake in the first place, Tanya, was in my *attachment* to your sister."

Tatiana looked at Gandhi. He said nothing.

She wiped her tears. Could it be that her father was *afraid* of loving? That he had learned, early on, that it could *hurt* if you loved someone and that person was then gone?

The thought made her miserable. It felt to her like the truth, coming out of darkness, bright as it could be. Her father was *afraid!* Afraid to love! Afraid of being disappointed again, afraid of being deserted, lonely again.

She nodded to Gandhi through her teary eyes. "I think I can see what you mean, when you talk of walking in someone else's shoes."

Gandhi nodded. "It's a phrase which we all use, but rarely do we try to really put ourselves in other people's shoes," he smiled, "or in their sandals."

Tatiana smiled. She remembered how much her father respected her. He really did. Yet any compliment he would give, if ever, was never to her face. Alexandra told her once that her father said, "You should learn from Tanya! She knows where everything is. She is thorough and organized, unlike you!"

Though it was not the warmest of compliments, and though it was used to rebuke Alexandra, Tatiana nevertheless clung to that comment. It made her feel that her father valued her.

She suddenly thought of her father's last letter. 'Good-bye, and thank you, sweet children. Forgive me for causing you to suffer—especially you, dear darling Tanya.'

He called her 'dear darling Tanya.'

Surely, she thought, that was an expression of endearment? Of true affection? Was it not?

Tears flooded her eyes again. She shook her head, "But he was so cold! So cold! So distant and remote! I always tried to please him! And he was *never* pleased!"

Gandhi's eyes became moist.

Tatiana bit her lip again, "I hate that I could never have brought myself to simply ask him, 'Papa, do you love me?' 'Am I important to you?' 'Do you approve of me?'"

Gandhi nodded. He hesitated for a moment but then said, "Do you ever speak to him?"

"Speak to him?"

"Yes. I speak to my parents often, in my mind of course. My mother often gives me patience, and my

448

father always encourages me to do what is right."

"But," Tatiana hesitated, "isn't it *delusional?*"

"It probably is," Gandhi smiled, "but it nevertheless *helps* me, which is more important. And the word you used, 'delusional', isn't an insult. If I had a penny for each time I was called delusional, I would have been a rich man by now!"

Tatiana smiled. Yet the thought of *speaking* to her father alarmed her.

She stood up. She wished to change the subject. "Do tell me, Mohandas, how did your campaign end—the nonviolent campaign in South Africa?"

Gandhi smiled. "Eventually we exhausted the government!"

His grin was wide, and Tatiana could not stop herself from laughing, "Yes?"

"Oh yes! It took four more years after your father died. But in 1914 the government decided to cancel and repeal the Asiatic Law, which essentially made all the Asiatics living in South Africa equal, at least under the law, to the Europeans. It was a great sense of accomplishment, to see the hundreds of Indians released from the jail. It gave us a sense of respect to ourselves!"

Tatiana nodded, "And then you decided to leave South Africa?"

Gandhi murmured, "India called me home, after nearly twenty years away. But South Africa was excellent for me, as it gave me the playing ground to practice nonviolence. And with its success I knew what could be done in India. Mind you, thanks to your father, I became a little bit of a personage—a well-known figure—in India. Which surprised me when I returned."

Tatiana did not understand, "Thanks to my father?"

Gandhi smiled, "No one had known in India who the South African lawyer Mohandas Gandhi was! Until the circulation of '*A Letter to a Hindu.*' Me having written the preface, and having the blessing from your father to print it, made me quite well known. But there was more to your father helping me in my quest."

Tatiana looked at Gandhi curiously.

"It was due to your father, and the encouragement I received from him while I was in London in 1909, that I wrote my first book, *Indian Home Rule,* on the steamer back to South Africa. I felt as if your father was pushing me to write the book. That book, infused with the spirit of your father, created the foundation for me in India among the activists and the socially minded."

"But I understood it was banned in India, wasn't it?"

Gandhi smiled appreciatively, "Oh it was. But that calamity proved to be a service, actually. It being banned helped the book get circulated illegally, which gave it a greater appeal, if you understand what I mean. The British have done a great service to me through banning the book!"

Tatiana smiled.

Gandhi smiled cordially, "Now, if you *were* to speak to your father, what would you tell him?"

Tatiana smiled, "You don't give up, do you?"

Gandhi smiled back, "Not when the battle is

important."

Tatiana looked at him, "And this battle is important?"

"Making peace with one's parents may be one of the most important battles one can make, Tatiana. If we wish to see peace in the world, it must begin in ourselves first. And peace in ourselves must go through the journey of understanding our parents, their own difficulties, their own shortcomings. As children we take too much responsibility onto ourselves. Most often the things we blame ourselves for had actually nothing to do with us!"

Tatiana took a deep breath. "I see," she said.

They both remained quiet for a long moment.

Tatiana smiled grimly, "You certainly listen!"

Gandhi shrugged his shoulders.

Tatiana looked at him helplessly.

Gandhi murmured, "'Papa, do you love me? Am I important to you? Do you approve of me?'"

Tatiana felt her throat tightening. She closed her eyes. A wave of emotions rattled her, and she opened her eyes instantly.

Gandhi sat there, his eyes closed.

She looked around the room, hoping for some distraction. She noticed a drawing of her father on the wall, one that she drew decades before. It brought tears to her eyes. She scolded herself for being so emotional, now, at the age of 67. She was not a young girl; she should know how to control her emotions.

She closed her eyes and took a deep breath in. She suddenly heard her father's voice, "Tanya."

She opened her eyes, alarmed. Gandhi was sitting there with his eyes closed.

She felt her heart beating fast. Her fist tightened. She wetted her lips and closed her eyes again, slowly, fearfully.

"Tanya?"

"Papa?"

"Tanya! Tanyushka! Of course I love you. What a silly question!"

"Papa!"

"Tanyushka. I always loved you. I always approved of you. Do you remember how you used to come into my study as a young girl, how I used to talk to you? You always had the brightest eyes. So clever!"

"Papa!"

Tatiana wiped her tears. She did not want to open her eyes.

"Yes, Tanyushka. You were. I have always loved you."

"Why did you not *tell* me then, Papa?"

"Oh Tanyushka… I was lacking the power. I was afraid to speak this way. I was afraid that the moment I would say that, something bad would happen to you. That you would get hurt. I was foolish. I should have told you. I should have told you many times."

Tatiana's tears streamed down her face.

She hesitated, but then said, in her head, "And you never approved of my marriage, Papa! And you never approved of my parenting!"

"Tanyushka... Sweet Tanyushka... How foolish of me... Your home was a safe haven for me. I was impressed by how you raised little Anya. And by your choice of Sukhotin. He was a good man."

"He loved me, Papa!"

"He did. I was very pleased to see your marriage, Tanyushka. Oh Tanyushka, my little Tanya... I was so happy for you."

"But why did you not *tell* me that? One warm word, Papa! I did not ask for much!"

"Tanyushka... How could I give you what I did not have?"

Tatiana opened her eyes, puzzled, wondering, 'What I did not have?' She closed her eyes again.

"Of course, Tanyushka! I was tormented myself! I was self-deprecating, upset with myself over the smallest of things. You longed for love, affection, warmth—all of which I could not give, because I did not have them!"

Tatiana frowned, "That is not true, Papa. You treated Masha with warmth. You said she was—"

Tatiana burst into a long, howling sob, "You said she was your favorite daughter!"

Silence followed. Then she heard the voice again, grief-stricken and quiet, "Tanyushka. I was so foolish... So erroneous...! What an unfortunate behavior. I loved you no less. I loved each of you children so greatly, words could not express—"

"But you loved Masha the most. I remember when she was dying, you hugged her, Papa—you never hugged me! You hugged her and embraced her in bed. I wished—"

She sobbed and sobbed, unable to stop herself. "I wished I was her, Papa! I wanted to die in your arms like her!"

"Oh, Tanya... Tanyushka... I should have hugged you! Why was I so uncomfortable? I should have hugged you! I should have hugged you and never let you out of my embrace. I am so sorry! I am so sorry to hear of your suffering...."

Tatiana's eyes kept welling. She sobbed and sobbed. Something in her father's words—in him saying that he was sorry—*moved* her. It *shook* her. It shook the mountains of blame and resentment and anger. It broke something that felt unbreakable within her, a stronghold of pain.

Tatiana opened her eyes and saw Gandhi through her tears, sitting calmly, his eyes closed. Somehow his posture calmed her. She was afraid he would be concerned with her state. But he sat there, unperturbed, unfazed.

She took a napkin from the table and wiped her tears. She closed her eyes and nodded to herself.

"Yes Papa, you should have told me. You should have hugged me. You should have made me feel like I wasn't stupid. You wrote of my *frivolity*...."

"I am so sorry, Tanyushka. I am so terribly sorry."

"And you criticized me *all the time!* You made me think that you valued my *help*, but that you didn't—"

She broke into a long howl, her shoulders shaking, her chin quivering uncontrollably, "You valued me for my *help*, not for being me! I felt that it was only because I could assist you that you cared for me! Not because you cared for me for being who I am."

"Tanyushka... Tanyushka... My Tanyushka... I am so sorry. I am so terribly sorry...."

"I was no less good than Masha! I was not less smart, not less kind—"

"Shhh... Tanyushka. You were *you*. Perfectly, wonderfully *you*. My little Tanya! You needed not prove yourself to me!"

"Exactly, Papa. That is what Masha did all the time. She was *independent*. She was the first to have the courage to get married and leave, even though she was younger. And you *valued* that. I *saw* that in your eyes! But I... I..."

She cried, her howl shrieking, her throat hurting, "I did not want to disappoint you by leaving you!"

"Tanyushka... I am so sorry. How much you have suffered, it pains me to hear.... I am so sorry, so, so sorry...."

"Papa...."

Tatiana gasped for air, breathing in short, deep inhales.

"Tanyushka, I *approve* of you. You are *important* to me—and you always were! And I *love* you. Hear me, Tanyushka. I love you, daughter of mine, I love you."

She cried and cried. Time stood still.

After what felt to Tatiana like a long time, she got up. She wiped her tears. She felt a little self-conscious of having bellowed like that. She howled like a baby.

But then, as she walked to the kitchen with the teapot, she remembered her father's nickname, "Leo the Howler."

Her poor father.

She heard Gandhi getting up from the couch in the living room.

She put the kettle on, they might have a chance to drink one more cup of tea. Her thoughts turned to her father. It was only in his writings that her father could express love. How much empathy he displayed toward Natasha in '*War and Peace*'! How much compassion he had toward Anna in '*Anna Karenina*'! Perhaps this was why she loved him so much as an author. Because there, in his books, he could pour out all his sentiments and wisdom, his kindness and empathy, his love of others—all of which were difficult for him to express in real relationships. She suddenly felt for him.

She waited for the water to boil. She thought of Gandhi's choice of words, calling her father "an orphan." How interesting was it that she had always refused to see her father that way? As if she—by recognizing that he indeed *was* an orphan—would lose her sense of righteousness! As if it would minimize her own pain. As if acknowledging her father's suffering would diminish her own.

Gandhi appeared at the door of the kitchen and looked at Tatiana. She blushed and looked away, afraid of what he may say.

But Gandhi said nothing and just smiled.

"I'm sorry," she said, "I didn't mean to—"

"When I was young," Gandhi interrupted her, "I once stole some money. My father, I knew, would have been very upset with me, had he known. At first I thought of never revealing it. But overtime I could not live with myself. So I wrote on a piece of paper, 'Father, I stole some money. I am sorry. Do punish me as you find fit.'"

Gandhi's eyes shone, "Do you know what his reaction was?"

Tatiana shook her head 'no.'

"He *cried*. He did not beat me. He did not scold me. He did not rebuke me, he just cried and cried." Gandhi's eyes watered, "I sat there, near his bed, and saw the tears falling from his eyes. What courage! What a brave man! He had taught me more in that moment of grace than he had taught me in his whole lifetime."

Tatiana smiled at him. So delicate, she thought, are human beings. Over the years, since she had begun following Gandhi's undertakings in the papers, she had thought him to be somewhat like her father: dignified, strong, never erring. But he too, the great Gandhi, was also once a child who looked up to his father. She was not lonely in longing for her father's approval and fearing his rebukes.

She breathed in and gestured with her head toward the living room, "Thank you for that."

Gandhi nodded, "Thank you. I feel honored for having the chance to meet you."

Tatiana brushed the compliment off and shrugged her shoulders.

"I mean it," Gandhi said.

Tatiana smiled. She noted again how perceptive he was. She looked at him, "I wish you luck with your struggle. The whole world is watching you."

Gandhi smiled, not knowing what to say. A bond of intimacy had been created between the two of them in these few hours. He did not want to leave. "I will tell my wife, Kasturba, about our encounter. She would be very pleased."

"I understand she is a great influence on you?"

"Oh, the greatest. Without Kasturba there would have not been a Mohandas Gandhi!"

Tatiana laughed. The water was almost boiling in the kettle.

They heard a knock on the door. Tatiana noticed she did not want him to leave. She approached the door mumbling, "But the tea!"

The lady, Mirabehn, was standing there, alone.

Tatiana was about to say something, when Gandhi came to the door, "Alright, alright! I am coming." He looked at Mirabehn with a twinkle, "Thank you for not forgetting me."

Tatiana heard the kettle blowing. She ran to the kitchen to turn it off. She then came back to the door with a heavy heart, not wanting to say goodbye. Gandhi looked at her and shook his head slowly, smiling his endearing smile, "Oh Mrs. Sukhotin! I do wish to thank you for a most charming reunion."

Tatiana pondered his choice of the word, 'reunion.' Feeling pain over his departure she murmured, "The pleasure was all mine, Mr. Gandhi." She looked at Mirabehn, "Thank you for letting me have him."

Mirabehn smiled. She nodded in appreciation to Tatiana.

Gandhi pressed his palms together and nodded gently. Tatiana smiled and did the same.

Gandhi said, "I do not suppose you'd wish to join us for the dinner with the great 'benefactor'?"

Tatiana smiled at his mischievous smile. "No, thank you. I'll skip the pleasure."

"And would you not like to join me for an impromptu waving to the audience downstairs?"

Tatiana was appalled, "No! Thank you!"

The three of them laughed.

Gandhi looked at her, "If you ever come to India…."

"And if you ever come again to Europe."

They giggled sheepishly like shy children.

Then Gandhi nodded, sighed, and gestured to Mirabehn to head downstairs. As she did, Gandhi smiled again at Tatiana. She smiled back to him, and he began descending the stairs.

Tatiana followed him with her eyes. Only when she

heard the building's main door open did she close the door to her apartment. She heard, from the street, a huge roar and the distinct sound of magnesium flashes, sounding like fireworks. She rushed to the window and peaked from behind the curtain.

She saw Gandhi and Mirabehn, surrounded by an audience that covered the length of the street. Several police guards stood by Gandhi, blocking the people from getting too close to him. She saw some people on the balconies of the building across the street, and some even in the trees. She suddenly realized just how popular her guest was. She saw several cameras, as well as two large film cameras, facing Gandhi. He smiled and nodded his head at the crowds.

Tatiana saw his small demeanor, his gaunt frame, and thought how unlikely he was to be a public figure. He was shy by nature. She could see it in his movement.

One of the camera man approached Gandhi and placed a large carbon ring microphone in front of him. Gandhi began saying something, and the crowd quieted.

Tatiana opened the window slightly to hear what he was saying. The words in their entirety were to appear the following day in the newspaper, with a photograph of Gandhi standing near the building:

> "It was a pleasure for me to visit the Tolstoy Museum, which is but a humble depository to the man who had so greatly influenced human kind. I was pleased to find such a precious Museum in Rome.
>
> Forty years ago I read Tolstoy's masterpiece, *'The Kingdom of God Is Within You.'* Before I read the book I was a votary of violence. After I

read it, my lack of faith in non-violence vanished. I would recommend this book to every Italian, and every member of civilization hoping for a better future for mankind.

To me Tolstoy was a great example. He practiced what he preached. His simplicity was extraordinary. Tolstoy strove uncompromisingly to follow truth as he saw it. He was the greatest advocate of non-violence in his age. No one in the world had tried to follow non-violence as sincerely as he did.

To me personally Tolstoy was the first to appreciate our movement in South Africa and India. It was he who had prophesied in his letter to me that I was leading a movement that was destined to bring a message of hope to the downtrodden people of the earth. And for that I will be forever grateful for him."

Tatiana had tears in her eyes as Gandhi finished his impromptu speech. The reporters began asking Gandhi questions, but he raised his hand apologetically and said, "Unfortunately I do not have the time to answer questions…."

The reporters nevertheless proceeded, "Are you disappointed from the Round Table Talks in Britain?" "What did you think of King George the Fifth?" "What did you like most about Italy?"

Yet Gandhi waved his hand, "I do apologize!" and followed Mirabehn and the guards to the black car surrounded by a ring of bodyguards. Mirabehn and he then disappeared inside the car, and the three cars began moving slowly through the street, some guards remaining outside to push people away from the road to let the car go through.

Tatiana closed the window, blocking the cold November air from entering her warm apartment. She sighed to herself. She couldn't wait to tell Anya about the encounter.

She walked slowly to the kitchen, poured the hot water into the teapot, and went to the living room. She then poured herself a cup of tea. She brought it to her mouth and smelled it, chamomile, allowing the warmth of the cup to heat her hands.

She looked at her father's drawing in the corner of the room. "Rest, Papa," she murmured, "your work was not in vain."

EPILOGUE

Mahatma Mohandas Gandhi saw his life's dream of liberating India from British rule without the use of violence, come to fruition in 1947. He was 77-years-old. His once 'impossible' dream that the British would just 'pull out' of India *voluntarily*, became the reality of 300 million Indians.

Not everyone in India, however, were pleased with his methods. Some Hindus saw his concessions toward the neighboring Muslim Pakistan in a negative light. In 1948 a Hindu fanatic assassinated Gandhi. He was 78 years old at his death.

Gandhi mentioned Tolstoy and the influence he had on him throughout his life, citing him often in his speeches and articles. As late as three days before his assassination, Gandhi was mentioning Tolstoy's writings to his followers.

Following the assassination, in the well-covered trial that followed in Delhi, the assassin received a death sentence.

From Rome, 84-year-old Tatiana Sukhotin-Tolstoy, read the news, grief-stricken. The assassination of Gandhi tormented her. But so did the punishment of death that was given to the assassin. She decided to write a letter to the Indian Prime Minister, Jawaharlal Nerhu. The letter stated:

> "While I strongly condemn the deed of the assassin, I strictly oppose the death penalty given to him. I personally know that Mr. Gandhi himself would have frowned upon this verdict. As it is well known, Gandhi was a strict Tolstoyan. And as the daughter of Leo Tolstoy and his former secretary, I know that Tolstoy had always—and under all circumstances—opposed capital punishment.
>
> Gandhi, if he could, would have raised his voice to prevent an act of violence toward that criminal. I therefore call you urgently to substitute the punishment with imprisonment or any other punishment your courts find fit.
>
> Yours,
>
> Tatiana Tolstoy-Sukhotin."

Tatiana's letter did not yield the action she had hoped for. However, through her many books, Tatiana Tolstoy-Sukhotin was able to further the cause of nonviolence, as well as the legacy of her father. She authored several books, including *On My Father, Childhood, Adolescence, Flashes of Memory, Years with*

My Father, Friends and Guests of Yasnaya Polyana and *Letters from the Revolution.* Through all of these books Tatiana Tolstoy-Sukhotin was able to leave an impressive legacy in her own right.

Tatiana died in 1950, at age 85, surrounded by her daughter, son-in-law and four grandchildren. She was buried in the Protestant cemetery in Rome.

After her death, an entry was found in her diary, summing up her life:

> "I have lived an incredibly and undeservedly happy and interesting life. And successful too."

> —Tatiana Tolstoy-Sukhotin

* * *

"Nothing is impossible for pure love."

—Mahatma Gandhi

"Love and be loved! That is the only reality in the world, all else is folly!"

—Leo Tolstoy

—THE END—

"My Father," pencil drawing by Tatiana Tolstoy, 1909.

PHOTO CREDITS

CLAIM YOUR GIFT!

Thank you for purchasing this novel. For a special behind-the-scenes e-book, including historical background on which *Her Father's Daughter* was based please visit:

Books.click/Daughter

* * *

This e-book companion includes group discussion ideas, unique photographs and much more!

JOIN OUR ONLINE BOOK CLUB!

Book club members receive free books and the hottest pre-release novels. To join our exclusive online book club and discuss *Her Father's Daughter* with likeminded readers, please visit:

Books.click/DuboisBookclub

* * *

We look forward to see you in our bookclub family!

RATE THIS BOOK!

We thank you for taking a quick moment to rate this book online. Let others know what you thought at this easy link!

Books.click/DaughterRating

The author has requested that we include the following personal email address below. Readers are invited to contact author Caroline Dubois directly at the following address. The author attempts to answer each and every email from dedicated readers.

AuthorCarolineDubois1@gmail.com

NOVELS BY CAROLINE DUBOIS:

All the Uncried Tears

The Stolen Violin

The Sisterhood

Her Father's Daughter

The Friendship

Islam

The Secret Earpiece